THOSE WHO
REMAIN

for Ray —

THOSE WHO REMAIN

Remembrance and Reunion After War

RUTH W. CROCKER

ELM GROVE

For information, address
Elm Grove Press
PO Box 153
Old Mystic, CT 06372

Published 2014

18 17 16 15 14   1 2 3 4 5

ISBN: 978-1-940863-00-9

Library of Congress Control Number: 2014931739

Cover Design by Sheila Cowley

*For David and those who
served with him.*

Untitled

To think.
wonder if, when, where,
I go to do;
It takes the thinking fear,
all inside becomes you
and you become whole
to like the finding.
Time passes—
And if it stops to pass
it won't hurt or bother
except those who remain
to think.

 —Captain David R. Crocker, Jr,
  Cu Chi Province, Vietnam, 1969

PART ONE
THE BURIED PAST

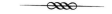

Truly nothing is to be expected but the unexpected!
—Alice James (1891)

On May 17, 1969, when I was twenty-three, my husband, Captain David Rockwell Crocker, Jr., was killed in the Vietnam War.

We had married on the day after his graduation from West Point in June 1966. Three years later, after six months in Vietnam, he was mortally wounded while inspecting a deserted Viet Cong bunker. He had entered the small dark enclosure with his first sergeant along with a Vietnamese translator, and another soldier—a conscientious objector—carrying a bulky radio.

There are speculations about what happened next in the bunker. Possibly an unseen wire like fishing twine, strung overhead, connected to the trigger on a booby trap; probably the antenna, projecting up from the radio, pressed against the wire. The explosion sent earth, human flesh, glass, bamboo and shrapnel in all directions. Dave survived for a few hours with fatal wounds to his chest and neck. The others died at the scene.

1

I thought it was impossible for such a thing to happen.

Perhaps I was naïve to this potential consequence of going to war because I believed in peace and that having such a belief would protect us like a charm. If I didn't believe in war, how could my love be cleaved from me like this? It was as if a guillotine had cut off my limbs. He was my source of love and adoration from whom I had learned everything I knew about being in love. How could I keep him with me after this? Could I live for both of us? I tried to inhale the vapors of his spirit from the air because I wanted to believe that he had merely been dispersed into the atmosphere. I kept looking up at the sky for a sign or a trace.

June 9, 1966, Mystic, Connecticut

At least this is what I imagine that I was thinking back then in the dishevelment of grief.

I'm not certain that we actually *can* think when leveled by such tragedy. Every portion of mind and body is bundled unwillingly into a one-person rocket that blasts off for unknown territory. Every landing is undesirable because he's not there. I was willing to go anywhere, do anything, if I could sooth the stabbing pain in my heart. Less than two months after Dave's death, Neil Armstrong walked on the moon and I yearned to be up there, too. Perhaps I could feel closer to Dave again, wherever his soul was, in an air-less atmosphere. Tragedy pierces the heart and takes up residence. Grief intrudes like an invisible boulder and lodges in the chest, an unshakable reminder that someone who loved me is lost and nothing can retrieve him.

Him—the one who had been so full of life and laughter; his body lithe and muscular after years of training as a gymnast; his love letters written in flowing script with a fountain pen; his blue eyes and loving glances; his hand in mine; his love my first.

Stephen Levine says in *Unattended Sorrow,* that when we love someone, they become a mirror for our heart. They reflect back to us the place within us that *is* love. When that mirror is shattered through death or separation, we may feel as though love itself has died.

Did I change when he died? My face still bore faint scars of teenage acne, my hair was still long and blonde sweeping to my waist. My eyes were still blue. Outwardly, I looked the same but things were different now. Deep within my cells emergency lights flashed, begging for help, screaming for an exit. Tears felt like unsatisfying expressions of other more trivial sadness; a distraction from thinking. Can we really *comprehend* during such a time? I believed I was thinking, and that's what counts. My impression—that I was still able to make a decision—is what saved me back then.

I see that slim twenty-three year old with the long straight hair, suddenly awakened from her stricken state by an epiphany. He will not be buried, she decided. He'll be cremated. And instead, his letters—the reminders of his devotion—will go in the coffin. The funeral director agreed with her plan. This new idea gave her a sliver of hope that she could survive. She felt a modicum of control over an uncontrollable situation as she hunted through her closet, loaded boxes into her car, drove to the funeral home. She ran up the wooden steps for fear of being discovered and thwarted in her plan, her arms full of treasures. She entered the Victorian style parlor to lay hundreds of letters and photographs in the coffin. Finally, she covered them with her wedding dress and his army uniforms. By this time, his body was already on its way to the crematorium. The next day she stood next to the gravesite and received a folded American flag, relieved that his body wasn't there to be lowered into the earth.

How astonishing, the mechanisms by which we help ourselves survive. Back then, after all that thinking, I wished for amnesia to save me from the pain of remembering.

Flash forward to All Saints Day, November 1st, 2011. I'm back at Elm Grove Cemetery in Mystic, Connecticut, where the funeral took place forty-two years ago.

Thousands of days have passed since May 1969, summer fall winter spring days. I can smile here today, but I avoided this place for years. Now it's almost comforting with light and shadow playing amid the garden rooms created by ancient specimen trees. Hedgerows of rhododendrons stand next to mountain laurels and burnished copper beeches. Hydrangeas bulge with faded blue and pink, lacy baubles—all performing a counterpoint against austerity.

A cemetery full of trees feels more *alive*. Even today on a clear autumn day, I don't have the sense of walking around on top of hundreds of dead people, many of my relatives included. It's a pleasant place possessed with quiet perpetuity.

Dave's elaborate military funeral was held here next to a giant sugar maple. Could the architects of this place have known how perfect these trees would look after centuries of growth? These trees, like Edwardian ladies and gentlemen holding great umbrellas, had sent their roots down, down and out without disturbing generations of residents, the forefathers, mothers and children of the area who are committed here. Except for the presence of headstones dating back to the eighteenth century, it could be a perfect spot for picnics—but beware of the small, discreet signs that say "no picnicking." There are limits to enjoying life here.

Usually I come to prune the pink azalea bush next to my grandparents' grave and water the red and white geraniums where my parents and brothers are buried. I've sat in my car under spring rain next to the Mallory family crypt and learned lines for a play, and I've worked on an essay leaning against a headstone with no worry about distractions or phone calls. Once I saw a red fox zip by, weaving between the grave markers. Gradually, over the years, I was drawn back to the single gravesite next to the maple tree. On some days I'd seek it out, just to be sure I could find it.

Now I'm on a mission that might seem counterintuitive; I've arranged to dig something up rather than to bury. The weather for my exceptional event is partly cloudy, windy and a chilling fifty degrees with the slanted sun of New England autumn glancing around the bare branches of trees like slim swords of light. It feels more like a cemetery than other days.

I didn't choose this particular date, All Saints' Day, for its spiritual aspects. I prefer the soft, generous light of June to be digging in the earth, but I have postponed and postponed the actual *doing* of this act I said I would never do.

When my young bereaved self buried the coffin full of treasure more than forty years ago, I said, "This is for eternity. I will never dig this up and never set my eyes on these beloved things again." And Mr. Ed, the funeral director, reinforced my decision with, "Just remember you can't dig this up. This is permanent." That was in May, 1969. Not until 2009 did another opposing idea intervene.

Some can't believe that those were my words and my reaction back then. I was young, naïve and devastated. That's why I decided to bury all that precious memorabilia. How could I do such a thing? How could I have had even one clear thought? Never mind such an elaborate plan. How could I manage my new condition of sudden widow-hood? As Stephanie Ericsson describes in *Companion Through the Darkness,* "Grief means not being able to read more than two sentences at a time. It is walking into rooms with intention that suddenly vanishes." Survival after Dave's death depended on harnessing my imagination and coming up with a way to live with an unsolvable problem; it was a stopgap solution to keep myself alive just for one day, and then the next. This is why I decided to bury all the things that I thought would be painful to look at from that point forward.

Was I courageous? I don't recall thinking about my courage, only his. Maybe it was just a way to manage pain in that moment. I look back over the early years after his death and see how I put myself in vulnerable, scary situations—camping on mountains pummeled by snow, traveling alone, trusting strangers, careless with my personal safety—but always accompanied by ambition to survive. I remember, two months after his death, climbing up Mount Washington in New Hampshire for seven hours and hiking back down that same evening, feeling too lonely and pained by the beautiful vistas at the top to want to stay. Or perhaps I couldn't make myself slow down and stop.

There was little or no analysis of my motives back then, only an enduring image of the small altar of things underground in the coffin dedicated to his memory. I didn't understand grief or the circuitous process of healing. I didn't realize back then that I had put something in place that would allow me a more gradual awakening to his absence, a private, personal action to hold my place in the midst of the public spectacle of his military funeral and throngs of mourners. After burying his love letters in the cemetery, I tried to close my mind to any images of my former happiness as if to protect myself from stepping into quicksand. The letters and our deep love were safe for eternity.

In 1969, the year of Dave's death, psychiatrist Elizabeth Kubler-Ross, published a landmark book on death and dying that mapped out five stages of grief: denial, anger, bargaining, depression and acceptance. She considered them to be navigation tools to help the dying and the bereaved identify feelings and normalize the grieving process. I discovered this book in the 1970s and it left me with an image of a pair of hands: palms pushing away in rejection (denial), moving to becoming a fist (anger), then to a handshake (bargaining), on to holding one's head (depression), and finally to prayer (acceptance).

I couldn't see myself among these images and was glad to know that, by the time I read the book, Kubler-Ross was emphasizing that there is no typical loss and therefore no linear progression through grief. Best of all was her notion that grief itself heals. It is a constellation of normal feelings on the path to healing. The idea that I was normal even though I still suffered from sadness and loneliness made me feel better.

Anger and depression are the only states that I can connect to my journey. It was impossible to deny Dave's death at any point. There was nothing to bargain for, and acceptance seemed weak and unsavory. If I could add another state of mind to this list, it would be forgiveness. When I could forgive, not accept, but forgive, everyone with any assumed culpability in relation to his death, I felt a sense of grace returned to me. It would take more than thirty-five years, but insight comes in its own time.

I might have been helped along by an old memory, a scene,

from childhood. Eight years before Dave's death, when I was fourteen, my youngest brother had died at home after a long illness. A debilitating grand mal seizure disorder began when he was twelve months old. The seizures, along with the side-effects of treatment with Phenobarbital and Dilantin, left him unable to speak or walk by the time he died at age seven. His sickbed occupied the middle of our family living room for the last three years of his life.

Danny and his condition were a part of our normal daily life during my childhood and I never gave up hope that he would "get better." But, he worsened and died. Shortly afterwards, his bed, his clothes and his toys were put away out of sight. I don't remember speaking of him except as an innocent with an unexplainable illness who was now in Heaven. My parents wore their sadness with quiet composure and life continued on after the funeral. My father wrote in his diary and sat next to the fireplace at night reading the Bible—sometimes out loud to me and my two remaining brothers as we did our homework. My mother cleaned every inch of the house, filling storage boxes with Danny's things, as if she could organize and purge her grief through housework.

One scuffed, white leather baby shoe remained on a bookshelf in the living room next to the Encyclopedia Britannica. "We'll have the shoe bronzed someday," my mother said. Perhaps it was in that living room that I learned my first practical lesson in the grief recovery process: to put things away out of sight. After that, to control the triggers of memory, go to school, continue forward, remember the hours you comforted him and the songs you sang, remember the hope that surrounded him. Most important: put things away. Don't leave the wedding table set in denial of reality like Miss Havisham in Charles Dickens' *Great Expectations.*

Becoming a writer is about becoming conscious.
—Anne Lamott, *Bird by Bird* (1994)

My decision to disinter the coffin with the letters was pre-ceded by years of writing journals, notes, biographical plays about heroic women, and fiction. Unconsciously I was looking for the pipeline between my mind and heart, but I didn't start with the intention of writing my own experience. The act of writing, however, built my courage and afforded a different and tantalizing mental challenge; it stimulated the urge to question and reconsider my life. This led me toward reversing what I thought was an inviolable decision at the time it was made. Writing, re-writing, and re-thinking untangled the old original idea that lay like a brittle nest, settled in a corner of my mind.

Burying his letters was my way of saying, "I'll never look back. I cannot look back. I don't want to remember how much he loved me." But, through unwrapping and teasing out my memories years later, I revisited, reviewed and revised my life. I began to separate the situation and the story. To paraphrase Franz Kafka, "[writing is] an axe for the frozen sea within us."

Are there others for whom the act of writing created an urgency to return to a cemetery and dig up personal effects? Not many have admitted to such a thing except for the British poet, Dante Rossetti in the nineteenth century. Grave robbing was popular back then, too, so his entourage might have been over-looked as just another band of enterprising marauders. Rossetti and I were separated by a century, but we vibrated on a simi-lar wave length in the face of death. He had buried important words, too.

In October 1869, Rosetti hired a group of men to travel at

night to Highgate Cemetery in England to retrieve a rotting notebook of poems from the grave of his beloved wife Elizabeth Siddal. His is the only example I could find of another grief-stricken person who buried, and then later decided to retrieve, significant documents from a coffin. Rosetti's example made me feel a little less fickle about my change of mind, but he waited only eight years after her death rather than forty and he didn't attend the exhumation.

I will be here for this one.

Another important difference between my experience and Rosetti's is that my beloved was not buried with his letters and poems. After his cremation, I delivered Dave's ashes to his favorite spot in the Swiss Alps, to be mingled with scree, snow, wild flowers, and the occasional footprints of rock climbers and mountain goats.

For four decades, I wasn't ready to change my mind about re-seeing the letters, his words, and whatever else I had placed in the coffin. What changed for me? Perhaps I'm rationalizing, that I don't remember as well as I would like the intense devotion and the pages of description inscribed in the hundreds of letters written over four years whenever he was away from me. Until 2009 when I changed my mind, I felt as if I held all his words within myself in an ark of tenderness, without needing to see them again. And, then—a twist, a knot, an interruption emerged in my chain, my rosary, of remembrance. I sensed it first in my ear; something like the sound of a butterfly wing against the wind, something I had to listen hard for in order to decipher. What did he say? What did he describe in his letters about his last six months in war? How did he describe his love for me? This flicker of thought reversed the electrical current in my body. Without a snap, pop or sparks flying, I simply changed my mind.

"I'll never dig them up"—became—"I will dig them up."

This is not to say that I wasn't both scared and excited by the idea. Digging up a real grave in a real cemetery is complicated. There are rules and regulations about such activities in the twenty-first century. And what about her? That young woman who said, "This is for eternity." Can she handle this?

Women never have young minds.
They are born three thousand years old.

—Shelagh Delaney, *A Taste of Honey*, (1958)

My grandmother once told me that if you flew over Elm Grove Cemetery like a bird, you'd see that it was laid out in the shape of a giant, spreading elm tree between the entrance and the Mystic River. She said the dirt roads and pathways sweeping out from the main road are like long fingers that outline the trunk and spreading branches. Now she's buried here among the branches along with my grandfather, my parents and two of my three brothers. I remember my mother joking that we own a lot of property at Elm Grove and therefore should be able to plant whatever we wanted—possibly referring to trees and shrubs. She bought an entire condominium of eight gravesites when my father died in 1981, even though our family was shrinking in numbers, as if she was expecting some influx into—or out of—the family. I like to think that she supported my idea to bury treasure.

I visualize the layer of vaults under the earth here like hundreds of containers in a giant ant farm. Are any of the others full of treasure like mine? Mini pyramids with no pharaoh, valuables preserved for the non-life after or protected from life ever after. As I stand above the military-issued bronze plaque bearing Dave's name, rank and place of death (because everyone thought that *he* was buried here) I want x-ray vision to peer down into the ground, six feet under to see my box and all that was committed here long ago, especially his words in those letters. Are they dry and fresh or have the worms gotten in to do their duty? The apple tree his parents had planted right after the funeral is long gone, but a white rose bush planted by my mother flourished in its place until last year.

When I changed my mind, when permanence became impermanence, my mental image changed: I saw the box open, sitting on the earth in the sunlight, the metal lid propped against the maple tree; I visualized envelopes addressed to me from West Point, Fort Belvoir, Texas, California, Vietnam— wherever he had been apart from me. I became as determined to look back as I had been years before to leave my treasure undisturbed. I became ravenously curious to see again those most intimate details of my earlier life. And I wanted to do it before another year dissolved into winter. After watching forty years of seasons change, I could lose my fragile courage before the ground freezes and I'll have to wait until next spring to try again.

My change of heart and mind required an official exhumation which does not sound as discreet as I would like. If the digging up could be accomplished without creating a big deal, a big event, the act would be more palatable to another voice in my head who occasionally screams, *what are you doing?* I wanted a secular experience, something neutral, somewhere between reverence and irreverence. No crowds, no sentimental observers. Only those who must be here because of the legal and physical requirements, the funeral director and the digging crew, and those to whom I don't have to explain why I want to do it now. Perhaps I am embarrassed and even afraid. I imagined massive earthmovers and giant, noisy dump trucks whenever thoughts came about the actual "digging up."

Finally, my entourage at the cemetery was small and included my son, Noah, along with John, the funeral director, his assistant, Brian, and the grave diggers, Moe and Jay, with their tiny backhoe and two shovels. My older brother came but stayed back away from the scene, standing with his hands in his pockets, arms tight against his sides in the chilling wind. Perhaps he was trying to locate a position on the continuum between, "How could you want to do such a thing," and "I guess you need to see again what's down there."

I understand that one could be reticent to attend such an event, so my invitation was open-ended, not compulsory. If I could have taken a shovel and gone at it in the middle of the night like Rosetti's gang, I would have, but I know my limits. I'm probably not capable of more than a pet burial or the transplanting of perennials. I needed a crew.

The digging down to the concrete slab took place on Halloween, 2011, the eve of the official exhumation. That's when Noah and I got to know Moe and Jay as we watched them dig. Jay, mid-thirties with spiky brown hair and a square, rugged body was on his cell phone, sitting inside a small black dump truck parked next to the gravesite when we arrived. He jumped out and picked up a shovel as we got out of our car and approached the site. Moe, perched on the world's smallest backhoe, weighed in at about 250 pounds. He looked like an over-sized toddler on a tricycle with his chubby knees spayed out to either side as he maneuvered the tiny, whirring machine around and between the gravestones. As he turned and dug and dumped the earth to one side, he glanced down and around, manipulating the levers controlling the bucket as eloquently as an orchestra conductor. But when he dismounted to inspect his work and his feet touched the ground, he lumbered like a great sea turtle out of its element, losing grace and speed on land. He lurched about and appeared to be without a center of gravity, teetering near the edge of the deepening rectangular hole, grabbing the backhoe bucket at the last moment to save himself from falling in.

Conversation with strangers in such a setting can be awkward. I don't think Moe and Jay expected visitors, but I needed to break the ice and speak with these guys who were bringing my new decision to fruition. I was also curious to see the whole process and take my place as the instigator of this event.

"Hi, I'm Ruth—the owner—of this spot—I guess you could say. This is my son, Noah. Nice weather for Halloween," I said, approaching the hole.

They smiled and introduced themselves, continuing to peck away at the earth.

They are local boys with deep southeast Connecticut accents; those folks who say "Linder" instead of "Linda" and "cah" instead of "car." Jay spat on his hand and smoothed his hair down when Noah showed them his video camera and said he would like to film the process. They both loved the idea of being in a movie.

Noah, thirty-three at the time of this event, is older than Dave was when he was killed in Vietnam at age twenty-five. Noah is not Dave's son. He arrived in my second marriage. But coincidently he has a likeness of spirit and heart and the same way of holding a person in his gaze, listening intently. It took five years of floundering in relationships after Dave's death to find someone with whom I wanted to be a couple again and create a family. I looked into the eyes of many men to see if my first love was there, but he always eluded me.

Dave's parents welcomed Noah like their own grandchild. They encouraged me to get on with my life, have another relationship and children. Noah played on the tire-swing hanging from the giant maple tree in their back yard just like their other grandchildren and, like them, he called them "Mee-maw" and "Pop-pop." As kind and loving as Noah's father was though, I left the marriage after twenty-one years, soon after I began the written examination of my life. I was determined to move forward in my quest to unpack my story, but I did not yet know the goal of the story or what the main character (me) would choose to do.

Neither Moe nor Jay knew why the grave was being dug up or what was down there. They leaned against their shovels, curious and quiet, as I explained about the letters and memorabilia and they seemed relieved to know that they were not digging up a casket containing a body. They relaxed and began regaling us with cemetery minutiae: practical, humorous tales of life with picks and shovels, different sizes of backhoes for different jobs, the discovery of campers in dense bushes along with lovers who thought they had found privacy, the moving of rocks, the mowing of grass, the thawing of frozen ground for winter funerals, the accidental breaking of sacred statuary. My favorite story was the one about the undertaker dropping his pocket watch in the grave during a funeral. They had to re-dig the hole by hand and sift the dirt with an old window screen to find the watch.

"How do you know exactly where to dig when you re-dig?" I asked.

"Sonar," said Jay. "We wave a sonar wand over the area and mark the spot. Of course there's a map, too, with everyone's name on it."

Moe chuckled that they did think it was a little spooky to be digging up a grave on Halloween. "But, this is what we do," he said, climbing back up to his perch on the back hoe. "They tell us to dig and we dig." He appeared to sit up a little straighter as Noah moved in with the camera for a close-up.

Jay had been a pizza deliveryman before he started working for the cemetery. He said he used to deliver pizza to the staff at Mystic Manor, the nursing home my family built and ran for almost fifty years before we sold it in 2006.

"It was a nice place, even if it was a nursing home, "he said. "I didn't hear people yelling 'nurse! nurse!' like I did in some places. I prefer this job, though," he continued, reaching for a shovel. "More job security and we work in the daytime."

Anyone driving by the cemetery could wonder what this convivial foursome was doing, standing around a partially dug hole, talking and smiling as the clouds moved in.

Moe's cell phone alarm rang.

"Twelve o' Clock. Time for lunch," he said. "We only get a half hour."

Suddenly both were in a hurry and I had seen enough of the digging. The temperature was dropping and the wind had picked up. Dry brown leaves were starting to whip against our legs. The trick-or-treaters would be at our door soon and now we were only twenty-four hours away from the exhumation. I could not (or would not) evaluate my decision anymore, although Noah kept gently pointing me back towards my emotions with questions like, "Are you sure you want to do this?" with his camera trained on me. I kept coming up with answers that sounded heroic but thin to my ear, like this one.

"Yes. We're in too far now. There's no turning back. Of course, that's part of the problem. I'm really doing the unimaginable—going back to the past. I'm not going to crumble up and die if it's not okay. It has to be okay—whatever it is."

I was on the path to reconnection. Maybe this time tomorrow I'd be basking in all of Dave's words again; I'd be reminded of everything I didn't remember deciding to put in the box when I'd made my lightning decision in 1969. On this day I didn't feel the brunt of the pain in my heart as I did the day I had decided to bury everything. Now there were flutters of promise, exhilaration, anticipation—almost like the time I expected *him* to return.

Welcome back—letters, pictures, special clothes! So glad to see and touch you again after so long. This is what I hoped to say. *Perhaps there will be a little mildew* was the worst fear I would allow myself to have.

I didn't linger on disturbing "what if?" fantasies of the condition of the contents. I saw my little altar created with the white tulle and lace of my wedding gown, his spit-shined combat boots, the gray cardboard letter boxes—the kind that hold hundreds of four by nine inch envelopes—all perfectly arranged, tied up with blue ribbons. More curious to me were my feelings of self-consciousness because I had tucked these items in the coffin in the privacy of the funeral home and, now, whatever was down there would be revealed to everyone present at the exhumation. I felt an awkward shyness as if I were about to invite them all into my bedroom and pull open my dresser drawers. And what would I do with the contents that were revealed? I saw myself carefully taking apart the layers, gingerly parting the uniforms and clothing to retrieve the boxes of letters. The coffin would be reburied immediately. Would I take everything home to peruse? I could not leap that far into the future even though it was only hours away.

"Is there anything new you want to put down there before they close it up and put it back?" Noah asked as we sat on the couch at home that evening.

This question had never occurred to me. There is that folded flag shaped like a tri-cornered hat in its plastic case. Why keep it in the closet? I had wanted to pop it in the coffin at the funeral. But by the time the honor guard presented it to me the lid had been supposedly closed forever and I couldn't move. My feet had grown roots into the ground like all the surrounding trees.

When Noah and I returned to the cemetery the next day, November 1st, at 12:30pm, Moe and Jay had finished digging down to the cement vault enclosing the casket. The top slab, a thick, gray, dirt-stained rectangle, was only about three feet down. Not as deep as I expected. Perhaps the expression "six feet under" applies to the bottom of the whole affair. As we approached, Moe and Jay were leaning over the edge of the hole, struggling to lift and pull up this heavy looking top-piece which seemed to have no handles or anything to grab. A running dialogue ricocheted between the two about types of vaults.

"Old-fashioned!" one spurted to the other as they gasped, grunted and pulled. "Look at that. No sealant in the four corners, your basic concrete slabs propped together."

"They used to use slate in the really old days and that cracks eventually," said Moe, a third generation gravedigger, breathing hard. "Then the whole thing caves in and you've got a wicked indentation in the ground. Got my rider mower stuck in one of them indentations once. I had a helluva time gettin' out of there."

Our conversation about common things, the nuts and bolts of graveyard work, was pleasant and desensitizing, humorous and warming in comparison with my mission. I enjoyed listening to the secular aspects of burial rites from two guys wearing Nikes, sweat pants and hooded sweatshirts; they weren't sacrilegious— just human.

They finally gave up on ceremony and leapt down into the hole, lifting and tugging the slab out with heaving effort, pushing it up and over to one side, revealing the gray metal coffin within.

A week before, John, the funeral director, had told me that the official time of the exhumation would be 1:00pm, November 1st and he would have vault experts standing by in case it had been sealed in some mysterious unexpected fashion. I wondered, *glue, cement, or Krypton? Some ancient fusion that necessitated a vault-cracking device?* He had also mentioned that this could add to the price of the procedure. He said he wouldn't charge for his services, the permits and paperwork, but the total cost might get up to about $3000 for everything mechanical if specialists had to be brought in. The concept of a price tag on this adventure was incongruous. For $3000 I could pay for one and a half root canals or a dental implant or spend a few days in the Virgin Islands. How could I put a price on this? Three thousand dollars averages out to about $75 a year for all the time it sat in underground storage. *A bargain*, I thought.

John continued, "Once the vault is open, we will bring the coffin up to the surface, open the lid and everyone will step back so you can have privacy to look and take what you want. Spend as long as necessary perusing the contents. Then, you leave and we lower the coffin back down, replace the slab and the dirt."

It sounded formal and very respectful, even reverential, almost as if there was a protocol in the funeral home files even for this apparently rare event. Here was the art of reassurance at work, making people feel as if this is a normal occasion that happens every day. I imagined myself wearing a scarf and turning away after viewing the contents with my eyes looking up to the sky or down at the surrounding headstones—like Greer Garson in an old black-and-white movie. I didn't think of practical things like bringing a bag or a box to put things in. I still felt a level of unreality that I was actually doing this and it was happening now.

By the time Brian and John arrived in the funeral home station wagon to join us precisely at 1:00pm at the gravesite, the formalities had been dispensed with. They jumped out of their car and rushed to the edge of the hole just as Moe and Jay, with a lot of grunting and manhandling, were dragging the heavy rectangle of concrete up and out to the side. *Where are those vault crackers and slab lifters?* I wondered, glancing around to other parts of the cemetery. Maybe they're discreetly poised behind a hedge. Perhaps John simply wanted to normalize and demystify the practical aspects of exhumation when he said, "we do this all the time."

With the slab finally removed, everyone stepped to the edge and peered down into the hole. I instantly recognized the ghastly rectangular box and I also noticed the rust spots on the outside of the gray metal lid. John thought the rust was unusual and asked me if it had been raining on the day of the funeral.

"No. It was warm and sunny that whole week."

I remember wearing a navy blue, sleeve-less A-line dress and sunlight streaming through the maple tree above me during the funeral. The weather was too nice that day.

Other than the rust, and the aged, blistered look of something that had been underground for four decades, the coffin was exactly as I remembered—utilitarian, metallic, army issue, gun-metal gray. The U.S. government paid for the whole package: burial site, vault, coffin, transport from Vietnam to Mystic, funeral service, honor guard, the riflemen for the salute, bugler, Bronze Star medals, Purple Heart and the help of a survivor's assistant. Except for hitching a ride on a military transport plane to Europe that summer when I went to deliver Dave's ashes to Switzerland, I paid my own travel expenses. It was a point of honor for me. From now on I would take care of both of us.

Getting the box up out of the vault was not quite the delicate, solemn, controlled operation I had imagined either; not the Hallmark channel TV event that John had intimated with only the cawing of crows and the thin creaking sound of the winch raising the coffin to disturb the tableau. I visualized straps placed underneath the box and a little crane gently hoisting it up. But there were no straps and no winch. Moe and Jay jumped back in the hole and just pulled it up and out with their bare hands (with difficulty—it was a small hole for two big men and a coffin). They finally lifted it far enough to prop it on the edges of the concrete sides of the vault. Then Jay began to search for the latch. He stretched his body out over the coffin and ran his fingers all around the edges of the lid with no success.

"We need Brian," John said. "He's the expert."

Brian, wearing a long-sleeved dress shirt and khaki pants, stepped forward into the work zone. He cupped his chin with one hand and stood in quiet concentration leaning down to study the under-edge of the lid. "Hold my foot," he said to Moe and then dropped both hands down onto the top of the coffin with the other foot on the ground next to the hole. Poised for a moment as if in flight, he cantilevered himself out over the top, supporting himself with one hand pressed down and using the fingertips of his other hand to feel around the edge and read the braille of hidden latches.

John turned to me and whispered, "Brian is the in-house expert on closure devices. He knows all the lids."

Perhaps he wanted to reassure me that, again, this was normal. I was impressed by Brian's agility and perseverance. I felt the whole crew supporting my project.

I've known Brian for a long time—almost thirty years. Both his parents spent the end of their lives as residents at our nursing home. Brian usually came to pick up the bodies of deceased patients so they could be held in the funeral home morgue until their designated funeral home collected them. The State of Connecticut requires that bodies be removed ASAP from any nursing home without its own official morgue.

Brian once shared with me that our "graduates" (the deceased) looked better and healthier than those he picked up at other facilities. I've wondered what else he does at the funeral home besides opening and closing coffins, but it seemed an indiscreet question to ask. I've seen him standing neat and trim in a black suit and overcoat to greet mourners coming to visiting hours, and later sweeping up cigarette butts around the front entrance. He weeds in summer months on his hands and knees in the pachysandra that grows next to the nineteenth century building that contains the reception area on the first floor, and a coffin and urn display on the second floor. Both nursing homes and funeral homes need key people with versatility, like Brian.

Brian located the latch but couldn't move it.

"Do you mind if we use a hammer?" John asked me in his softest undertaker's tone.

"Go for it," I said.

I had been flitting back in my memory to the time when John told me that exhumations are not a big deal and I was glad that what was happening in front of me was unfolding like a simple, down home event. John had organized my mother's funeral with me when she died in January 2008. He is a warm, amicable person with a good sense of humor. Perhaps it was the combination of his relaxed style and wandering through the coffin display at the funeral home that caused me to blurt out the story of Dave's death and my percolating desire to dig up the coffin. Until that conversation with John I wasn't sure if an exhumation to find a bunch of letters was even possible, even if I wanted to—and I wasn't sure I wanted to.

"You can experience eternal rest in just about any way you want these days," John said back in 2008 as we sat in his office amid a display of urns for cremated remains. We smiled together at urns that were wood and ceramic replicas of cowboy boots and golf bags next to a miniature guitar case.

I was surprised when John said, "We dig graves up all the time. Sometimes the family wants to move the body. Sometimes it's an investigation of some sort. The last guy we dug up had been down there forty years and he just had a little mold on his cheek. His clothes were perfect. With no body down there—it's a cinch."

I was reassured, but it still took three more years to bring me to this moment, ready to unearth and relive the past.

Now, in 2011, on All Saints' Day, the clanging of the hammer against metal broke my reverie. I came back to the present and the obstinate creaking of the lid as it was pried open with the contents about to be revealed.

In memory each of us is an artist: each of us creates.

—Patricia Hampl, *A Romantic Education* (1981)

What would Dave think of what I did back in 1969—and what I'm doing now? The only way I can ask is to stare into a picture of him and conjure his quick wit and decisiveness. He always seemed to know what to do.

In this photo, he stands above the rest wearing earphones with a mouthpiece attached. A wire runs down his shirt from his ear to a radio held by someone else. There was always a radio—a big clunky box with a tall spike antenna. His face is blurred, but I know by the set of his chin and the height of his cheeks pressing up beneath his eyes that he's amused by something.

He's standing on top of his track, an armored personnel carrier, a big box-shaped, thirteen to fifteen ton amalgamation of dusty green metal, traveling on tracks with wheels inside and a machine gun on top. All those around him are identically dressed in olive drab fatigues and sitting on similar armored vehicles lined up in a formation pointed in the same direction. I know it's his track because *To the Alps* is scrawled in red paint on the side. The visible side panels of the six tracks in the front of the line are labeled "U.S. Army" in big, white, block letters. The rest behind are a blur of green blobs of metal with human forms poking up from the top of each one. It is an ocean of young men perched on war machines disappearing into a dusty mist.

The landscape is indeterminate—a flat, windless place without jungle, palm trees or rice paddies in sight. The thickened fog in the background is probably dust emanating from the scorched earth of the dry season. This was not a vacation photo, but it's almost muscle beach with sleeves rolled up and chests exposed to the humidity and baking, broiling sun. It was a naked war compared to twenty-first century standards of protective garb for combat.

His shirt is unbuttoned down the front and the sleeves hang at his wrists. The V formed at his neck shows darker, tanned skin below his Adam's apple which is more prominent now because he's thinner than in earlier pictures, much thinner than when I had seen him in the flesh months before this picture was taken.

Dave Crocker, center, 1969

His face, the line of his jaw, the handsome boyishness, his muscular shoulders—all stir my memory of being in his embrace.

He clutches something small and black in his right hand in front of his chest. A mystery object; something one needs to conduct war? His breast pockets bulge with unknown things—maybe his small Rollei camera with which he took hundreds of slides of landscape, bomb craters, and villages. The guys closest to him are smiling, a meandering river of teenage faces streaming out below and beyond him, all looking in the direction of the camera as if a joke had passed from him or the photographer. There are 120 soldiers in an infantry company and perhaps they are all there spread out beyond the reaches of this picture but all within the gaze of their leader, the smiling captain who holds the little black thing.

To the left and the right and off into the distance these anonymous youth look more serious. Some faces are out of focus but still telegraph a grim, tired expression. Who could possibly *want* to be in this picture?

All the guns and rocket launchers on their vehicles are pointed in the same direction, all at a right angle to their faces.

There is suspense within the order and power of their mass as if, like a tight school of fish, they could suddenly dart off in all directions, this sea of young men with helmets and bare heads stretching back to a horizon blurred by a dusty mist. They are a flock of sameness at an indeterminate time of day like a cattle drive in an old western. It could be dawn and they are "moving out" or late afternoon on their way back "home"—some protective position in which to eat and sleep.

At my first reunion in 2006 with the surviving men in this picture, no one was able to read this particular photo and say, "Oh yeah, I remember that day. We were..." This could be a stock photo for a war which consisted of relentless incursions into "enemy territory," mass destruction of terrain to encroach on the enemy, and then return to a place where they circled their wagons in relative safety. The man in charge, in this case the captain, could call in fire power from the air or artillery back-up from surrounding units if the largely invisible foe was too close for comfort. It is oddly comforting to study this picture from decades ago and conjure what happened; to excavate my deep love for this young man who transformed my world, introduced me to sensual love, to devotion, to military life, and war, and suddenly disappeared.

I think he would agree with my decision to dig up the letters.

Dick Nash gave me this photograph. "I want you to have this," he said, when we met at my first reunion in 2006 of the 22nd Infantry Regiment Society with some of the soldiers of *Alpha Company*, guys now in their sixties and seventies. When the picture was taken in 1969, Dick was a twenty-one year old first lieutenant and platoon leader. He's somewhere on one of those vehicles. "This is my favorite photo of Captain Dave," he said in his mid-western accent, his eyes crinkling with his smile. "But darned if I can't remember where we were or what we were doing."

Moving out, Vietnam, 1969

"This is how I remember him," he continued, with tears welling up as he studied the picture. "Good-humored, ready to laugh, but always watching out over us, always ready to help us get through. He was the one who should've come back. Hard to believe he was only twenty-five. He was older than most of us. We called him 'the old man.' He was everything to us—captain, counselor, protector."

I heard similar tributes over and over in my recent meetings at reunions with some of the guys presumably in this picture. I didn't know any of these men when they spent their days in the jungles of Vietnam with Dave—except their names may be in some of the long-buried letters. Now, almost four decades later, we've met because some of them posted tributes to their long-dead captain on the virtual "Wall" and Dave's younger brother, Tom, discovered them and sent them on to me.

"I knew about you," Dick said. "I always wondered what happened to you. Dave showed us your picture. He was discreet about his personal life and didn't speak much about it, but he was proud of you."

At reunions I've attended since my first in 2006, the men of Alpha Company have recounted story after story of life alongside Dave in Vietnam. When they returned to civilian life they said they tried to quietly melt into their communities. They stayed mute about their experiences for years in spite of the flashbacks and nightmares. It wasn't a war to be associated with. They were told not to wear their uniforms when they traveled from their re-entry port in the United States to their hometowns. In spite of their wearing civilian clothes, some were still recognized as returning soldiers.

"I don't know how they guessed we were just back from Vietnam, "said Joe, describing his arrival at San Francisco Airport in 1969. "These two guys took after us and taunted us asking how many Viet Cong we'd killed. We didn't say a word. It was scary."

Others who wore their uniforms home saw onlookers turn away and parents pulling their children close as if to protect them when they walked by.

No previous war in our history evoked so much publically expressed opposition. The stories told by these young men returning from Vietnam is echoed in Michael A. Bellesiles' *A People's History of the U.S. Military: Ordinary Soldiers Reflect on Their Experience of War, from the American Revolution to Afghanistan*:

"When the soldiers came home from Vietnam, they did not find a warm welcome, but generally encountered a willed indifference if not open hostility, as most Americans did not want to hear about what was clearly a defeat for the United States. The psychological impact of the Vietnam War on those who served exceeded that of any previous American war, as thousands of veterans suffered from what was slowly being diagnosed as post-traumatic stress disorder. These veterans did not find the same

government support that had been granted the GIs after World War II. Not only did they not receive the full benefits of the GI Bill, they also found the Veterans Administration hospitals suffering from budget cuts and poor management. Those who served in Vietnam would continue to pay the price for many years to come."

It's not surprising how long it took for stories and first-person accounts of the Vietnam War to come forth for both soldiers and surviving family members. As I re-examine this stained and grainy photograph, a picture of

Vietnam 1969

a man appreciated and revered by so many, I feel the mystery of how I met and married someone almost of a different culture. I went from a family in which adults spoke daily against war, to life on a military base as the wife of an army officer. The tragic ending is mixed with the transformative experience of having known and loved him. As terrible as it was to lose him, I don't regret any aspect of our relationship. Nothing in my youth and extended family pointed the way to our extraordinary love story. Or did it?

PART TWO
THE POWER OF MEMORY

Breed is stronger than pasture
—George Eliot, *The Mill on the Floss* (1860)

The roots of pacifism in my family bubbled up from our ancestors who were Rogerene Quakers—those free-spirited people who opposed organized religion, starting in the eighteenth century, and were persecuted by the New England Congregationalists. Our branch of Quakers, followers of John Rogers, were tarred and feathered for refusing to participate in the church services mandated by the Congregational Church. My mother spoke often about the Rogerenes with pride to anyone in listening distance. It was the vocal backdrop to my playtime growing up as I glued shells on cigar boxes or sewed doll clothes.

Our house was busy and chaotic, and somewhat resembled a MASH unit with all the paraphernalia related to the nursing homes my family operated; sheets, bandages, gallon jugs of disinfectants and medications, towels, basins, crutches, canes, walkers and wheelchairs were always within reach. My mother wanted me to be a doctor. As a nurse, she saw physicians as possessors of power, prestige and a steady income. She worked hard and thought I should go right to the top of the health care ladder.

Our living room was lined with bookcases stuffed with medical textbooks from the days of her nurses' training. When I felt the need to be titillated or shocked I could pull down *Diseases of the Human Eye* or *Obstetrics and Childbirth* from a shelf. The practice of medicine seemed violent to me as I pored over pictures of abdominal surgery techniques and Caesarean births. But, these pages were also resting places for pressed flowers put there by my mother and grandmother; I might find flat, papery faded violets or an oval of browned carnation surrounded by the pink ribbons of an ancient corsage preserved against a depiction of treatment for a bi-lateral hernia.

This juxtaposition of romance and reality led me to think that medical illustration might be close enough to the action and perhaps an acceptable compromise to my mother's aspirations for my future. The thought of touching wounds or handling blood-soaked bandages horrified me. I preferred copying pictures of hands, ears and feet from the pictures of more intact human specimens. But, at age eighteen, before I was launched in any particular direction in a profession, I fell in love with a man destined for war by his chosen profession in the military.

When Dave was killed, it was not my first close-up experience with death. Besides witnessing the death of my youngest brother, I had glimpsed the shrouded bodies of patients carried from the nursing home my family owned even if the deed was always done with great discretion. The doors of the other resident rooms were closed and children and visitors were rounded up and herded to a place out of view.

But, losing Dave was my first brush with *war*—in which courage, ethics, smartness, physical health, youth and faith have nothing to do with survival.

———∞∞∞———

The family—that dear octopus from whose tentacles we never quite escape, nor, in our inmost hearts, ever quite wish to.
—Dodie Smith, *Dear Octopus* (1938)

How do we survive these up-close experiences with death? Where did the seeds of my survival notions come from? Perhaps from the stories I heard in childhood; oft repeated stories about our relatives, about personified animals who behaved like people (especially in the tales of Thornton Burgess), and people who behaved like beasts (relatives included). Gruffy Bear, Reddy Fox and Peter Rabbit were as present in my life as Sleeping Beauty, Pinocchio, and my great uncle Tom who sold homemade chocolate ice cream from a barge in 1895 to other family members attending a Peace Meeting next to the Mystic River. Stories flowed in a constant stream; as present as cooking, eating and teeth brushing.

Family stories held a higher status than the "facts" we learned in school. Tales abounded about our relatives who sold everything they owned to "go out west," or those who became missionaries in Africa, or sailed on whaling ships or survived shipwrecks. I didn't see much of the world outside our small town in Connecticut when I was growing up but I heard about it.

In *The Healing Power of Stories*, Daniel Taylor describes stories as vessels for carrying meaning. He says the stories we grow up with tell us what we can do in the world and whether or not we have choices. Family tales told in my childhood usually had a dramatic, sometimes incomprehensible, rising action. My grandmother might say, "one minute Uncle Joel was calm and sweet, and the next minute he was so angry he was smashing all the windows in the house with a hammer." But they would usually end in a whirl of coherence and redemption; someone stopped him, calmed him, and usually prayed with him, creating almost a moment of transcendence (even though my grandmother would usually add a caveat that it was wise to be careful around people like Uncle Joel).

They were stories of hard luck, survival, and adventure involving whales, wars, cruelty, scary forests and eccentric farmers. There was little romance. The dominant theme was overcoming obstacles. Both at home and in Sunday school, stories were imbued with catastrophic events in which characters had the will to persevere because there was an imagined end affected by choices. In the words of Taylor, "If I can imagine nothing, I can do nothing." Imagination leads the way to coherence.

One of the painful aspects of the Vietnam era was the incongruence of story that spiraled on during and long after the war. Even though most who served in the war were drafted, they became objects of derision when they returned because they had served in the *wrong war*. The reception some received negated their personal stories of heroism and survival and created a gap between them and the larger community. Meaning and coherence is created by connection with a larger story: the collective consciousness. Otherwise the personal story can remain an isolated episode of pain even if many people are living the same story simultaneously.

I did not meet another Vietnam widow until 1999, thirty years after Dave's death, when I met filmmaker Barbara Sonneborn, at a writing conference. Her film *Regret to Inform*, nominated for an Academy Award, describes her experience of going to Vietnam to find the place where her husband was killed and interviewing and sharing stories with both American and Vietnamese widows. She became a filmmaker in order to find congruence through the storytelling process and her effort created a vivid testament to the legacy of war. She discovered, in her quest, that she needed to go to the last place her love had existed on earth. She eventually went to Vietnam and found the spot where he had died.

Recovery after living through war or the loss of a loved one becomes a quest, but at the starting point we don't know the true goal of the quest. It is discovered during the journey. I didn't know that I would dig up the buried letters when I started to write this story. Action reveals the need within. The act of writing, thinking, revising, speaking about Dave, and speaking about myself to describe my story, revealed to me who I had been and how I was transformed by his death. I learned that living itself is an act of faith. We create and discover the meaning of life through our stories. But the stories have to be unearthed, contemplated and considered with compassion.

There were also sacred stories from my Sunday school days that shaped my notions about survival and choices. Stories about problem solving, magic, serendipity and perseverance like Daniel in the lion's den, Jesus and the multiplication of loaves and fishes, Moses in the bulrushes, and Mary on the donkey headed to Bethlehem.

Growing up in rural Connecticut in the 1950s, I attended a fundamentalist church with my father in Quakertown, an area in Ledyard. Sometimes going to church in my hat, gloves and best dress was a bit like going to the circus. The main event of every worship service was music and lots of "praising" as people stood up spontaneously to say, "praise the Lord" and "amen." There was a piano on either side at the front of the church and, behind the lectern, on a raised platform like a stage, an orchestra of shiny gold trumpets and trombones, along with clarinets, violins, flutes, accordions—whatever instrument anyone could play. Every Sunday morning was a jam session of old hymns.

There was no sermon. Brother Fred nodded with closed

eyes behind the pulpit causing me to wonder how anyone could sleep sitting directly in front of the music-makers. Members of the congregation would mumble the names of the sick and needy during the praising periods and ask for blessings. Some people, overtaken by the Holy Spirit, rolled on the floor in the aisle while speaking in tongues, an odd language over which the speaker supposedly has no control. For me, it seemed like a curious explosion of emotion in these adults who were otherwise meek and shy. Kids didn't "know" this language, but grown-ups acquired the ability with a direct transmission from God and apparently felt better afterwards. When they recovered and climbed back into their pew, they would be smiling and perspiring. I'm not sure what anyone expected, but they seemed happily exhausted as if they'd run a marathon. Perhaps this made up for the forbidden dancing, smoking, movies and television. My father sang fervently at these services, but never participated in the more emotional physical prostration and tongue-speaking, fainting and praising. I didn't understand my father's restraint but I appreciated it—and we had a black and white TV at home.

As a teenager I moved on to the Methodist Church because they had a musical summer camp and a youth group where we danced the limbo on Sunday evenings after our teen service. This church offered an intermediate step on my journey to a larger world of ideas. Chester, the minister, was a storyteller. His face resembled that of Mister Bluster, the puppet from the *Howdy Doody Show*, with sagging cheeks that made his chin appear to move separately up and down when he spoke.

One story concerned a man who was found dead on the desert. Chester lowered his voice to a whisper as he described the body discovered within yards of a lush oasis where the man almost reached shade and water, if only he wasn't carrying excess baggage. In spite of intense heat, he wore a raincoat and galoshes and hugged a heavy suitcase containing the long braided leather whip by which he had been thrashed, legal briefs from an old lawsuit, and thick packets of letters tied with twine. Chester liked to remind us that we choose our burdens. His stories resonated with my need to be free—of something—even at the tender age of fifteen.

By the time I was able to string words into sentences as a small child and ask my father to 'tell me a story,' Dave was already a world traveler by age five. His father was an Army Colonel and among the first group of American military to enter Japan at the beginning of the occupation after World War II. The family had joined him there in 1947. Dave said that his parents loved military life, even the frequent moving. Much of the time they moved together, except during the war, and felt lucky to enjoy so many different cultures. From Japan they would go on to Germany and Pakistan.

I would experience such places only in stories and wait for visitors to arrive at our house from exotic places. People like Cousin Clara.

Clara was a skyscraper of a woman. As I leaned my head back at age five or six to see up to her face beneath her felt hat, she seemed impossibly tall. It could have been the way she strode up to me each time like a politician on the campaign trail and reached down to give my hand a brusque shake: "Do you remember me, child? I'm your cousin Clara …fifth cousin once removed."

Dr. Clara McGuigen was one of the first women to graduate from Philadelphia College of Medicine. Perhaps Clara was the person my mother was thinking of when she decided that I should be a doctor. She eventually became medical director of the Mystic Oral School for the Deaf until she retired in the early 1950s. Whenever she returned to Mystic she visited the school first, and then came to our house to reveal her latest findings in the reconstruction of the family line and history, and to share stories with my mother and grandmother. All three prided themselves on remembering. Some stories were embellished and turned this way or that to suit them or to fit the characters whom the stories were about, but genealogical data about the family approached accuracy by necessity because, as Gram said, "One was either born or not born."

Clara arrived at our house periodically at her own whim, about every three months, always wearing a long wool coat regardless of the season, to check her latest data collections with my grandmother and have a meal with us. She usually brought a deaf child with her—not the same one each time. They were always boys.

I learned that deaf children are not silent or quiet, especially if they read lips. The children who came with Clara were current students at the Oral School. The school sat on an important limb in the scaffolding of the family tree because it had been started by another relative, ancestor Jonathan Whipple, in the nineteenth century when he discovered that his infant son was deaf. Jonathan devised a method of reading lips for young children and news of his success spread rapidly across the country. Eventually he organized a boarding school and boys and girls with hearing impairments arrived in droves to learn lip reading and oral expression.

With their varying levels of hearing sensation, the children Clara brought to our house often spoke—or made sounds— in loud, wild tones. I became accustomed to this vocal music because my job was to entertain and speak with the visiting child while my grandmother talked to Clara about the latest discoveries in her genealogical quest.

Clara always arrived in her own automobile, a blue 1949 Dodge. My older brother, Bob, a lover of anything with wheels, was usually the first to see the car enter the driveway.

"Clara's here!" he shouted with eyes wide at the window. "She's parking the car! Just look at that *car!*" We stood with our noses to the glass straining to see. Bob was painfully shy and would disappear when it was time for introductions. He lurked in the yard hiding behind bushes until everyone was in the house after which he emerged to spend the rest of the afternoon examining the head and tail lights, touching the glimmering silver bumpers, running his hands over the curves of metal. I brimmed with curiosity about the new kid.

"They need to get out in public and communicate especially with children who *can* hear," Clara said about the child in tow.

While my brother and I scrutinized Clara's parking of the car from the window, she often appeared to give some last minute instructions to her passenger with her hands flitting up and around her face. She had campaigned against sign language as the single mode of communication for the deaf. "They've got to read lips if they're going to communicate with everyone," she said. She even battled State lawmakers when they wanted to make sign language the official education method for the deaf throughout Connecticut. But my grandmother was convinced that Clara used to sign when she had to. Clara was held up among all the women in the family as very clever and advanced.

"She knows what she wants and she gets it," said Gram. "She slept on the steps of Buckingham Palace and ate pork and beans out of a can just to see Elizabeth II leave for the Coronation." This story lingered for years in our house without benefit of fact-checking.

Eventually, they would get out of the car and Clara would lead the child by the hand over the bluestone walkway between the driveway and the house. I was at the door ready to greet my new charge. Clara walked right up and loomed over me, as usual.

"Ruth, this is Jimmy and be sure that he can see your lips when you speak to him," she said. I nodded and smiled to the boy who was about my size and took him away by the hand to the kitchen or living room, curious to attempt communication. Sometimes we joined my brother outside to look at Clara's car, but mostly I remember wandering around the house and the yard looking for things to do.

Jimmy pointed at things and laughed with a howling, hooting sound. He craned his neck and concentrated on my face when I spoke. I exaggerated words with my lips, trying to be understood. Other kids on other visits would pull me by the shoulder to turn my face to them when they spoke. Sometimes Clara asked me to play my violin and she would place the boy's hand on the satiny wood body of the instrument as I drew the bow across the strings. He would grin and raise his eyebrows as I launched into the "Carnival of Venice" or "Beautiful Dreamer," unlike my brother whose face scrunched up in pain when I played.

"He can't hear it but he can feel it!" said Clara, as Jimmy's shoulders rose, his eyes rolled up and his smile broadened with my squeakiest tones.

I was curious about the murmurings between Clara and my grandmother. Sometimes I positioned myself at the bookcase behind Gram's chair where I silently pulled out books, one after the other, to show the boy while trying to catch the conversation between the two.

They sat side by side in armchairs and talked with lots of head nodding and occasional bursts like, "my goodness! You don't say!" Clara would eventually open a large black satchel like a doctor's bag and reach in to pull out bits of paper and notebooks with lists of names and sketches of circles connected by lines. These were her maps of the ancestors and descendents in the family. It was Clara who explained how my parents descended from two brothers—Noah and Jabez Whipple—and were therefore fifth cousins. She and my grandmother were fourth cousins in the Noah Whipple line. Noah had thirty-two children with the aid of four wives, so Clara had her work cut out for her tracking down all those descendents.

I discerned from these periodic meetings that my grandmother also *knew* things. She possessed knowledge. She remembered things. As I grew up in the presence of her prodigious memory, I assumed that memories were somehow secure and would always be accessible. Gram was a vault of information—a raconteur of reminiscence. She moved slowly without wasting a single motion from her chair to the stove to the table but her mind was always out in front nimbly fashioning a new familial connection from Clara's research linking one story with another. Even if I didn't understand, it sounded interesting. Our family seemed like the spores of mushrooms, blown by the winds of chance, fanning out to fertile opportunities and taking root further and further beyond the woods behind our house. Clara was our official mycologist.

"So … that's how Big Wilma came into the picture. Wilma was adopted by the Coates family when her parents died in the flu epidemic of 1918 and Albert was working on the milk run with her uncle Ernie. Albert got Wilma into trouble and they had Little Wilma," said Gram, as she passed the plate of molasses cookies to Clara.

Hours later, when my mother came home from the nursing home in front of our house, the family business, Gram would repeat everything. She would describe all the latest family connections that Clara had uncovered. As I listened to the repetition, I realized that she rendered an even more keyed up version of connections between people and distant places. The stories were re-fingered, re-remembered, perhaps a bit re-touched.

"Clara got out to Waukesha, Wisconsin, last month and tracked down those Whipples who went out to attend Bible Training School in 1926. They stayed out there, for a time. Came back poor as church mice. You remember—that's where Muriel got the smallpox as a baby. Almost blinded her," said Gram.

This would lead to another story and on and on.

After years of pushing away certain memories, I never thought I would feel an imperative *to remember*. I avoided thoughts of my brief life with Dave from our initial meeting on a blind date until his death four years later. I remember how I accomplished almost total repression. I would avoid speaking about that time and if an image came to mind of the two of us doing something enjoyable together—laughing at a joke, eating with friends in a restaurant, spending hours in bed on our honeymoon, organizing an apartment together after another move—I would block the image and try to think of something else. Silence was a way to survive. When I returned to college after his death and moved into a Boston commune in the early seventies, it was not an atmosphere in which to speak about anything related to the Vietnam War. The topic was so repressed that I never knew what had been the experience of my housemates at that time with the war—their deferments, lottery numbers or opinions.

It was painful to remember Dave's bright blue eyes and his quirky blend of interests: rock climbing, sewing his own camping gear, shopping for household appliances, poetry, photography, music, diving. His twenty-five years on earth had been crammed with interests and activities—and fun.

I became skilled at selective memory. Some scenes persisted, like the first time we met, as if they had been burned into place. But without the restorative process of rumination and reflection the rest was locked out. Or so I thought.

People who study memory say that what happened to us in the past determines what we understand about our daily encounters in life today. Memories are there somewhere in our body as records of *how we experienced events*, not replicas of the events themselves. Retrieving memories, when the motivation to remember finally arrives, is more important than we imagine; it is essential for an understanding of history—ours and our historical time. A memory can be off kilter or not quite accurate, but it still forms the foundation for our most strongly-held beliefs.

I also think that my experience of Dave's death occurred at an age when remembering did not hold the same value that memories have for me today. To worry about forgetting seemed irrelevant back in 1969. How could I forget? The memory of him felt cemented in my soul. I focused on staying in motion to survive. I had to lean into activities in order to want to continue. Before his death, all my dreams and aspirations were connected with his. I was a novice and he was an expert. His goals were more formed and vivid than mine. I was infused with his confidence and his world of camping, ice climbing and exercise as well as his love of Danish teak furniture, music and writing. He was good at everything he tried. Without him, the world felt common and vacant. I couldn't dwell on him without meeting his absence. And there was no way to tell the story without bringing up the war that no one wanted to talk about—especially me.

The burial of his letters accomplished a separation from painful reminders. I thought I wouldn't need them because every day he was in my sunrise and sunset. Each time I saw something he would like, it was a stab to my heart, unless I pretended I *was* him. Now I loved *for him* the wildness of mountains, glaciers, camping in snow and rock climbing. I had lost my source of ado-ration and desire. The only solution was to keep moving with him on my shoulder.

Psychologists say that this lack of ability or desire to dif-ferentiate and accept the intolerable state of being bereft of the other is a normal condition of grief.

It's good to know that something was normal.

The Vietnam War cut a swath of confusion through the 1960s and 70s followed by a cloak of silence. Returning veterans felt alienated from both the war and from civilian soci-ety. It was difficult to know, even years later, with whom the experience could be shared. A member of Dave's unit who had worked with him every day for months as his track driver in Vietnam, wrote to me in 2007 for the first time:

"I have meant to contact the Captain's family since 1973. Initially, I didn't have the courage because I felt such a strong loss of a person who was my hero. How could anything I did make it easier for the family? As time passed, I didn't want to intrude and rekindle bad memories. Eventually, my past seemed to have slipped into a closet... It is now about 38 years later and I have an opportunity to thank the Crocker Family ...for all that the Captain meant to me. He is truly my hero, but more importantly [he] was my friend. I wish I could tell him what he meant to me. I look in the mirror and see an old guy looking back at me; however, my mind is still like I was nineteen years old. I see the pictures of us in an old album and ...the fallen friends are ageless and frozen in time just like my memories."

I was grateful when I finally met Phil, the writer of the words above, on my first trip to the Vietnam Memorial in 2008. His memories and those of others created for me a new history for Dave. Through their descriptions and stories, I saw Dave living his last, intense six months on earth.

We never imagine that we will forget the details of powerful moments in our life, but there is a translucent skin that forms over some memories. I'm sure it's essential for our survival. But when it became imperative to remember more clearly, Cousin Clara and my grandmother stepped forward from the past and became my mentors in memory excavation. They had been like pearl divers, exhilarated by the challenge and delighted by their finds.

Conjuring my grandmother who taught me to read as she braided my hair every morning, and remembering her wisdom and superstitions, her toughness and lack of sentimentality, helped to thaw the icebergs in my history. Regardless of the accuracy of her stories and sentiments, she delighted in remembering and had a lot to say about everything past, present and future. Her efforts to console me about Dave's death up until her death in 1972 were laced with loving, hard-nosed pragmatism. She was not afraid to speak out and she didn't use euphemisms. About war she would say: "...and don't think you're going to survive because you're smart. It's just damn luck. Remember that."

This was oddly comforting to me, even after Dave's death. He *was* smart. He wasn't reckless. He was in the wrong place at the wrong time in a wrong war.

I remember the back and forth between Clara and Gram as they explored one clue after another in their quest to piece together the family history. Even the tableau of the two of them speaking with their heads close together inspires me to think that I can recover—or unwrap—memories. I believe that my body remembers even if my brain lags behind. An action, a movement is often connected to a thought if I'm paying attention. The smell of wet wool revives my memory of Clara's rough handshake and her long coat. The sound of a tennis racket socking against a ball and the impact that runs up my forearm can bring back a lightning flash image of Dave lobbing back a serve with precision. I'm grateful now for the desire to remember, without the feeling that I am broken, and the sense that I am whole.

Writing is finally the best conjurer of all. Thoughts bubble up and I wonder, "...is this how I felt? Can I smell the wood smoke from the campfire? What was the sound of the zipper on the door of our tent?"

Clara and my grandmother generated energy when they shared memories. Their voices brightened, their hands flashed about their faces and fluttered down to Clara's notes. Clara eventually wrote the definitive book about the Whipple family history and genealogy: *The Antecedents and Descendants of Noah Whipple of the Rogerene Community at Quakertown, Connecticut.* She went all the way to Japan to have it published in the early 1950s. Coincidentally, she probably arrived in Tokyo not long after the Crocker family had left Japan for their next duty station.

My grandmother had loads of advice for me, "If you want to remember something, use your head. If you want to do something, get off your dime and do it ... don't try to *be* something because you already *are* something ... practice your violin ... people who *are* something can play a musical instrument."

Out of mercy, I won't play my violin, but I am intent on remembering.

PART THREE
DOWN TO THE ROOTS

Adaptable as human beings are and have to be,
I sometimes sympathize with the chameleon who had
a nervous breakdown on a patchwork quilt.

—John Stephen Strange, *Unquiet Grave* (1949)

For all the talk against war in my family, I had the impression that we lived perilously close to the edge of violence and extreme behavior most of the time. I remember those stories repeated again and again about Uncle Joel smashing all the windows in his house with a hammer in a fit of rage until I thought I could hear the breaking glass and visualize the flying hammerhead. What about our peaceful forbears, the Rogerene Quakers, on which our pacifism was based and who set the precedent for Conscientious Objection in our family? Stories abounded about their legacy as abolitionists, free thinkers and their openness to allowing women to speak in Quaker meetings even as early as the eighteenth century. Was our branch of the family on a different tack?

In 1904, Anna B. Williams published an account of the history of the Rogerenes, a religious sect founded by John Rogers in

1720 in Southeastern Connecticut. A century later, in 1860, our local newspaper the *New London Day* (still in circulation today), published an article saying that "The Rogerenes despised the authority of law." Williams used letters responding to this article and other historical material to establish who these dissenters were who had been portrayed to their own and succeeding times as *brainless enthusiasts.*

Williams' account describes them as consistent Christians with a religious practice depending not upon observance of rituals or of days, but upon love to God and neighbor. They maintained that "civil government had no right to dictate in matters of religion... The divine commands regarding religion as set forth in the New Testament they would strictly obey, but they would, 'for conscience's sake,' obey no command of men in this regard."

They stood for uniform peace and encouraged their followers to forgive their enemies and return good for evil. By the end of the nineteenth century, the remainders in the group had moved to an area about two-miles square in the southeastern part of the present town of Ledyard. By this time the merciless intolerance that had brought this sect into existence was finished. They built a meeting house and a school and partially isolated themselves from the rest of society—at least in regard to their belief in disavowing material trappings of society and continued rejection of the old laws of force and retaliation. Both of my parents were born at home in this region.

This was Quakertown, the first church that I knew as a child, where I attended services with my father. The stories of the peaceful rebellion of this group against authority reaching back for two hundred years was probably the inspiration for my version of "civil disobedience" when I buried the letters instead of Dave.

Life was not all peace and love at our house, though, in the 1950s. Stories of violence during my father's childhood came back in longer and longer sequences over the course of my childhood, especially after I stopped being dumbstruck by them and started asking questions. Stories like my father's recollection of the day he decided he had to do something to stop his deranged stepfather from abusing him and the rest of the family. Bits and pieces of my father's life collected like beach glass over the years until they coalesced into a collage that seemed to define him; an amalgamation of deep spiritual faith and the residues of tragedy, poverty and family violence.

During one telling he said: "I was ten years old and up in a tree outside the front door of our house. My stepfather and Joe Prosser were talking and laughing and then I heard him say that he had figured out how he was going to 'eliminate' me. After they left I climbed down and got my hunting rifle and went back up that tree. I was going to wait for him and kill him first."

I think this was originally an overheard story, one that I heard from behind a door or at a table where adults thought that kids weren't listening or wouldn't understand; a fragment that I used to explain my father's temper outbursts when I was growing up. I was shocked to think that my father believed that someone wanted to kill him. Perhaps I thought that living through that experience explained his mood swings; his silence in one moment and sudden storming out of the house in a rage, or his fists flying and one of us kids a human rope stretched between him and Gram, while she yelled, "Don't touch that child!"

People talked about each other. One family member often told a story to explain another's behavior. Perhaps it was a symptom of the fuzzy boundaries between people, but I'm sure it helped me survive or gave perspective on some of the scary behavior swarming around. I might have overheard Great Aunt Mary, as she sat crocheting with my grandmother, explaining the roots of my father's violent behavior, telling and re-telling the tragic story of the death of dad's biological father in a hit-and-run automobile accident in 1923 and then his mother's marriage to this man who people thought was a savior but turned out to be a demon.

"Treated terrible, he was, him and all the kids in the family by that maniac stepfather. They'd be out in the snow in their bare feet looking for food. I used to take them in," Aunt Mary said as fine cotton thread flew into intricate patterns between her fingers.

One cousin described how the stepfather attempted to poison the whole family with arsenic in a stew and how another time he tried to drag his three daughters into a pile of burning brush. Ten years after that incident, my father finally orchestrated his arrest and institutionalization in a local mental hospital. After that, my father became the hero in the story and was called "the Prince" by his siblings.

The whole epic with the hunting rifle was finally told from beginning to end in 1980 when I was thirty-four and my father was paralyzed from the chest down after an accident. Four months earlier he had fallen three stories off the roof of a house he was building. He was sixty-one and would die within the year from his injuries.

"Tell me again about your stepfather and the gun," I said. It seemed important to get this story straight after all these years. We were eye-to-eye, me on the couch and him in a wheelchair. How I wished that he could jump up and rant and rave again.

He held his arms tight against his body, clasped his hands in his lap and looked down at the floor as he told me that he had sat all day in a tree with that rifle, waiting.

"It gave me time to think, sitting up there," he said. "And

finally I decided that if I pulled the trigger, it would determine my life from that point on. I'd never be free. If I killed him my life would be set in stone. I'd be a murderer. I'd be as bad as he was. It would be the end of any potential I had."

The notion that hope and belief in the future was stronger than fear and revenge in the moment sounded familiar. Here was tangible evidence of the theme of resilience that flowed like an underground river in our chaotic family. There was an echo, too, of those peace-seeking ancestors who desired to meet evil with goodness.

Aspects of my life seemed not lived by me first hand but told to me—reiterated by relatives, acquaintances and books. Perhaps my daily life did not seem as riveting to me as everything that happened to other people. Maybe I heard over and over, *this is nothing, much worse things happen to other people.* When Dave died, I could not think of anything worse. This disaster could not be measured against anything with any tool in my possession when I was twenty-three, but burying the letters and carrying his ashes to the Eiger served me for many tragedies to follow. I knew that I could survive almost anything as long as I could imagine what I needed to do.

We find what we search for—
or, if we don't find it, we become it.

—Jessamyn West, *Love is Not What You Think* (1959)

I would like to put a stethoscope to the walls of my parents' house on Main Street in Old Mystic, Connecticut, tuning in to 1955, and listen to the buzz and hum of my family. I know we practiced a peculiar kind of isolationism—possibly remnants of the Quakertown sect. That could account for some of my innocence and naiveté about the outside world. My brothers and I usually walked home from elementary school for lunch but when some school function required us to bring a bag lunch, I couldn't enter the concept. I would lie to the teacher and the other kids and say I wasn't hungry that day. It was as if I didn't want to share that aspect of my home life, even if we ate perfectly good food at home. Or perhaps we didn't have paper bags or make sandwiches. Or maybe, even at age eight or nine, I wanted to hide my private life.

Socializing with kids outside of school was discouraged. My mother said that we kids didn't *need* friends. Other kids could be a *bad influence*, according to her. The Averys were loud-speaking Methodists, the Polinskis were Polish Catholics, the McGoogins had some ambiguity about who was the uncle and who was the father of five kids in their house, and the Sebastians had very dark skin; all these were subjects of speculation among adults in our house. My parents would not have required us to attend school except that it was the age of lurking truant officers and my parents had no time for home schooling. "Schools are just institutions," my mother said. This was reassurance because school intimidated me with its order, rules and smart kids with lacy anklet socks and Buster Brown shoes. It felt better to pretend that school wasn't that important.

"Just get through it so you can go to college," my mother said.

A passing missionary might accuse us of ancestor worship, a belief in family so strong that it bordered on paganism. God is good, but family is best. *Family members must stick together and protect each other from the outside world at all costs* was probably cross-stitched onto a sampler and hung somewhere in the house.

I was the second child, and only daughter, of four children

born to Jacob Austin Whipple and Estella Elizabeth Ashcroft, aka Bob and Stella. The fact that any of us came into existence always seemed a kind of miracle because I often heard my mother say: "Why in the world would anyone want to go through pregnancy and childbirth—avoid it." She loved us once we were out of her womb, but not before. Her belief in the family lineage and the roots of our heritage bordered on obsession and perhaps she consented to the rigors of childbearing just to keep the world populated with the family name. In reality, though, there is no story: we just kept happening in her life. Birth control was hit or miss in those days long before the pill. Her campaign against childbirth did have some trickle-down effect, I was the only offspring to produce a grandchild.

They ain't no feelin' in the world like takin' on somebody wilted and near bout gone, and you do what you can, and then all a-sudden the pore thang starts to put out new growth and git well.

—Olive Ann Burns, *Cold Sassy Tree* (1984)

I grew up in a nursing home, our family business. Most people cringe at the thought of them—those sad, inhumane depots for the dilapidated old and sick. But my mother and her mother thrived on caring for the elderly and infirm. With her great business sense, Mom often said: "We'll never run out of old people." In the beginning, we even lived in the nursing home. My mother laughed about the temerity of the State Health Inspector who arrived so early one morning that he came up to their bedroom in the attic to wake her and my father.

My family began with the rest home model, taking in those folks without family, who couldn't take care of themselves or live alone, people with paralysis or incurable illnesses, and those who were salvaged from the poor farm or the State (mental) hospital—the crazy house as the locals called it. Besides old people, we were surrounded by animals. There were chickens and pigs for food, usually a dog of mixed heritage for protection and companionship, and, on one census report by my older brother, thirty-nine cats patrolling for rats, mice and snakes.

My mother didn't believe that the people who came to live in our nursing home should be separated from their pets especially if the creature was a cat. We were forever trying to find a hiding place for "John," Lucy Main's twenty-eight pound white angora cat, or "Alfonso," the yapping beagle, when the State Health Department made their surprise inspections.

It was not a lucrative business, nor was it exotic or sensational. It was endless, messy, poignant, sad, sometimes humorous and bittersweet. But it was guaranteed employment for a nurse like my mother who wanted to be self-employed. She was determined to succeed and handled the messiest, goriest emergency with calm skill—and she loved old, fragile and demented people. Possibly she liked them better than children but I've forgiven her for that.

My parents also owned a mobile home park near by—called a "trailer park" in the '50s because they were truly trailers, houses on wheels that moved. Now they're called manufactured homes and people don't haul them around the country. The park was dubbed "Whipple's Folly" by most people in the area because it was literally hewn from a mountain of stones left by a passing glacier during the ice age, dug into the side of a hill embedded with rocks that is one of the highest and steepest points in Mystic. Sixty years later, however, the park is still there, owned by my older brother. This is more than can be said for many other businesses in town that have come and gone—even without the benefit of wheels.

The trailer park was a breeding ground for another type of *story* in my early life. Stories about how people lived. Until I finally saw the interior of a mobile home, I imagined the people inside like hot dogs in a package lying close to each other, one upon another. My favorite trailer park experience as a child of ten was visiting the small store with groceries and a soda fountain that my parents kept for a few years as a convenience for the park residents. At the store I met a girl my age named Diana. She lived in a shiny, metallic green trailer which looked like a toy house on wheels. My mother was not enthusiastic about my desire to fraternize with trailer park children. "Why do you need to go there?" Mom asked, referring to Diana's trailer, as if I wanted to go to a nightclub.

Diana's mother made us grilled cheese and tomato sandwiches in an electric frying pan in their tiny, immaculate kitchen. Diana's father, like most of the men living in the park, was in the navy and stationed at the submarine base in Groton. Their family life was different from ours. Her father came home with a lunch box every afternoon and sat in a chair and read the paper. Her mother was always there when we came inside, dusting, vacuuming, adjusting scatter rugs on the tiny living room floor. They seemed to do the same things everyday. They spoke quietly and never argued. No one appeared to be even thinking about throwing or breaking something. I felt calm in their small metal house. *This must be how regular people live,* I thought.

During my last visit to Diana's mobile home, I gazed at the knick knacks, mostly small ceramic poodles, on the shelves above the tiny black and white TV in their miniaturized living room, and wondered if they would fall off and break when the trailer was hitched to their car and it jiggled and bumped down the road to another park across the country. At that time my family lived under the slant ceilings in the garret under the roof of the nursing home, a castle-sized, eighteenth century house built for a sea captain, where nothing moved, even in a hurricane when the wind ripped the shutters off the windows. Twenty-five nursing home patients lived in the two floors below us. The great ramble of endless bedrooms smelled of plaster dust, old clothes, the occasional soiled sheet, baking pies and boiled vegetable steam wafting up from the kitchen.

My father eventually built a separate house for us behind the nursing home but I continued to think that we had an endless family, that all of those old people in various stages of disrepair sitting or lying in room after room were somehow members of the family. Their lives were linked to ours like rescued pets. At mealtimes, as my brothers and I sat at a picnic table outside the back door, Mom told stories like that of Jennie Wolff who came to live with us because she had developed the habit of taking off her clothes in public places, or Ned Durfee who was so filthy when he arrived that, during his first bath, each time they thought they were getting down to skin color, it was just another set of long underwear (according to my mother). She laughed uproariously at this even though she had been one of the nurses up to her elbows in soapsuds trying to get down to his skin whereupon they discovered a nest of body lice in his navel. Ned's delousing procedure would be dinner table conversation for the next meal.

Nature alone cures…What nursing has to do…is to put the
patient in the best condition for nature to act upon him.

—Florence Nightingale, *Notes on Nursing* (1859)

Nothing was more natural to my mother than being a nurse. Her mother had trained as a licensed practical nurse in the 1920s and gone out to provide care in people's homes when they were sick, injured or giving birth. My mother tagged along and by the time she was eight years old, she "sat" with people confined to their bed. Few people could pay in cash in the 1930s and early 40s, and much of my grandmother's service was paid on the barter system. Eggs, chickens and vegetables swapped for time and talent. One elderly woman in Mystic had money, though, and she offered to pay my mother's tuition at Rhode Island Hospital School of Nursing affiliated with Brown University if Stella agreed to go and become a registered nurse.

The beginning of the nursing home dynasty was related to that story. One weekend in 1940 my mother came home on furlough from nursing school and there was an elderly person in her bed. Gram had brought all her patients into her home while my grandfather recuperated from a leg amputation. They renamed their house on the hill overlooking Mystic, Pleasant View Home, and from that point those who needed care came to them.

Both my grandmother and my mother died as patients in the last iteration of the business, a 100-bed skilled nursing facility rebuilt in 1967 close to the site of the original *Pleasant View*. In 2006, when I finally sold the business "lock, stock and barrel" as my grandmother would have said, we were one of the last family-owned-and-operated stand-alone skilled nursing facilities in Connecticut. The rest had been swallowed by nationalized chains. Our family had been in the nursing home business for almost seventy years. It had evolved from a private home stuffed with beds to a small hospital with private rooms providing skilled long-term and post-operative care.

The oddest fact of all was that, although I was the only member of the family who did *not* want to be involved in the nursing home, and with no desire to be a doctor or a nurse, I ended up running the place during its final fifteen years. I had earned a master's degree in counseling and a PhD in nutrition, and had my own career with no idea that I would ever administer the nursing home. But, as a member of the family tag team, I finally caved in to a sense of dutiful fatalism and accepted the seat of honor as administrator.

I was not bad at nursing home administration, even though it was no pleasure to deal with the State Health Department bureaucracy. Decades of association with the health care environment had permeated my DNA. I had grown up surrounded by models of leadership—including Dave. To my surprise, I could manage the unwieldy staff of nurses, aides, housekeepers, launderers, cooks, kitchen aides, dishwashers, maintenance workers, recreation specialists, physical therapists, bookkeepers, doctors, psychologists, and consultants, some of whom had worked for my family their entire working lives. The building buzzed like a hive, two to three hundred people (including residents, staff and visiting family members) at every moment of the day and night with all their needs and wants, abilities and disabilities.

We were a fine, well-respected establishment right to the end. But daily life continued to remind me of scenes from the movie *The King of Hearts* at its best and worst moments. There was the occasional demented person escaping outside into a snow drift or a kitchen worker on drugs attacking the dishwashing machine with a butter knife or a nurse aide who needed to be rescued from her abusive boyfriend. I also had my mother in a bed down the hall as a patient with dementia for most of my tenure and that added an element of surrealism. Her twenty-five pound black angora cat, Madame Queen, lived with her there until the end.

Taking charge of the nursing home also facilitated my continued healing from the tragic deaths of Dave, my father and two of my brothers by demanding a broad sense of humor. I was living an old inherited story. I could hear my mother laughing long ago at absurdities rather than complaining. The memory and lessons of leaders before me in my family, Dave included, came to me as I grappled with managing people, emergencies, paperwork and the authoritarian bureaucrats of the Health Department. It's not so far from life in the military.

While I grew up in a small New England village, surrounded by elderly people and listening to my mother describe the cleaning and bandaging of bedsores, Dave had already lived in Japan with his family in the late 1940s. In the early 1950s, as an elementary school age child, he explored the forests in remote Wildflecken, Germany, where his father was the commanding officer.

Dave had his own brush with the medical world in 1960, five years before I met him. He was riding in a car that was hit broadside and he was thrown through a side window. The car flipped over and landed on him. Warned that he may not walk again, he recovered completely and entered West Point Military Academy two years later where he excelled in gymnastics, especially floor exercise.

My only reference for West Point was the film *The Long Gray Line* starring Tyrone Power and Maureen O'Hara from 1955 and a subsequent television series in the late 1950s. I thought it was a fictional place until my first date there with Dave in 1965.

Growing up in Old Mystic, with both parents and my grandmother working in the nursing homes and trailer park, my brothers and I roamed our territory, an area in easy view of the horizon on Long Island Sound and up-river from the larger town of Mystic which had several streets rather than just one. Mystic means "tidal water" in the Pequot Indian language, the place where salt and fresh water mingle. Old Mystic, wrested from the Pequots in 1654, was a simple, working-class village with one main street studded with mill houses and a few homes built before the Revolutionary War. Antique houses from the seventeenth century were not quaint, fashionable places to live in the fifties and sixties. People lived in them because they had to, or because their family had always lived there. The houses, many in need of paint, were built without insulation and often without indoor toilets. I remember hoping that I wouldn't have to go to the bathroom when we visited certain people without indoor plumbing. Outhouses were favorite resting places for black snakes laying in wait for large water rats. These muskrat-sized rats were common in the houses and basements up and down the river, unless you had a dog and a lot of cats.

Most of our neighbors on Main Street were Polish and many of them lived in nineteenth century mill houses. The Prakniak, Woycik, Robak and Volinsky children (there were lots of kids) all attended the Old Mystic School with us. Some of the women in town still worked at the Sirtex fabric dye mill next to the river across the street from our house. At the mill, they dyed cloth and dumped used dye into the river which flowed down past Mystic and into Long Island Sound. Most of the men who formerly worked at the mill had migrated to better paying jobs, especially at General Dynamics, or 'Electric Boat,' as it was called locally, building submarines. The weaving, dyeing, thread-making, silk, velvet and button mills throughout the northeast were disappearing and moving to the south but new jobs were plentiful in the northeast building jet engines and submarines for the growing military-industrial complex.

We had only to walk out our front door and cross the street to reach the tainted headwaters of the Mystic River. My brothers and I played daily in the muddy tributaries and nailed together bulky rafts to float on the multi-colored waters created by the discarded dye from the mill. Some days we navigated through floating potatoes, rotting cabbages and salad greens dumped in the river by a grocery store upstream. The building of the rafts was my favorite part. But once they were built there was peer pressure to get in the thing and see if it would float. I was secretly afraid of being washed down river and drowning. My mother and grandmother filled us with cautionary tales about the dangers of water, snakes, rabid dogs, and "bad" kids.

I kept a blue leather diary with a lock and key and tore out the pages upon which I had written too much about certain things. I wrote frequently about my father's displays of temper. I wondered how a person could get so angry so fast and then suddenly become quiet and somber. He erupted like a volcano over sometimes indiscernible events. I wrote that he was like a blast furnace who needed to keep his door closed. I was afraid of him but also riveted by his temper and by trying to understand *why* he behaved like an ogre. I felt embarrassed and sad when I later read my renditions of his displays of extreme and uncontrolled rage. I remember writing something like: "Daddy is angry about a broken water pipe in the nursing home. Daddy has taken a big hammer and smashed down the whole wall. People are trying to get out of his way. Now he's throwing pieces of the wall every

which way and yelling. People are running out of the room."
Compelled to record the event, perhaps to wrest control of it on
the page, I would write while hiding in a corner or under a table.

The stories about why he was the way he was didn't help
when I was in front of his anger. I was afraid for myself and
everyone around me. Writing was how I dealt with things that
were difficult or incomprehensible to me. But I never saved those
observations and stories. On better days, I tore out the grotesque
and scary passages.

I had some general thoughts about my father's temper
besides the psychological damage done to him by his stepfather.
One was that his life was full of uncontrolled crises: Something
was always breaking, or shutting down or blowing up, and he
had to fix everything. Nothing was permanent or stayed fixed
for very long. During the summer months there was a race to
build and fix and repair new buildings, old buildings, machines,
snow plows, furnaces. In the winter he was thawing frozen water
pipes, plowing snow and picking up nursing home staff who
couldn't get out of their driveways and get to work in a blizzard.

There were no snow days or holidays in the nursing home
business. We never closed. All of these details could push anyone over the brink. Violence and rage were understandable in
these situations. *Leave it to Beaver* had not yet established a norm
of the *ideal* family. And Mr. Cleaver worked in an office somewhere, not with his hands like my father, while Mrs. Cleaver
wore white cotton gloves rather than surgical gloves and cleaned
table tops rather than people's bottoms.

My father also had aspirations for higher education. I'm sure
this added to his frustration. He had left school at age twelve to
shoe horses during the Great Depression. Then during World
War II he took advantage of the opportunity to obtain his high
school diploma in the Navy. He read the Encyclopedia Britannica
at home every night and eventually enrolled in a local college in

the early 1950s when I was eight or nine where he took German, English, Art History and Music Appreciation. He still worked as much as before, performing all the maintenance of the trailer park and nursing homes, but now he would miraculously appear at times in a suit and hat and overcoat carrying a pile of books and notebooks. He was happy at school and never lost his temper (or so I'm told), and received nothing below an *A*- (or so I'm told). As a child, I remained a perpetual observer of my father. I watched for changes in attitude, mood and clothing; staying alert to what might happen next.

I met Dave when I was eighteen and his life, growing up as an Army brat, seemed the opposite of the chaos that I had grown up in. My first introduction to his family was at Fort Dix where they lived in officers' quarters filled with hand-painted Japanese screens, brass pitchers and plates bought in Pakistan, and candles and ceramics from Germany. Military home life appeared organized and precise—civilized even—without eruptions of violence and moody behavior among family members. Meals were convivial and pleasant with no talk of wounds or sickness.

His father, Colonel David R. Crocker, Sr., sat at the head of a dining table set with antique china and crystal at dinner each evening telling funny stories about the pranks played by cadets at West Point, like the replacing of long ceremonial saber blades with butter knives just before a military parade. We all laughed at the humiliation of the unlucky targeted cadet when swords were drawn with precise choreography. Dad Crocker was a master storyteller with a deep, resonant voice. I was amazed to be suddenly part of a calm, jovial family. *Perhaps they know something about peace*, I thought.

During that summer of 1965 when I met the Crocker family

for the first time, Dave was on a short leave between his third and fourth year at West Point. He had decided to bring me home to meet the family rather than take a trip he'd planned to visit Angel Falls in Venezuela. We were falling deeper and deeper in love and spent every evening after dinner in the intimacy of my car in some secluded spot.

Even though his father had graduated from West Point, Dave was not immediately selected when he applied. After high school, he entered the army for basic training at Fort Jackson and received his appointment as a result of the competitive Army Reserve examination and eventually attended the USMA Preparatory School at Fort Belvoir, Virginia. Dave had wanted to attend West Point since the age of ten, and when he was finally accepted in the summer of 1962, he wrote in one of his detailed weekly letters to his parents on July 3rd:

"We have been here only three days now. When we first arrived we were stupid, scared plebes; now we're just stupid plebes. Dad, you probably know exactly what we are doing—drill, clothing formations, lectures, showers ...things shouldn't have changed too much from the time you were here except that it may be easier now. The swearing in on the first day is quite impressive even though it is simple. It made me feel really proud. I've wanted to come here for seven years and now that I'm here, although I hesitate to say it for fear someone might see it, I already like this. Some of it seems a little silly, but it's all in the game."

West Point prep school had been a competitive, demanding experience with many dismissals as a result of the relentless weeding out of those less qualified academically and physically. Still, Dave took the risk of an emergency leave to go from Virginia to New York to be with his grandmother just before her death in February 1962—because the rest of the family was in Pakistan. It was the first time he had dealt with the death of a close family member, and I recognize the authenticity of his words, his desire to try to share an experience even if only through description of location and behavior, as he relates the scene to his parents, far away:

"On Tuesday I received a telegram from Aunt Marion about Nana. They gave me emergency leave and I arrived in New York at 1:30am. On Wednesday Nana and I talked as much as was possible, and I stayed at the hospital with her for a few hours. Thursday I stayed with her, but she was unable to talk. Friday morning I had to come back here. I don't quite know what to say about it all, but she is at peace now. I am leaving it to Aunt Marian to write more than I have, she will be able to explain so much better. Boppa [grandpa] seemed to take it as well as could be expected. I am afraid I am at a loss as to what else I should say."

Dave would go on to excel at West Point and share the details of his life with his family through frequent letters, even describing the personalities, hair styles and bodies of young women he met on dates. His friends described him as having an irrepressible will to succeed, a mischievous side, a ready willingness to help, and determination to make a bleak situation cheerful with an unselfish sharing of his talents for the good of the group. His description in the West Point yearbook of 1966, *The Howitzer,* said:

"Camping, scuba diving, mountain climbing, music, philosophy, thought, knowledge, athletics, hard-work—these are some of the things that help Dave live life to the fullest. Dave was always able to distinguish that which he valued and that which mattered not. He was a source of strength and encouragement for those of us not so fortunate. His consideration, understanding and respect for the rights of others make Dave a true friend."

In my junior year in high school in 1962, I was not even close to the launching pad that sent people like rockets to the galaxy of careers. The concept of future seemed like a place to which the mode of transportation, other than the shoe leather express, was nebulous. Like childbirth, I didn't know exactly what made it happen. I had no premonition of war and little knowledge of the world outside our New England province. At school, we sat on the floor in the corridors at the end of the school day and sang our rendition of Bob Dylan's new hit song "Don't Think Twice, It's All Right." Some of us would eventually imagine that a flower stuck in the barrel of a gun could stop a bullet—perhaps a war.

We were embroiled in an electrified age, brimming with stories about "us" and "them," differentiating ourselves from parents and adults but without knowing what was real or the truths of the historical time we lived in. We were hordes of kids jettisoned from the playgrounds and family rooms of the fifties, trained on stories of Dick, Jane, Spot and Puff, nourished by meatloaf and mashed potatoes, and propelled headlong into the sixties still lugging our Lincoln Logs and Revlon Dolls. We were naïve and emboldened just the same and eventually formed up in disarrayed clumps to be shot out of a cannon into the *happenings* of the seventies. Meanwhile, the bumpy landscape of the sixties was strewn with burgeoning war, assassinations, protests, and race riots.

Who was I in the midst of all this? Can I look back and visualize the scenic views and rest stops along my narrative path? I was a girl who grew up in a small New England town, in an entrepreneurial family, proud of its pacifism (family violence didn't count) *and* anchored to the land all the way back to the pilgrims and the Rogerene Quakers. How could I end up a war widow at age twenty-three in 1969 and never see it coming? That story was so hard to believe it seemed as if it happened to someone else, some third person. Each time I filled out a form afterward that asked for marital status—single, married, widowed—it was a jarring exercise to realize that all traces of Dave and the couple we had been for four years were gone except for our books, furniture, wedding presents and a buried casket of love letters.

PART FOUR
LAUNCHED INTO HISTORY

———∞———

The future is plump with promise.

—Maya Angelou, *All God's Children Need Traveling Shoes* (1986)

When I graduated from high school in 1964 with vague dreams of going to art school, dreams of doing *something* on my own, going *somewhere*, my parents discouraged the *going away* outside of their physical comfort zone, their territory.

"Go to this nice little community college, five minutes from home," they said.

So I did. And, in spite of the good intentions of my family to keep me close to home, I met Dave in my freshman year of college when he visited the area by chance. He would eventually invite me completely out of their protective grasp and put my story on an unimagined tack. Those monumental parental fears, that the child will be plunged into grief and unhappiness, are the unpreventable consequences, especially when a love story is part of the picture. The troubles of the historical time in which one lives are like the power of water to get in somehow and wreak havoc.

At Stonington High School, in the southeast corner of

Connecticut, and in close proximity to the Naval Submarine Base in Groton and General Dynamics (where they build submarines), Vietnam was a word, not even a place, wavering in the background. News about the "conflict" in Southeast Asia vacillated between the growing threat to the security of the West by the Communists and continuous reassurance to the American people that the U.S. military role would be limited to providing training and logistical support to South Vietnam.

Then there was the overthrow and assassination of South Vietnam's president Ngo Dinh Diem, followed soon after by President Kennedy's decision on October 2, 1963, to begin withdrawal of U.S. forces; and then, fifty days later, Kennedy's assassination on November 22nd.

I was sixteen in 1963 and the true north of my life was my academic resurrection. After my brother's death when I was fourteen, I suddenly had time for school and it became a distraction from my grief. I won first prize in the regional science fair, received the history prize and became art editor of the yearbook. I went from the bottom of the class to what I considered the top. The school guidance counselor, Miss Nineer, was still not impressed. She confided to me in her office that I was "...not college material and don't even think about it." Later high school reunions with my former classmates, some of whom went on to receive advanced degrees like me, revealed that this was her standard line to most students. I thought she had x-ray vision and could see the real me.

My mother's response was: "What's wrong with that woman?" Here was a blatant example of the *us* and *them* stories. Miss Nineer's evaluation helped to soften my aspiration to go away to school. My mother believed in me even if she rejected my choices, but deep down I was afraid that Miss Nineer was right; I might not make it in higher education. Finally, I had no problem being accepted into my parents' college choice for me.

Mitchell Junior College was the greatest social adventure I had known so far and only ten miles from home. I gave up my dream of art school, near or distant.

Each time I got behind the wheel of my car to drive to school I felt exhilarating freedom. My family became the home away from home for the new, homesick friends I made who lived on campus. I met Ilana, fresh from Israel, who described countries I'd never thought about. We're still close friends, fifty years later. My parents didn't monitor my life or perhaps they did, but it seemed easy to slip out to dances and parties. They were busy planning to build a new state-of-the-art nursing home. I came and went at home and felt like a college coed. Independent, at last. I kept an eye on my grandmother and her physical decline and occasionally provided her favorite foods on the "forbidden" list like her beloved fried whole belly clams.

I loved the teachers at Mitchell Junior College. They talked and lectured with enthusiasm. *Oxford University or Harvard couldn't be better than this*, I thought. College life sparkled with new ideas, interesting people and a fabulous library. Even the red beanie cap that freshmen wore pleased me. At least I was now part of a group outside my family. In high school one of my cousins from Quakertown was the school librarian and her eyebrows had lifted at every reading choice I made. It might have been *Cheaper by the Dozen, Nancy Drew* or Thomas Hardy. I never knew exactly what Cousin Connie considered acceptable reading material. When Connie was at the front desk, there were many books I didn't even have the courage to check out. I read *Tess of the D'Urbervilles* sitting in the cramped stacks out of her sight simply to avoid *the look* over her glasses. College offered anonymity and privacy. None of my relatives worked there as far as I knew.

I barely had what could be construed as a boyfriend in high school—just a few infatuations with low mileage and poor return. Even the Sadie Hawkins dance where girls could invite boys was a disappointing thud in my dating life. The one boy in my class who seemed cute, friendly and polite in the hallways of school became a terrified mute when we arrived at the fake barn setting in our red plaid and denim outfits. And when I did find someone else with a little more enthusiasm, I always halted progress at the passionate kissing stage. I carried my grandmother's obscure warnings about sex and the mysterious arrival of babies around in my head. I could hear her even if she was miles away.

The first kiss was planted by Joe Giavanni in the middle of a Halloween party at a neighbor's house when I was sixteen. Just before we got off the couch to dunk for apples, he turned and pecked me on the lips. I had anticipated this for years, but it was not the romantic, titillating moment described in *American Girl Magazine*. Most things took more time in those days, but Joe's kiss hit target with a quick *thwack*. I remember his Roman nose sailing away from my face afterwards at lightning speed in the direction of our host's mother who was chaperoning the party. There was little time to feel anything except his warm breath in my face for a moment, like a freight train flying by, and I knew there was no possibility for any future with Joe because of his last name. "Sounds like a foreigner," my grandmother said. But he did have the dubious honor of being *the one* in regard to the first kiss and I almost missed it. Joe never rose to fame in my household except as "that Italian." Romance, or even having a boyfriend approved of by the family firm, seemed a distant possibility.

Lyndon B. Johnson campaigned for the presidency during July of 1964 and some friends piled into my 1958 Chevy convertible with me to see him go by in a motorcade going to an event at General Dynamics. A handful of protestors with posters against the conflict in Vietnam were hustled away by the State Police before Johnson arrived. He would be handily re-elected after he made the claim: "We still seek no wider war." Little did we know that the path to war was being paved even as we squealed with excitement just to see him zip by in a limousine.

Howard Zinn describes in his book *A People's History of the United States*, that Johnson used a murky set of events in August 1964, set in the Gulf of Tonkin, to launch a full-scale attack on Vietnam. Zinn says that President Johnson and Secretary of Defense Robert McNamara told the American public that North Vietnamese torpedo boats launched two unprovoked attacks on American destroyers. The Gulf of Tonkin incident, which turned the deadly tide in Vietnam, was apparently a jumbled misinterpretation of information that was not agreed upon even by eyewitnesses.

McNamara offers in his memoir, *In Retrospect*, published in 1998, an almost concise statement to settle decades of controversy about how the conflict was magnified into a war. He says that the evidence of the crucial "second attack" in the Gulf of Tonkin was "not supportable," but that the Johnson administration used it to justify subsequent military actions and to create a pretext for Congress to authorize expanded force levels in Vietnam.

While McNamara does pass the blame to Johnson, and eventually Nixon, for the way they used their authority, McNamara's memoir is worth reading. He spins out a compelling narrative that reads like a ship's log describing—with chilling forthrightness—all the paths that coalesced into a dubious war. It leaves the reader mourning the way choices were made, resulting in more than 58,000 Americans killed during the war, more than

300,000 wounded or missing in action and countless others who suffered the effects of Agent Orange and PTSD afterwards. The estimates of Vietnamese war dead range from 2.1 million to 3.8 million.

Dave and I met on blind date at the U.S. Coast Guard Academy in New London, Connecticut, in March 1965, the same month that U.S. ground troops were beginning to move into Vietnam in droves. He was in New London on a cadet "exchange weekend" from West Point—the one weekend per year during which cadets from all the service academies—Annapolis, the Air Force Academy, the Coast Guard Academy and West Point—are sent voluntarily to visit and convene with those who they might otherwise only meet as rivals on the football field.

Part of this intercultural experience for the cadets was also the possibility of a date with a young lady from the area. This is where I entered the picture. I accepted an invitation to spend an afternoon and evening with a West Point cadet, but only as a big favor to a college friend.

"Please, you have to do this for me," Linda pleaded. "All you have to do is meet him. We'll go have a pizza. You don't have to spend that much time with him. We'll double-date, so you don't even have to be alone with him. It's really, really *bad* if Leo can't find him a date."

Linda was tiny and disturbingly perfect in appearance. Her thick, blond hair formed a smooth cap on her head and flipped up at the ends, forming a circle of curls at her neckline. She looked like a cover model for a teen magazine with her matching sweater and cardigan set and big blue eyes. Horseback riding was her passion and she once showed me a room in her house fluttering with blue ribbons and shelves stacked with flashing gold and silver trophies.

"I ride English style," she said.

We had known each other in high school but hadn't been friends. Sometimes I would see her at school after she changed into her cream-colored riding pants and leather boots and waited for a ride to the stable where she trained every afternoon, or I would pass her in the hall on my way down to the art room to finish a poster for a drama club production. She smelled like leather cleaner and I smelled like chalk dust and oil paint. She was someone I observed in high school but never imagined having anything in common with. She lived in town with her horse. I lived in the country with a lot of cats.

We were thrown together in our college commuting experience, both attending Mitchell. Every day one picked the other up at home and we embarked on a friendship forged by necessity as we drove to school. She mainly spoke on our twenty-minute ride about how much fun it was to date "Coasties"—local slang for Coast Guard cadets. The Coast Guard Academy was in the next town and Linda had entered the dating scene there as a "young lady available to escort cadets at formal events." This was how she met Leo, a burly twenty-year-old who seemed to bulge out of his uniform, especially his collar. Every trip to and from school was peppered with "Leo said ...," and "Leo did ...," and often, "I think Leo is very serious about me."

Linda convinced me that I should follow her example and join them with a cadet for double-dates. In hindsight, after listening to Linda and Leo in the back seat on some of our dates, I think she wanted a chaperone more than a dating partner. Up in the front seat I would eventually hear from the back: "Leo, stop that. Not now Leo. Leo, I said *no!*" in small, determined, continuous sound bites.

My dating experience with Coast Guard cadets left me

ambivalent, even if they were local celebrities, considered by other women at my college to be gods in uniform. I felt uncomfortable with their rigid and mannered behavior and starched polish. I had difficulty carrying on an easy conversation with most of them. Their mouths barely moved when they spoke and they seemed corseted in their uniforms. At a distance there is a romantic heroic austerity about cadets in their regalia, but up close I always felt underdressed and too much of a frail contrast unless I wore gloves, hat, nylons, high-heels and possibly a long-line girdle under a coordinated outfit.

The one Coast Guard cadet I fell for in my first semester at Mitchell was terrible at conversation, as usual, but an excellent kisser. He was handsome, polite and mysteriously silent; a tall, fair-haired, well-groomed Viking smelling of shoe polish and English Leather Aftershave. We graduated to solo dates after several double dates with Linda and Leo and spent hours on our twice weekly trysts in my car in unlighted areas outside the main gates to the academy. The silent petting and kissing was enjoyable but it seemed odd that we never went to public places together—not even the pizza parlor down the street. We continued for weeks in our tantalizing but private dating life. Then, one day, as I sat in the anteroom to the women's bathroom at Mitchell where all the latest news and gossip was exchanged, one of my classmates plopped down in the seat next to me. She leaned in and spoke in a conspiratorial tone.

"So—you're going out with Doug. Did you know he got a girl pregnant and she's living on the Cape until she has the baby? I heard they're getting married when he graduates. It's a big secret. Cadets can't get married, you know, until they graduate. He'd get thrown out if they found out about him." She rattled on as if she worked for the FBI.

I barely knew her. What was it my mother always said in this situation? *They're just jealous. They don't know anything about you.* I went to the pay phone outside and dialed Doug's number in his dormitory. *I'll check the facts.* By chance, he answered. Cadets were usually not that easy to track down.

"Someone just told me that you already have a girlfriend and that she's pregnant on Cape Cod," I said.

"Uh...someone told you that?"

"Is it true?"

"Well—uh—I guess it sort of is."

"Okay. That's it then," and I hung up. This had been one of our longer conversations. I was shaken to think I'd been duped. My role was instantly clear. I had been just an understudy. All the private parking and alone time suddenly made sense. I was a stand-in for the real star who was off giving birth somewhere. On Cape Cod no less. I never even imagined that people *gave* birth on Cape Cod.

That same semester my philosophy professor told our class that those who were believers in organized religion would be agnostics and atheists by the end of his course. At seventeen, my experience with Cadet Doug felt life-hardening. I welcomed Mr. Mugge's introduction to a larger world of ideas—beyond my family's usual explanation of difficulties by saying they were "God's will." Acknowledging my hurt feelings and profound disappointment with Cadet Doug heightened my realization that I had been a believer, but also a real sucker.

The stories in my philosophy class would save me, though. Reading the Greek philosophers, Hegel, Kant, Kierkegaard and others was liberating and therapeutic. These two streams of stories combined, one based on faith and the Bible and the other on new (to me), more secular ideas, was exciting. Philosophy 101 offered infatuation with no fear of rejection. When Kierkegaard said, one is not a Christian, one is always becoming a Christian. I said, *yes!. Forget about boyfriends. Remember Chester and his story of the guy who died on the desert. I'm going to learn philosophy and study ideas and figure out how to think.* My understanding of life, death and how to live was suddenly flipped on its head. I hadn't lost faith, I had gained a new way to think about it.

I never saw or spoke to Doug again or dated another Coastie and I was less than enthusiastic when Linda started to badger me the following semester to be a date for a West Point cadet for the cadet exchange weekend. He would be Leo's roommate for the weekend. From Wednesday to Friday that week in the car, she harangued me about being Miss Anonymous on Saturday.

"Why are you so worried about pleasing Leo all the time?" I said. "Cadets are a bunch of spoiled brats."

But I finally gave in. We had three more months of commuting ahead of us. *What the heck—I'll keep the peace.*

Linda and Leo were already in the back seat when Dave opened the front passenger side door and climbed into my car. He wore civilian clothes, a cotton shirt and chino pants. His hair was dark and short, very short. *He* was short, only three inches taller than me, and his eyes deep blue. He told me later that he had never met someone with waist-length hair like mine. We started with outward appearances and worked our way in.

Leo was in uniform and locked in an embrace with Linda as I could see in the rear view mirror.

"Stop it Leo! Not now," Linda said, pushing him away.

Dave seemed to ignore the scene behind us. He smiled at me, "So what shall we do?"

In the Northeast we are accustomed to quick changes in the weather. We might even become immune or callous to the transformations, the clouds forming up and the tides pushing and pulling on the shore. Nothing changed perceptibly that after-noon. It was still a warm March day with gaudy, green buds on maple trees and daffodils crisp and fresh under an even sky. But unknown to me, everything was about to change. There was not a discernible fork in the road, but meeting Dave created a new direction. I was about to leave the obscurity of a hometown existence for unimagined territory with no warning or foresight.

The four of us sat in silence for a moment in the car. Leo didn't have a plan for our double date except: "Some place private where we can relax." This eliminated the bowling alley and we weren't dressed for golf or tennis. I suggested a spot along the Mystic River where we could walk and watch shore birds. As soon as we arrived, Leo, armed with a blanket, coaxed Linda off into the woods and I was suddenly alone with a stranger, but he wasn't terrified or mute or aggressive.

"Leo said you like to sing and play guitar," said Dave. "Tell me about that and what music you like."

As we walked along the river next to the marsh grass, Dave picked up small stones or a piece of clam shell and skipped them three or four times over the surface of the water. He handed me a stone: "Here, you try." Mine were clunkers, never getting beyond the first skip, but I had never been good at athletic competition.

Conversation was easy. He described his project of catalog-ing all his favorite music and putting it on reel-to-reel tapes. He liked Wagner and said someday he wanted to go to the Wagner Music Festival in Bayreuth, Germany. I thought I had heard of Wagner but never listened to his music. As we navigated the boggy marsh between the road and the river he described the sports program at West Point and how he discovered gymnastics as a "plebe," a first year student. I learned eventually on a future date that he was an Eastern States champion gymnast in floor exercise competition—Olympic material. I shared that I had not been able to take ballet lessons until I had a driver's license and could take myself to classes and I was already in toe shoes after only two years.

There was a tender shyness between us and somehow we were hand in hand within the hour. We came in earshot of where Linda and Leo had camped in the woods and could hear Leo pleading "Oh c'mon Linda. Just once?" and Linda's reply: "Stop it, Leo!"

We made some noise to let them know we were in range. Dave made quacking sounds. He even excelled in duck imitations. There was a small kiss exchanged between us before rousting Linda and Leo from their lair and Dave and I continued on to my parents' house for dinner. Yes. I was already spellbound, but mostly with intense curiosity about this person, this boy/man, who was without pretense, slim and muscular, articulate and kind. I was flattered, too. He had mistaken me for someone in another category—someone perfect like Linda.

What do we tell each other, at this age, with our brief histories? We both came from families with four children. He had already spent a year in the army before going to West Point. He spent his last year at George Mason High School living with a family friend, an elderly woman, in Falls Church, Virginia, because his family was stationed in Rawalpindi, Pakistan. His father's brother, a retired army officer who I remember as sad, quiet and prematurely gray, had spent two years in a German POW camp in WWII. His mother's sister, Marion, had been a "ferry pilot" during the war and shuttled military planes between air bases. Now she was a counselor in a women's prison in upstate New York and a fanatical tennis player. His grandfather had been a botanist.

Just before entering West Point, after finishing Army Prep School, Dave had hitched a ride on Air Force One to Paris on his way to visit his family in Pakistan. He told his family that it might be *his* personal plane someday. He spoke about his life growing up on military posts all over the world including Japan, Germany and Pakistan. We were opposites. Me—born and raised in southeastern Connecticut where my parents had been too busy running various businesses to go anywhere, with family roots so deep in one spot that the concept of Dave's family moving every two to three years, especially to foreign countries, could have cast him in a suspicious light. "A globetrotter," my grandmother might say, which is what her family had said about her eventual husband before he went to war in France and came back a broken, but marriageable, hero in 1918. Instead, my grandmother, my parents and my brothers, were impressed beyond measure with Dave's demeanor, his curiosity and soft-spoken answers to their questions.

Looking back, I see a bright, clear-eyed young man, standing in my parents' living room crowded with books, furniture and Victorian clutter. I imagine he spoke easily with my father, probably addressing him as "sir." And my father probably asked him with enthusiasm about the history of West Point and the kinds of classes taken by cadets. My father was probably impressed by his manners and intelligent answers, something he had

David R. Crocker, Jr, USMA class of 1966

dreamed for his own children. There's no doubt that my mother spoke about the new nursing home they planned to build over the next year and she probably reiterated the Whipple legacy in the local area starting with John Whipple who signed the Declaration of Independence and then moved on up to Noah Whipple, the stone mason with the thirty-two children. She possibly tossed in our descent from the Rogerene Quakers, too.

Back in that living room, my grandmother, slowed by a stroke, probably watched with rapt attention from the chair we called her "command post" in front of the hearth. Her eyes would have followed him around the room as she took mental notes for her summary opinion after he left. My older brother Bob, home from college for the weekend, was possibly curious about the content of engineering courses at West Point. My younger brother Sam, always in need of the limelight, likely convinced everyone to listen to him play the piano and sing *Meet Me in St. Louis*.

Eventually that evening we moved into a too small dining room where seven of us pressed elbow to elbow around an oval, cherry wood table laden with what amounted to a traditional Thanksgiving dinner, even though it was March: roast turkey with stuffing, butternut squash, apple pie. Dave slipped easily into this noisy, eccentric family.

My parents probably did not express their concerns that day about the activities in Vietnam. Nor did they challenge what Dave's career choices represented even though they would battle to help my brothers obtain Conscientious Objector status. I remember my father saying that evening after Dave returned to the Coast Guard Academy that he was "a high quality young man."

———⊂∞⊃———

*Our first love-letter...the dread of saying too much
is so nicely balanced by the fear of saying too little.
Hope borders on presumption, and fear on reproach.*

—L.E. Landon, *Romance and Reality* (1831)

Dave's first letter arrived on the Tuesday after our Saturday blind date. He invited me to West Point the following weekend. We both jumped into constant letter writing to each other. The thoughts and dreams I had previously written in my diary now appeared on my pages dedicated to him. Emily Dickinson once described to Mabel Loomis Todd that "A letter always feels to me like Immortality because it is the mind alone without corporeal friend." I realize now that much of the unbearable grief that followed his death for years afterwards was related to this sense of losing him *and* that continuous stream of communication. Whenever I was without him, because of the interruptions of military life, there were always letters from him and letters to write.

My parents had given me a new car, a burgundy Pontiac LeMans with a black interior, just before I started commuting to college in 1964. On my first visit to West Point, my parents led the way in their car and I followed. I saw parts of Connecticut and New York for the first time. Places with names even more exotic than Pawcatuck and Quaqatanuck on the eastern side of Connecticut. New names like Cos Cob, Tappan Zee, Bear Mountain. When we arrived at West Point after driving three hours, my parents lunched at the Hotel Thayer, just inside the gates, and left me for the weekend to get to know this stranger who had made such an impression on everyone; so much for my parents' mistrust of the outside world.

I was eighteen and naïve about anything that didn't involve nurses and sick people. West Point opened my eyes to a new world with its regimented pomp and ceremony, drills, parades and lists of rules and regulations. Perhaps I had seen some of this on television episodes of *The Long Gray Line,* but thought it was fiction. Young men dressed in classy archaic military uniforms, gray waist length jackets glinting with gold braid and buttons, and chalk white pants, all marching in formations flowing by like synchronized swimmers on a giant stage of green turf. Smiling young women fluttered about in pastel dresses, white gloves and pillbox hats like a flock of exotic migrating birds, preening on the edges of the parade ground.

The Hotel Thayer, a sort of demilitarized zone for visitors, provided rooms especially reserved for cadet dates. Each suite stuffed ten young women into two rooms with an adjoining bath. Cadets were strictly forbidden above the main floor of the hotel but there was a mezzanine to walk through with one's escort where well-lit, jewelry display cases contained samples of "miniatures," the traditional service academy engagement ring.

Weekends at the Thayer would be my first experience in dormitory living. We were called 'cadet drags' (a young woman escorted by a cadet). I was not as sensitive to the derogatory nature of this expression as I was confused; what does this mean to be *a drag* and how could you drag someone with all their rules against touching in public? During my weekends at the Hotel Thayer I received a crash course, not just about the culture of West Point, but about the lives of other young women living through happiness and disappointments; being more or less in love; choosing between a career and marriage (marriage being the number one choice of most).

In hindsight, I was more Zen than ambitious. I had no plan to marry or even a concept of marriage. I was just enjoying the attentions of a nice guy and my new independence away from *the family firm* albeit in a highly structured experience. From arrival until departure during our initial weekends together, activities were planned as if we were royal princesses on safari. Corn flakes were served in fine china in the breakfast room of the hotel on Saturday morning, followed by watching the cadet dress parade. Lunch was back at the hotel without the cadets (they were not released from duty until the afternoon), a walk around the grounds, a visit to the field house, a snack, a social event with other drags and cadets, curfew at 9:00pm for cadets, worship services in the chapel on Sunday morning, departure.

There was the occasional scandal whispered about in our suite such as a secret marriage or pregnancy resulting in a tribunal and dismissal for the cadet—if and when it came to light. How anyone had the opportunity for intimacy was a mystery to me in the early months. As we dressed and arranged our hairstyles between the beds in the crowded rooms, trying to avoid inhaling the occasional blast of hairspray, I heard a litany of rules. Don't try to take a cadet's arm. Don't take your gloves off in the Superintendent's house. Don't eat a chicken leg with your fingers.

The second wave of the women's movement was years away for some of us and I was still just getting up to speed on the normal life among females in the 1960s. I learned that, for most, their mothers were housewives rather than entrepreneurs and that some families took vacations together every year. I didn't overhear any conversations about birth control or sex or perhaps I didn't know what they were talking about.

I saw other women's scantily clad bodies for the first time during my Hotel Thayer experience as we jockeyed for space in front of bathroom mirrors to primp for the limited time we could spend with "our" cadet. They looked like Degas paintings from my art history book—certainly not like the diagrams in my mother's medical textbooks. Some appeared to be between girl and woman with tiny breasts and straight, thin bodies. Most were savvy about fashion, jewelry, hair products and rules for cadets.

Their matching luggage and clarity about their social position and future was impressive; to be an officer's wife was a career choice. Those focused on marriage and children were not the ones with whom I thought I could become friends. I didn't see children in my future. I wanted friends who were independent with a sense of adventure. Possibly my mother's horror stories about childbirth had left me terrified by the prospect of the physical experience of giving birth. I was a virgin and had not even thought of how or when I might be un-virgined.

I spent those weekends fascinated with the precision of cadets in dress parades on campus, observing their extraordinary discipline—like memorizing an elaborate definition of leather and blurting it out perfectly upon orders from someone of higher rank—and discovering how a sense of tradition and carefully orchestrated rituals seemed to make people into creatures who behaved differently than everyone else. And—in this place of mythical proportions—I was with someone of quality and substance who seemed dedicated to falling in love *with me*, wanting to know me and interested in my opinion. Blind dates are highly underrated.

Ladyclift, a local women's college, provided dates for cadets regularly. These were arranged by Mrs. Holland, the West Point social director, who kept an album of female prospects in her office. Meeting someone by her arrangement was described as, *going through the Holland Tunnel*, a process which sounded more arduous than romantic. Most Ladyclift women were on the fast track to matrimony, based on the gossip in our suite. Other women came from Bryn Mawr, Sarah Lawrence, Amherst, Swarthmore, Skidmore, or schools in Boston, New York. They walked out of the pages of *Seventeen* and *American Girl Magazine*;

smart, well-dressed, polite and bubbling with enthusiasm and sophistication. They were mentors, or at least models, for my new social life. I even learned that I could shave my legs with hair conditioner instead of soap in an emergency.

At the end of each evening, when the cadets had to return to their barracks by curfew, we 'drags' sat on our cots dressed in nightgowns with hair rolled in curlers, talking into the night. We were a chorus of innocents with no idea that our futures were being determined by background events still secret from the American public, rolling on as we sat giggling in a hotel at the gates of West Point.

Unknown to me and most of the world, *Operation Rolling Thunder*, the sustained American bombing of North Vietnam, had commenced on February 24, 1965; apparently, according to a current analysis of old information, this campaign was the result of the misconstrued incident in the Gulf of Tonkin. Following that, on March 8, 1965, two marine battalions, a total of about fifteen hundred marines, landed in Vietnam to defend Danang airfield. They were the first American combat troops to arrive in Vietnam—landing only one week before I met Dave for the first time.

Former Defense Secretary Robert McNamara said in his memoir, that the sustained U.S. bombing of North Vietnam began in 1965 with over 100 aircraft launched from carriers in the South China Sea and air bases in South Vietnam to strike an ammunition depot in North Vietnam. McNamara wrote that it would continue for three years and *drop more bombs on Vietnam than had been dropped on all of Europe in World War II.* Half a century later, the people of Vietnam are still suffering the consequences. PeaceTrees VietNam, an humanitarian organization, has found and detonated more than 80,000 pieces of unexploded ordinance in the small area of Quang Ngai Province alone, as of November 2012. They say there are a lot more to find before they are accidently stepped on, or dug up, by a child hunting for scrap metal.

The bombing would span the entire length of my relationship on earth with Dave.

When I started my weekend treks to West Point, it was the spring of Dave's third year. In West Point language: the year of the "cow." Cadet cows began to experience some lessening of the rigid control of the first two years. That winter of 1965 was the first year since 1802 that they were given a Christmas holiday. Perhaps this was also related to the specter of a burgeoning war. As Robert McNamara said, wars generate their own momentum and follow the law of unanticipated consequences. Vietnam was no exception.

I was oblivious to the fact that the fog of war was moving in my direction. I had other thoughts, like, *how could I be so adored by someone who seems to be almost royalty and here I am, all of a sudden, visiting West Point every other weekend?* My journal entries reveal my stunned surprise that I had met someone who seemed perfect. I listed my imperfections, lack of knowledge, lack of social skills, lack of self-confidence, lack of dating experience, residual facial scars from adolescent acne. At the same time, I was surprisingly optimistic considering my habit of self-deprecation. After my Coast Guard dating experience, I wasn't ready to trust guys who looked too good to be true. But, regarding Dave, I was still clearly a romantic and thought that Prince Valiant had finally come to his senses and pushed Princess Aleta aside— for me!

I was eighteen when we met. He was twenty-one with his life set in high gear on a career path. He had dreamed of going to West Point, like his father. Now he was in the lock-step of a military career where his future would be determined by the extent to which he could meet the challenges, first as a cadet and eventually as an army infantry officer, a dream that would erode as he advanced in his responsibilities. Just before he left for Vietnam, he began to speak about leaving the army after his five-year obligation was finished. He said it was not his father's army.

Dave had an elegant esteem for his father. Never had I seen such respect and comradeship between a father and son as I observed when I eventually met his parents. The humor and deference between them belonged in some ancient, epic poem of a great leader bringing along his beloved namesake in a noble cause. Dave had learned confidence, discipline, and loving respect, growing up in his peripatetic family who loved army life.

The differences between us were immense, but we fell towards each other as if pushed from opposite wings backstage into the same play. How else could we explain our chance meeting and our curious comfort with each other? And on top of all that, he was handsome, athletic, and chivalrous and ready to find a companion, to be in love. Traveling, hiking, camping, mountain climbing, military life and being a couple were new concepts for me. I could not see myself beyond my next art project and even that was fuzzy.

"I'm lucky to find you," he said when he kissed me on our first date at West Point.

West Point, 1966

How was I so fortunate to find this extraordinary person? I felt like a freshly promoted goddess of a new religion. Soon after our first date he announced in a letter that he had fallen 'in like' with me. Dave had codes, but they were more fun than my grandmother's, who liked to spell certain words in a sentence as if it preserved a secret.

"Do you know that your name means 'companion' in Hebrew? It's from the story of Ruth in the Bible," he said, "and David means 'beloved.' Those will be our special names for each other from now on. Okay with you?"

"Sure," I said in amazement. It was the most romantic idea I'd ever heard. This was right on keel with every dreamy fantasy I'd ever had and I liked the biblical associations, even if my college philosophy class had caused me to square off against my Protestant religious education. Dave's mother confided later that Dave had been spurned by a "Catholic girl" and that, much to their dismay, he had even considered converting to the Roman Catholic faith; an unpleasant idea for them. *His parents are just like Gram*, I thought; I felt right at home.

Dave was deeply romantic. He would eventually have "Companion to Beloved" and "Beloved to Companion" inscribed on the inside of our wedding bands.

Cadets were not allowed to have their own cars on campus until the spring of their senior year and Dave was already dreaming about the dark blue, Jaguar XK-E he would buy at the annual senior cadet car show in 1966. Thanks to his parents' financial foresight in saving for their children's education—they bought stock in Chesebrough-Ponds in the early 1950s—and the fact that West Point was tuition-free and cadets were paid a pittance (but had little to spend it on), Dave would graduate with a nest egg of about $20,000. The Jag cost $6000 in 1966.

That car was probably the only Jaguar to receive a spit shine. He understood popular culture. An XK-E of the same year, model and color is now part of the permanent collection of the Museum of Modern Art in New York City.

In his cadet life, Dave was careful to observe regulations and prided himself on never having to "walk the area," a disciplinary action involving hours of marching back and forth in an interior courtyard in full dress uniform carrying a rifle. He found ways to break the rules with discretion. I am one of the few females (if any) who briefly saw the interior of a cadet barracks long before the school was made co-educational. It was a stealth operation with me in a long, gray cadet overcoat along with Dave and three other cadets moving so fast that I don't remember what I saw except for two cots and dark wood paneling. Perhaps they won a bet among themselves but I wasn't there long enough even for a flash bulb to go off.

When Dave explained PDA (public display of affection), he said that it was one of the most common offenses resulting in punishment. If a cadet was caught holding hands with a date he could receive a punishment of twenty-two hours of "walking the area." Basically, physical contact in public, in any form, between male and female was not allowed. Even offering an arm to a date tottering on high heels while crossing a slippery road in the middle of a deluge was sketchy behavior on the part of the cadet. Only at dances were we allowed restrained physical contact in public. Waltzing without touching is difficult.

The one place of exception to the no-touch rule was Flirtation Walk. "Flirty" was a well-worn path winding along a steep bank between the campus and the Hudson River. It was a veritable Garden of Eden without snakes or fear of expulsion, visible by boat with binoculars if one was really curious about cadets pursuing romantic bliss, but fairly well-hidden when the trees were leafed out. As we walked along, Dave pointed out that the typewriter cases other cadets carried did not contain typewriters. They were stealth vehicles for picnics, radios, blankets, etc. He said Flirty was the only place at West Point where couples could behave like couples.

"This is where cadets can let their hair down, what little they have," he said, taking my hand.

Flirty was too public for Dave, though, and he was derisive about the activities we observed like some of the gray, army issue blankets off the path that looked like giant, undulating ant hills as couples tried to find a little privacy beneath them. We kissed and held hands as we walked on Flirty, but Dave thought it was too communal for more demonstrative affection. When he decided it was time to take our relationship to the next level, it wasn't going to happen lying under an army blanket at a forty-five degree angle to the Hudson River. It would be a camping trip with tents and sleeping bags outside the gates of West Point in Bear Mountain State Park with a gourmet picnic including thick porterhouse steaks provided by the cadet mess hall to cook over an open fire. I trusted him. Whatever he wanted to do seemed okay, but my fear of pregnancy severely hampered my pleasure in those early experiences. I was embarrassed to ask anyone about birth control, even my best friends. It was a time during which some of us blundered along, thinking we'd learn *somehow*, perhaps by divine intervention or luck.

When I consider what I didn't know—about love, sex, relationships, war—I cringe. My future was revealed moment to moment as if I was unwinding a surprise ball made from a long stream of paper with mystery gifts tucked in at twists and turns. I didn't have to do a thing except agree. Entering this story was like slipping into a fairy tale. The prince finds the princess, wakes her up, and the whole kingdom rejoices. And we always think it's meant to last.

Less than one year later, I stood in my bedroom at my parents' house staring at a box of bobbie pins on my dresser. The hands on my blue Baby Ben clock had never moved so slowly. Within the hour, I'd put on the voluminous, lacey wedding dress with an empire waist and three-quarter sleeves that my mother and I picked out at The Style Shoppe. Helen and Marilyn, my two best friends in high school, would arrive at 5:00pm to help me get into the thing—there must be one hundred tiny cloth-covered buttons up the back. There is something innocent and seductive about a long row of miniature fabric covered buttons on a beautiful dress, a pillbox hat with yards of Tulle veil, and long white gloves going up above the elbow and buttoning at the wrist. My hair would hang loose down to my waist.

My parents eloped when they married. Or rather, they got married and came home to announce the fact. My mother had been in nursing school and students were not allowed to marry until after graduation or risk expulsion. She didn't want to make an issue of the marriage in case someone at the school found out. It was October 1943, and my father was about to be shipped out to China on a navy oil freighter for two years. They were married by a justice of the peace in Providence, Rhode Island and marked the occasion by having a studio photograph taken. My mother has an ambiguous smile similar to the Mona Lisa. My father, in whose face I see my own, is beaming.

Dave's parents were married on June 14, 1940 and he would be born in the south on a military post in Macon, Georgia on December 20, 1943. After Dave's birth, his father left for war in the Pacific.

At the occasion of our wedding in 1966 my parents made up for all the ceremonies that had gone undetected and uncelebrated in the past century. I had nine bridesmaids and 250 guests and it all had to happen within twenty-four hours of Dave's graduation from West Point, in case his father could get compassionate leave and return from Vietnam. Our giant candlelight wedding was set for 8:30pm on a Thursday evening, to be followed by a

sit-down turkey dinner at the newly opened Seaman's Inn restaurant at Mystic Seaport Museum.

My mother always looked cool and calm, but after caring for
her for ten years at the end of her life I realize the price she paid
for that mild exterior. I resemble her style of worry—without
the high blood pressure. Or, let's say, I was like her. I think—or
I hope—I've improved, healed by experience and reflection. On
my wedding day I flitted from one worry to the next, trying to
anticipate everything that could go wrong: *I wonder if Gram will
be okay? She never wears real shoes and tonight she's going to wear
her big old fashioned gunboats with the square heels. I don't care how
they look but she has to get up all those steps to the church with her bad
knees. Will Dave's mom be okay without her husband or will he magically appear, flown in at the last moment?*

It was difficult to calculate how I had arrived at my wedding day back in 1966—so fast. *You're too young* I said to myself
(especially since no one else was saying it). *But he chose me,* my
romantic nature said, *and he even had Beloved to Companion
inscribed on the inside of my wedding band.* When I graduated
from high school I never imagined that exactly two years later
I'd be married. Parroting my mother and grandmother, I scoffed
at my classmates who married right after high school, and those
fledglings from Ladyclift flocking to the altar. I thought I was
different.

On Wednesday, June 8, 1966, my family and Dave's family
(except for his father) arrived in Mystic in the evening,
after attending West Point graduation. Hubert Humphrey had
given the commencement address and we were buoyed up by his
confidence of a resolution in Vietnam. We talked about it on the
three-hour drive home, arriving just in time for the wedding

rehearsal and dinner. The next day, while I fussed with my hair and obsessed on my anxieties, Dave and his classmates, those who returned with us to be in the wedding party, were off finding their tuxedos and possibly pondering their new status as 2nd Lieutenants, or maybe they were playing golf.

Did I know what was burbling in the background on my wedding day? The fact that Dave's father was in Vietnam from August 1965 to September 1966 as a high-ranking officer gave me an oblique reassurance that he might help to get this "conflict," this—whatever it was—over with. Like many people in the early 1960s, I was naïve about the on-going cauldron of violence in Southeast Asia. When I attended junior college from 1964 to 1966, it was barely a topic of discussion on campus. My parents talked about it at home but we lived in the submarine capital of the world, home of the USS Nautilus, the first nuclear powered attack submarine. Most people in town worked in some aspect of the defense industry. War protests were rare but usually violent in our region when they occurred. At the Center for Non-violence and Peace in nearby Voluntown, Connecticut, people dressed as Ku Klux Klan members wearing sheets met protesters against war with armed attacks.

The new Medicare legislation signed into law in 1965 dominated the conversation at home as my parents worked on plans for a new state-of-the-art nursing home. When they sold the old homes in 1960, they signed a non-compete agreement with the buyers in which they agreed to stay out of the nursing home business in Connecticut and Rhode Island for five years. They would survive on monthly payments from the new owners and rents from the trailer park while my mother planned her re-entry back into the nursing home business. Her plans included the whole family; my father would construct the building and we kids would be drafted into her health-care army.

My parents were adamant that my brothers would not be

drafted into the military. They were dubious and concerned about Vietnam. Members of my family had served in the military—my father in the Navy in World War II and my mother's father in the British Army in World War I where he fought in the Battle of the Somme. My father's infamous stepfather had served in the Spanish American war.

A survey made by the University of Michigan in June 1966 showed that 41 percent of people with only a grade school education wanted immediate withdrawal from Vietnam, while only 27 percent of college educated people supported immediate withdrawal. Looking back on the prevailing sentiments of the time, I hear the echo of my parents and grandmother, that this war could be a waste of time, money and lives.

The message to avoid war, and especially Vietnam, was so consistent in our house it may have desensitized me to the possibility that I could ever be touched by a war except in some peripheral way—like experiencing the absence of Dave's father at our wedding. Dad Crocker impressed me as an intelligent, knowing person, someone who could organize things and resolve conflicts. Perhaps he was clearing things up over there right at this very moment. Finally, he wasn't able to return for Dave's graduation and our wedding. We would not see him again until later that year just before Dave and I left for two years in Germany.

I asked my mother years later if she thought I was too young to marry at age nineteen and she said, "Your father and I did the same thing in 1943. It was the war. You don't have much choice about things during war-time. Besides, if I said no, you would have done it anyway."

My parents worked hard to help my brothers get deferments from military service. My older brother was easy because he suffered from allergies and asthma. After wheezing through one interview he was declared 4-F, unfit for military service. My younger brother, Sam, was a different story. He was a healthy toothsome specimen at age eighteen who would eventually die of AIDS at age thirty-nine, but the military did not know his predilections when his number came up in 1967. I'm not sure that Sam did either at the time.

I was already married and living in Germany when Sam received his draft notice. He chose to reject the military on the basis of his religious beliefs. To accomplish this, he had to prove that he had attended church as an active member over many years prior. That was easy enough. Sam had remained devoted to the Protestant faith since his first days of Sunday school, but my parents wanted to make sure his Conscientious Objector status wasn't derailed. When I cleared out my father's desk years later I found pages of notes in dad's handwriting with different scenarios and supporting Bible scriptures, each making a case against war. I don't know how these were used before the draft board but Sam received a status which took him permanently out of reach of the military. The result of his hearing was published in the local newspaper.

Sam told me eventually that a few days after his deferment became news he went to buy a car and met a member of the draft board who ridiculed him in front of everyone in the showroom for his lack of *patriotism*. In another instance, he was refused service at a restaurant and called a coward.

*I'm a universal patriot, if you could
understand me rightly: my country is the world.*

—Charlotte Bronte, *The Professor* (1846)

Patriotism. What is it? Is it only evidenced by full agreement to participate? In Sam's case, I can't imagine him holding a gun during his lifetime. He wouldn't even participate in the shooting of Coca-Cola bottles with an air rifle when we were children. I don't think it was due to a fear of death or injury on his part. Military deaths were handled so discreetly in years prior (compared to those in the more recent wars) that we barely knew they happened unless it was in your family.

Back in 1969, coffins containing dead soldiers arrived in town to be quietly slipped in the back door of the designated funeral home. Families were not informed where and when transfers of coffins took place. California? New Jersey? The next of kin was not encouraged or invited to be anywhere except at home, waiting for a call from the funeral director.

Today, coffins of dead soldiers are called *cases*. Perhaps it soothes the impact and sets death in war apart from regular, everyday death. Family members now have the opportunity to fly to Dover Air Force Base to watch from the tarmac as the flag-covered cases of loved ones are carried out of the belly of a C-17 airplane. In January 2010, Dover opened the "Center for Families of the Fallen," a $1.6 million, 6,000-square-foot space of soft lighting and earth-toned furniture for families to assemble before they step out on the tarmac. But what do we learn about war from experiencing this mollified version of death? Do we know more today about what we've signed up for than those who were conscripted in the past?

Back in 1966, our mid-week wedding went off without a hitch except for the moment when a gust of wind blew my veil of tulle into the spiny, prickly apple tree by our front door as I helped my grandmother into the car. I see myself clutched for a moment by that tree next to the driveway as if it wanted to hold me there. I was almost late for the candlelight ceremony. It took three bridesmaids to separate me from the branches.

Years later, Dave's mother and I would laugh together over a bottle of wine remembering my capture by the tree and, later, the stampede to buy drinks at the bar at the reception as people realized it was a "dry" wedding. My parents didn't drink alcohol and didn't worry about not offering it. Most of the wedding party was under the legal drinking age, including me. There was also the contingent of relatives from Quakertown who stood in clumps on the edges of the dance floor. If there had been dancing *and* alcohol, surely they were in hell.

Finally, Dave's best man 2nd Lieutenant Wesley Clark and some of the groomsmen, commandeered a bottle of champagne from somewhere for a wedding toast or so I remember. By that time it was midnight and I was on the border between beginning and ending, suddenly aware that my shoes felt much smaller. Dave's sister recalls that our wedding "glittered like a fairy tale." She remembers stepping out onto the deck behind the restaurant overlooking the Mystic River and breathing in the salty, warm air with Dave. He said, "It's the first and most beautiful wedding I've ever been to!"

We spent our wedding night at a nearby motel where I sobbed for the first hour. My brand new husband tried to comfort me, holding me, asking me quiet questions. I said it was worry and lack of sleep. I had taken final exams at college until the day before his graduation (the day before yesterday). But I remember a distinct feeling in my chest and a voice in my head saying: *I've done it. I've gotten married. I'm not just myself any more. I'm a different person.* Dave was resolute that we had made the best decision and soon, that night, I was relearning how to breathe.

I might sound disloyal to this man I adored, and I know it was something else—not him—that kept pelting the windows in my fairy tale castle. I loved being with Dave, but we were galloping at lightning speed on an obscure landscape. The truth was difficult to decipher in that historical time of the late 1960s. We thought we were making informed choices. I had no concept of the future, not even an inkling that the women's movement was just over the horizon. I thought I was liberated already, having been raised in a household where it was said that opportunities were unlimited (especially if I chose to become a doctor). There was also the old saw repeated over and over at home by my mother and grandmother: "Don't become an artist. You'll never make any money. Get an education. Have your own profession. Don't be dependent on a man, even a nice appearin' one."

From left – Best Man Wesley Clark, Dave, Ruth, Helen Giles Maid of Honor

And *poof*, I was married.

I had already taken a red pen to my journal and added "I" wherever the word "God" appeared. The entire message changed: "*I* want to do this and this and this, *"not "God* wants me to do this." My faith stories and my idea stories were converging into a torrent and I was on fire with a sense that I could do anything. At the same time I was giving over my independence by joining the military through marriage as well as becoming a "dependent." Something seethed in the background like the bubbling earth above a geyser about to erupt. Dave and his family were engulfed in it, a world where one was sent places and where one lived with layers of rules and authority. And now I was part of it, too. I didn't see myself as submissive or passive, and Dave was not macho or authoritative in any way (although he was incontrovertible that we would marry in June and not wait for his father to return from Vietnam in September). Events took on their own momentum.

I was *almost* convinced that we were doing the right thing. But what else was there to do? We would have to be married to go to Germany together in the fall and that's where Dave was going. Perhaps the energized shadow in the background of our love story was the specter of war looming and the question as to when and if Dave would have to go.

I remember 1965 and 1966 as a time of whitewater currents that pulled and pushed and finally swept us right over the falls. The poet C.K. Williams used the phrase "narrative dysfunction" to describe the process by which we lose track of a story, the story that tells us who we are supposed to be and how we are supposed to act. I had been handed a hastily written script titled: *Your New Life Story and it Starts Today*. How appropriate that at the end of 1966 we would be whisked off to a foreign country to begin our married life away from our families in an area called *The Wild Place*.

Two days before Thanksgiving in 1966, Dave and I left Fort Dix, New Jersey on an army transport plane bound for Frankfurt, Germany and ultimately, Wildflecken. We were headed for his first duty station as a 2nd Lieutenant in the infantry. I knew little about our destination except that winter was long, with snow from October to April, and that country was still rebuilding after World War II. When Dave had lived in Wildflecken as a child, his father was commandant of the post and they lived in a house with a view of hills on which nuns skied down from a local monastery. Dave made sleds from pieces of wax paper and all four siblings romped in the snow together throughout the long winters.

As we prepared to leave for Wildflecken, we packed our matching sets of blue and brown Samsonite luggage with winter clothes, Dave's uniforms and my dress-up clothes for social events. It was the fashion era of wool felt loden coats, A-line skirts ending just above the knees, empire waist dresses and pillbox hats. The rest of our worldly goods would not arrive for at least eight weeks. Our estimated time in Germany was two years or until Dave received orders to go to Vietnam.

"Take plenty of shoes," my mother-in-law advised. "You'll need shoes for all occasions." She loved footwear, especially spike heels, and wore them everywhere. They complimented her long, slim legs and smart dresses. She knew our destination in Europe, having spent most of the 1950s on U.S. military posts in Germany with her husband and children. I deferred to her experience and dedicated almost one whole suitcase to shoes. She showed me how to set a proper table with "eatables" on the left and "drinkables" on the right and how to organize a seating plan for dinner parties. Formal dining with lots of glasses and silverware was still mysterious territory. I had grown up *family style*.

She was a devoted and gregarious partner to her husband in military life and I felt complimented, if slightly embarrassed, one night before our departure for Germany to receive an intimate lecture about the facts of life, since I'd never heard such words from my own mother.

After she had had a few martinis we went upstairs to the room in which Dave and I stayed in their house. She took my hands in hers as we sat facing each other on the edge of the twin beds with white chenille coverlets and said: "Our men are doing difficult things. You have to be ready to give them whatever they need, whenever they need it. Sometimes Big Dave (her husband was named David, too) just—comes on to me. You have to be ready for anything."

I surmised that she was speaking about sex although I wasn't completely sure. But, considering her state of intoxication, I just nodded my head in affirmation and hugged her. Her allusions sounded interesting but I couldn't imagine a scenario like she described. Dave was almost as shy as I was, so far. I adored her attention and concern for me and Dave, though. Our relationship, the two "Ruth Crockers," would last until the end of her life in 2001. Her advice and genuine concern for my welfare continued uninterrupted after Dave's death.

She was also an intrepid shopper and her eyes became wistful as she described the china, porcelain, and wood carvings I would find all over Germany at bargain prices. The exchange rate was four Deutsch Marks to the dollar and she sent me off with her shopping list: Hummel figurines, Meerschaum pipes, Rosenthal china, fat candles carved and painted with forest scenes, wood carvings, and Italian glass—if I ever got to Italy.

When our plane touched down at Rhine-Main Air Force Base in Frankfurt, I saw from the window a multitude of vertical cranes. They were moving in every direction, lifting and swinging massive steel beams, stones and lumber. It was as if dozens of Erector Sets had been spilled out on the landscape. I had spent hours watching my father at work building and fixing when I was a child. People in Germany were at work everywhere—moving, carrying, hammering, and shoveling: reconstructing a broken country. How odd to think that only twenty years earlier we had been dropping bombs on this very spot. *This is Europe*, I thought as I scrutinized every view, every person. *I'm in a foreign country! I've arrived in the middle of my History of Western Civilization college text.*

The alpine town of Wildflecken, "the little wild place," at the border of northeastern Bavaria and southern Hesse, was another four-hour drive from Frankfurt. The long car ride lulled me to sleep after twenty-four hours of travel in cars and planes and I slept through the gradual change in scenery as we left the urban areas and drove deeper into forests approaching the border of what was then East Germany.

When I woke up I saw that the roadways had become smaller and rutted. Tall, narrow pine trees leaned into our path. During the Cold War, many roads in West Germany close to the border were intentionally left unimproved lest they turn into invasion expressways for the Red Army coming over the border. I had no sense of place except that the landscape was becoming denser, colder and wilder. As we climbed higher and higher on mountain switchbacks, we crossed the snow line and evergreens thickened with snow pressed in on both sides of the road.

Wildflecken was a soft palette of yellow-ochre light, gray buildings and whirling white when we arrived in the late afternoon. It was Thanksgiving eve but only in my thoughts and only as long as we were in the presence of other Americans. American military bases all over the world create the illusion, with traditional holiday symbols, that one is still in America. Outside the gates it might be Germany, Italy or Spain, but inside, it's always a Little America with paper cutouts of pilgrims and Tom Turkeys plastered everywhere. The military base at Wildflecken was exceptional because the post was shared with the German Army, the Bundeswehr, for training purposes. The German soldiers were housed in separate barracks on one end of the post, distinct from buildings and activities on the U.S. side, but it created a more "foreign" atmosphere than other military posts, or at least the few that I had experienced.

Here the roads were packed deep with a permanent winter snow cover. Studded tires crunched into the frozen crust as we drove through the entrance of the post and up the winding path to—I did not know what. Dave was unsure as to where we would stay because the place was bursting at the seams with incoming officers and enlisted men. We did not have assigned housing. He said we would live temporarily at the BOQ (Bachelor Officer's Quarters), a long building in a quadrangle of buildings built in 1937. It had been occupied by Nazi officers at some point. The German Army had originally established *Camp Wildflecken* as a training area and built housing and accommodations for 9,000 soldiers and 1,500 horses. During the Second World War, several Wehrmacht and Waffen-SS divisions were activated and trained for combat on this spot. Nearby there had been an ammunition factory and two POW camps, one for Russians and one for prisoners of French and Belgian origin. The U.S. Army took control of the entire area in 1945. Not much had physically changed since then.

———— ⌾⌾⌾ ————

Dave knew this place. Thirteen years earlier his father had been commanding officer of the same post. I imagined the adventurous boy of nine or ten who had roamed the post with friends and played in the forests. Dave had spent his infant and toddler years in Japan where his father had led the first U.S. military contingent into occupied Japan. Dave's first words were in Japanese, but Wildflecken was the place he wandered and explored as a child. He loved this spot and had requested it as his first duty station after West Point.

My first full day in the wild place was Thanksgiving Day and we bundled up for the short walk from our single room at the BOQ to the dining hall where I would meet hordes of soldiers. "We'll eat Thanksgiving dinner with the guys in the mess hall," Dave said. "It's a tradition."

After standing in the chow line, we sat down to eat on long benches and tables with hundreds of soldiers. They looked like natives from the same tribe of young men, slim and muscular, with very short hair and dressed identically in starched olive drab fatigues and spit-shined boots. This was my first mess hall holiday and my eyes glazed over at mountains of food in a long steam table and plates overflowing with turkey, gravy, mashed potatoes, grits, peas, collard greens, squash and cranberry sauce. The men, like an olive green sea around me, maintained a restrained decorum as they streamed smiling through the chow line and heaped their plates and trays with the traditional fare.

I was becoming familiar with the two states of being in the military, to be "at attention" and to be "at ease." Snappy salutes and clicking heels sounded wherever we went. The hierarchy is well defined. Soldiers and officers of lower rank must salute a higher ranking officer whenever they encounter each other and the highest ranking person gives the order to be *at ease*. I was to be addressed as *Ma'am*. Smiling and nodding with good posture seemed to be my protocol. I was growing up fast but I felt younger than ever and definitely part of a minority. I spotted few women in this cavernous hall. I found my place elbow to elbow at a long table of ravenous GIs as the room relaxed into the low-pitched, raucous sound of men happy to eat solid American style food.

Outside, the snowfall had become a blizzard. On our walk back to our temporary room, the deepening white was accented only by German soldiers in gray and U.S. soldiers in green, heads and caps turned down against the wind, as we twirled past on packed snow through the blinding swirls of snowflakes. But this is a new, different snow, I thought, *German* snow whipping against my skin. And when it calmed enough to allow me to smell the air, the scent was exotic and foreign— ozone mixed with diesel fuel, the aromas of nature mixed with industry, machines and effort. *You'll get used to this,* I thought.

We passed through the heavy wooden doors, the height of a goal post, at the entrance to the BOQ and trudged up the three flights of stairs to the hallway outside our room. Everything was a variation on the familiar. The tall toilet with a black seat enclosed in a tiny closet—the WC. The method of flushing the toilet with a long chain coming down from a box near the ceiling, the fact that toilets were separated from sink and bathtub in a different space. The beds with boards on either side, and a board in the middle if it was a double bed, like the ancient bundling beds of puritan times and the elongated pillows and puffy eiderdown clouds covered with duvets. We entered our room from a long hallway reminiscent of an old elementary school, lit by clear light bulbs that hung down from the center of the twelve-foot ceiling, and from light coming through the transom windows over each door opening on the hallway. There was no kitchen in the room or the building.

"Don't worry," said Dave, "it's just temporary. I'll get a camp stove at the PX and some equipment and we'll use the window sill for a refrigerator. It'll be like camping." I set myself to the task of organizing and decorating the campsite with what we had brought. At first I wasn't disturbed by our limited and impromptu living situation. I thought this was normal and I was distracted by a macabre fascination with the fact that SS officers had stayed here, maybe even slept in our room. We had lived in three places since our marriage six months earlier, and this setting won the prize for best film noir qualities. Except for the excess of steam heat, a Calvinist could agree to the plain walls, the heavy wood furniture and the single tall window curtained with coarse brown cloth and a sallow shade; a serious room for sleeping and boot polishing. I saw no other females in the building except for German women, nationals, employed by the U.S. military as secretaries and housekeepers, who came and went to offices on other floors. They were substantial Wagnerian women who dressed in layers of wool with thick stockings and sensible sturdy shoes.

Snow, wind and sleet continued to obliterate whatever view there was outside the window. Dave was full of anticipation to start his first job as a 2nd Lieutenant. He polished his combat boots to a mirror shine and asked me to sew on his new insignia, the unit crest of the 2nd Battalion 15th Infantry 3rd Division. I was happy to have something to do. He said he would be a platoon leader in charge of twenty men and would have to spend a lot of time training in the field. He was not permitted to say where he would be or what, precisely, he would do or for how long he would be away at any given time. I understood this discretion—or secrecy—as somehow normal but not pleasant. I knew he did not intend to keep me in the dark. These were simply the rules. I decided to focus on what I *could* learn: the currency and the language. And sooner or later I would embark on my own mission: serious shopping, somewhere, for my mother-in-law.

"Sorry," Dave said on his return from headquarters the next

day. "They're sending me out to the field tomorrow." He started to stuff underwear, socks and sundries into a duffle bag. I learned that *the field* is not a pasture, but a place where war is staged and practiced in seclusion.

"I picked up a camp stove. It's a good one—it'll be perfect for camping later—and we'll get you some groceries."

Okay. This must be normal. I guess army wives get used to this, but how odd to be left alone here.

The snow pelted the windowpanes as I contemplated that our third night in Germany would be our last together for two to three weeks. We started the night in one of the two twin beds. I felt self-conscious in our intimacy under the light of the transom window above the door. Dave was still jet lagged and in need of sleep before 4:00am reveille. He apologetically departed for the other bed at some point in the night. I awoke to darkness and the sound of starched clothes brushing against skin, the lacing of boots, the coat snapped up. I'm sure he was excited to finally begin his career. He left before sunrise with a quick, goodbye kiss as he hefted his green canvas bag over his shoulder. I pulled the eiderdown duvet up over my head against the mystery of it all.

The first day of my independent life dawned bright, clear, cold and silent except for the radiator. The steam heat which rumbled to a clanging start in the early morning hours had melted the frost on the inside of the window and I looked out to distant snowy mountains above and military troops marching around below. I thought about Heidi in her grandfather's chalet. If only I had those hard rolls she packed away in a napkin, the ones she saved for her grandmother. *Okay, I'm not Heidi, but, who am I? Now I'm a foreigner. Other people live here and I'd better*

get out and discover this place. I was clueless about what to do, where to go. I ventured out anyway but with a big trepidation about getting lost.

During the coming weeks I would receive detailed descriptions of where I could and could not go in order to avoid entering the five kilometer zone just before the border of East Germany. The warning was direct and severe on signs and documents "U.S. personnel do not go beyond this point." The consequences of wandering out of bounds were less clear except that it would create a big problem for Dave. Any aberrant behavior on the part of military dependents reflected on the soldier or officer to whom they were attached.

I learned that Wildflecken was a hardship post, not difficult to believe, a famed and feared Army Training Area, and a strategic location whose main function was training American and German troops against invasion by the Russians. Hardship also means that there are limited services and facilities, one movie theater, no shops or stores except the commissary and the PX (the military version of a department store), and a one-room library. A hardship posting also meant a place where sometimes dependents, family members like me, were not even permitted to be with their spouse during their tour of duty. I was one of the lucky ones.

The tiny hamlet of Wildflecken—the actual village—at the base of the hill was a vestige of pre-war Germany which had seen limited progress and reconstruction following the war. There was a post office, a Lutheran church, a bar frequented by U.S. soldiers, shops with sensible shoes and clothing, and two bakeries where fruit tarts glazed with gelatin sparkled like jewels in this otherwise austere setting.

A railroad station on the edge of the village had been a stopping point for displaced persons transported out of Poland during and following WWII. The local cemetery was sprinkled with black iron religious icons and Polish names. These were the graves of people who had died in the purgatory of the Displaced Persons camp including two hundred and three infants. The area felt medieval but not in a poetic sense. Rather, it seemed worn out and trampled by unseen beasts carrying the burdens of the past, and softened only by the fact that the Germans were glad we had come (or that was the prevailing myth). The presence of Americans and other allied forces was a charm, for some citizens, against the darkness of the past and the lingering menace of the present.

The architecture contributed to a somber mood. Most of the buildings on post were built just before World War II; they were gray, rectangular monoliths; identical five-story buildings with steep roofs to discourage snow accumulation. These looming stone structures with long dormer windows conveyed permanence like weathered repositories of old secrets, planted deeply into a landscape that swept down to farms and fields enriched by night soil.

Night soil is human excrement, the preferred fertilizer for local gardens and crop fields. It was collected from farm to farm and house to house in what Americans called honey wagons which rattled night and day over rutted village roads and farm lanes. Most homes in the area had outhouses. All the fresh vegetables in the commissary and grocery stores came from local farmers and the first advice to newcomers was: don't eat vegetables uncooked without first soaking them in disinfectant. Salad was out of the question. I wrote home:

Dear Family,

I'm in Germany! Hard to believe! It's beautiful, but lots of snow. Three feet and it's still snowing. There are so many people being sent here that we can't get housing for a while. I learned that Dave had to give a phony address, to say that we had someone to stay with, in order to bring me over with him. Otherwise, I would have had to stay in the U.S. and wait. But, don't worry. I've decided to look for something in town and get it set up before Dave gets back from the field. He was sent out right after Thanksgiving. I miss you already. How are the cats?

I wrote in my diary.

November 27, 1966: Dear Book, we've been here about four days now—Dave has been sent somewhere and I'm here by myself—not exactly happy about it either. It wouldn't be so bad if I could move to an apartment tomorrow, but I can't. I seem to be stuck. This place is Heidi-land—the Snow Queen's world— everything is white and cold. Looks like it will be an excellent week for writing to you, Book, with Dave away and me here playing house.

Later in the week I wrote with stoic commitment that I should count my blessings and if I could stop thinking about home in Connecticut, I'd be fine.

My recollection of being a young female of nineteen and a military dependent on a remote Army post was a combination of feeling different from everyone else and aware that I attracted attention without actually making contact with people. It was like the first day of school but without classmates or a class to go to. Soldiers whistled sometimes if I walked by unaccompanied and I stared straight ahead in confusion. I didn't know how an officer's wife was supposed to react. I felt conspicuous in my red loden coat, black boots and fur hat. So many young men, identically dressed and uninteresting except for the one I wanted to be with. I celebrated my twentieth birthday on

December tenth alone at the BOQ. Dave was still off in the field. Roaming the hallways I found a vending machine full of cookies and candy and discovered the German version of vanilla wafers, pronouncing them to be my birthday cake. Where would I find a dentist if my teeth fell apart?

In *The Stations of Solitude,* Alice Koller describes being solitary as being alone *well,* being alone luxuriously immersed in doing things of your own choice, aware of the fullness of your own presence rather than the absence of others. How to find things to do of my choice was my problem and I was acutely aware of Dave's absence.

I studied a German phrase book realizing that my five years of French was, if anything, a hindrance. When I tried to speak German, French words burbled up. At least it was a foreign language. Exploring the interior of buildings was warmer than walking outside, and upstairs in the BOQ I discovered an office labeled, "*HOUSING.*" I sprang into action.

"Excuse me, is this the housing office?" I asked an ample woman sitting behind a desk piled high with paper. Her name plate said Frau Diskau.

"Yah, and how can I help you?"

"My husband is Lt. Crocker and I would like to go out and look at some houses or apartments. We just arrived. He's in the field."

"Don't you vant to vait for him to come back?"

"No. He may not have much time to look with me and I'd like to start now. I'll surprise him."

She didn't smile, but her face smoothed out a bit as she raised her eyebrows and looked down at her paperwork.

"Vat area do you vant to live in?"

"I don't know. I don't know anything about the area," I

stammered, unprepared for her question. I had not seen even a map. "Where would you suggest?"

"Ve have a lot of people who need housing now, but, here, I'll give you some addresses. You vill have to go and look yourself."

"But, how do I find them?" I was beginning to wonder if I should wait for Dave. Back in Georgia, just before we came to Germany while he completed Ranger School and started Airborne training, I had arrived and found an apartment completely on my own. Why not in Germany? My biggest problems in Georgia were cockroaches and my perception of being followed by strange men—possibly a projection of my loneliness. Cockroaches could be exterminated and, against potential intruders, I barricaded the doors with furniture wherever I was and stayed in after dark. Germany seemed too cold for roaches and I felt fearless among the people. They seemed too busy, regimented and regulated to bother a young woman wandering around. I felt obvious *and* invisible.

I was desperate to *do* something. What could happen with all this snow and these busy people? The language seemed like a surmountable problem even though I spoke no German. I needed to *move*, to see this country. I had heard enough English language speakers to give me the false sense that everyone spoke a little English. Frau Diskau was either convinced by my temerity or more likely she didn't have time to talk me out of my crazy venture. I thought Dave would be pleased if I found us a place to live.

"I vill call a taxi for you. They will take you out to look and some of the drivers speak English. Here is a list of places to visit," she said.

I'm free, I thought. *I'll ride around in a taxi until I find a home.*

My cab driver was a small hat-less man with a kind, wrinkled face. I handed him my list of addresses from the back seat. His wispy hair matched the mounds of snow that had continued to accumulate since our arrival. I wondered if he was here, twenty-five years before, in the middle of a country at war. I stared at the back of his head, visible like a half-moon rising above the front seat, trying to think of something to say in German as we drove by rustic farms down small, unpaved roads and past wagons pulled by horses. This was my first introduction to the world outside the walls of the military post.

Clods of earth the color of black umber steamed under the hooves of cattle standing like sodden muddy statues in ancient barnyards. The cold winter air smelled like dark, moist soil, cow manure and diesel fuel. Orchards of dormant fruit trees formed black lace against the snowy hillsides. People trudged along the road pushing wheelbarrows or bent over under a sack on their shoulder. They paused, motionless, to look at us as we passed. I felt out of place in my warm taxi peering out at this archaic, rough landscape. It was fortunate that I knew nothing about the rest of Europe. Otherwise, I might have lamented that we should have been stationed in England or the south of France.

I tried to make conversation with my driver, resorting to English.

"I've never seen so much snow," I said, "even in New England where we have snow, but not this much."

"Ja, ja, schnee," he replied without glancing to look at me in his rear view mirror. We went back to silence.

The landlord at the first address spoke some English, enough for me to understand that it was an apartment heated by coal and attached to his house. He lived with a full-size St. Bernard who bounded out when I approached and met me almost nose to nose. My fear of dogs at that time was greater than my concern about working with a coal stove. A large black dog had bitten me on my first day of kindergarten and fifteen years later I was still working out my relationship with strange dogs. I was not as fearless as I thought.

"You see here, Miss, open little door, in goes scoop of coal from bucket. Close door. Coal comes every week. It's not so hard, a little dirty, but you get used to dat and you clean," the landlord explained.

"Danka—danka," I said as I backed away from the dog.

I knew farm landscape from growing up in Connecticut but these ruddy-faced, solid people with their snow-burned, cold water washed skin, their ancient tools and wagons, their language speckled with consonants and hard sounds, their earthy smells and big dogs—this was something new.

Visiting these places made me feel that I had rocketed back in time. It was how I imagined New England to be in the 1930s. The next house had an inside sink, but an outside toilet. I hadn't thought about plumbing and heating when we left the United States even though I knew there was at least one family in my hometown who still had an outhouse in the 1960s. Military housing on the post had all the amenities but nothing would be available for months. And besides, I liked the idea of living in a village among Germans.

The last address of the day was in the village of Brüchenau, about ten kilometers away. It was three rooms in the attic of a home close to the center of town. The German family who lived there spoke little English but somehow I understood that they liked Americans and felt secure in the presence of the U.S. Army. My soon to be landlady, Frau Schauka, indicated her fear of Russians coming from the east with furtive glances in an easterly direction. *"Americans, gute! Russians, nein!"*

The bathroom was downstairs and shared with the family, but the fact that toilet and sink were both inside the house seemed like a great leap forward. I reserved the apartment and returned that night to the BOQ full of a sense of accomplishment and less concerned that I knew no one except Dave. That night I thought about the Schauka family and their fear of invasion. It was incomprehensible to me.

Isolation was also a new concept. Amid the chaos of my upbringing, there was always someone around. Here, not only did most of the people around me speak another language, but those who spoke English lived a life unlike anything I had ever known. It's true that I grew up among nurses who wore uniforms back in Connecticut, but not with all this marching and saluting.

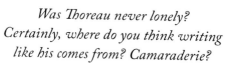

Was Thoreau never lonely?
Certainly, where do you think writing
like his comes from? Camaraderie?
—Jessamyn West, *Hide and Seek (1973)*

Dave had entered the busiest and most exciting time of his life—his first job as an army officer. If I had been a writer of something more than letters and nostalgic, philosophical diary entries, I might have thought I'd found nirvana; here was total solitude with no friends, no methods of communication, limited transportation and language barriers in every direction. Probably I could have sat with my pen and notebook and written a novel while waiting for Dave to come back. However, I was unable to sit, wait and delegate. I was my mother's daughter. I needed to act.

The next morning, as I contemplated how I would move

all the Samsonite to Brüchenau before Dave returned from the field, I had a visitor:

"Is anyone home? Whooh-ooh. Anyone there?" It was a female voice followed by a knock.

I opened the door and a young woman my age peered around the door frame. She seemed like an apparition with her long black winter coat, suede boots and fur hat.

"Well, ah HEARD you were here. You're Lt. Crocker's wife, aren't you? Ah couldn't believe it when ah learned you had arrived and we didn't know where you were!" she said.

Her name was Claudia, also the wife of a 2nd Lieutenant. She was from Texas and the soft twang of her all-American, southern accent felt like a warm bath.

"Someone said they thought y'all was German. They saw you from a distance in a red cape, and, well honey, you do look German with that blonde hair," she continued as she glanced around my makeshift camp, "but you're not, ah see, and you've been here all this time. You poor thing! You must be lonely. What on earth have y'all been doin' all this time?"

I was shocked to realize that what I had experienced was not what happened to everyone when they arrived. Dave had little chance to explain anything with his early departure to the field. And they, these others like me, had *seen* me. But who were they and where were they?

"I've been trying to find a place to live," I said.

"That's amazin' honey. You are *so* brave. Ah can't imagine tryin' to find something all by myself!" Claudia crooned at me. "I'm going to pick you up tomorrow for the Wives' Club Meeting. You need to meet some people, honey!"

That was the beginning of my association with other wives from all over the United States. At twenty I was one of the youngest. Most of them were pregnant with first or second children. I was about to enter the high and low experience of making friends fast and, just as quickly, saying goodbye as people moved on to their next duty station. The Christmas card list grew as friends came and went. Letters were the only connection after they moved on. But my fast and deep connection with these women didn't stick after Dave's death. I would let them fall away, too pained by the memory of the origin of our relationship as members of a couple. I lost my commonality with them and what could I speak about? Perhaps it was difficult for them to relate to me, too, out of fear. What could be more terrifying than to receive "the telegram"?

I did enjoy the camaraderie among wives, though. Being without our spouses for much of the time, we were more like a troop of girl scouts earning badges: cooking, cleaning, singing, playing cards, waxing floors, exchanging recipes, studying our Betty Crocker cookbooks for party menus, shopping, dieting and exercising. We occasionally spoke about what would happen when our husbands' orders might come, but never about war.

Within the week I moved our suitcases to Brüchenau to be ready for Dave's return. As a junior officer, he had to be continuously available when he wasn't completely off in the hinterland. Our car would not arrive for another two months and train or taxi was the only transportation to the post. Unknowingly, I was making his time away from me even longer with this extra commute.

Finally ensconced in my three-room attic castle in the house of Herr and Frau Schauka, I discovered a new torture: the cooking smells that drifted up from the kitchen below. I was not enthused about eating alone especially when the aroma from below conjured up big family meals. Isolation stirred up my obsessions about food. Five years earlier, in the months following my younger brother's death, I had stopped eating almost entirely for a time. Looking back at family pictures I realize that my mother had done the same thing. And her preoccupation with her own grief was possibly why she was not attentive to my diminishing size. Usually she was chiding me about being too thin, worried that I had some dormant TB bacillus waiting to attack. Perhaps I was a comfortable companion in grief for her. Eventually we could wear the same clothes until her size eight or nine was too big for me.

Now, above Frau Schauka's stove, I couldn't write or think. I dreamed of ham, mashed potatoes and fruit pies and the kitchen back in Connecticut. In my overheated attic when the smell of roasted meat, potatoes and vegetables wafted up from the kitchen below I paced back and forth until I had to leave and window shop in the town. I retaliated with my own cooking smell production as I made huge meals for Dave when he was able to come home, but dinner for two was not the same as the endless family meals I had prepared for ten or twelve or twenty with my mother and grandmother. I wanted to disappear from Germany and magically appear in Mystic in my apron.

But Frau Schauka saw me. Once when I was making my escape from the aroma of fried potatoes and apple cake she stopped me on the stairs. "*Kommen sie*—come in," she said, standing at her open door and gesturing with her hand. Her kitchen was tidy and small with stacks of painted earthen pottery bowls, tools for grating and slicing and a large wooden table in the center covered with flower-printed oil cloth. Her hands were dusty with flour and we sat with coffee and slices of poppy seed roll at the table where pieces of veal cutlets rested for the next round of pounding and seasoning.

Our friendship began around her table in a stilted mixture of German, English and sign language as she taught me all her variations of Weiner Schnitzel. While trying to communicate we pounded veal, dredged it in flour and egg, cooked and tasted. *My grandmother will never believe all the ways you can serve one piece of meat,* I thought. I sent the recipe home to my mother and grandmother.

In spite of Frau Schauka's kindness, the reality of our first German apartment was that it was too dark, too small, and too far from the military post for Dave. I filled my days with finding things to do; I walked, peered in shop windows, and visited a local elementary school where I wandered into a classroom after the children left and found a teacher eager to trade German lessons for English conversation.

Without books and without hearing my own language each day, I felt sorry for myself and then chastised myself in my journal: "Stop complaining—this is educational." I *had* gotten away from home, after all. A trip to the commissary (the military food store on post) to buy groceries could be extended to occupy an entire day. It was hard to admit that I hated the sloped ceilings and stuffiness of our attic, the place I had been so proud to find by myself. My new battle was against feeling useless. At night, when Dave returned, I rattled on about my day, but he was exhausted and had few questions about my hermit life.

In my sketchy memory, I see him entering the apartment and ducking his head to one side to avoid the sloped ceiling. He removes his hat and overcoat and sits down to start spit-shining his boots in silence. The table is set for two with china and silverware borrowed from Frau Schauka. He's ravenous after a long day and says he's happy that I continue to cook enough food for four people. His work is a mystery to me.

As a new officer overseeing classified details and maneuvers, he couldn't speak with any depth about his daily life. There was also the question of what was happening in Vietnam, the question we had decided, without saying it, to be silent about. What could I ask? *How's the war going these days?* Perhaps I was afraid to find out. We had lapsed into casual and limited conversation. During his intermittent trips to field exercises for days and weeks at a time, he would resume writing to me, and, again, it became the glue of our relationship as it had when we first met at West Point. He probably told me more in letters than he could in conversation.

I remember that they were long letters in his flowing script written with a fountain pen, describing the landscape, how much he missed me, impressions of his men and some details of his work. Those letters are with all the others, now, six feet under. Again I wonder what they would tell me. Will I be reminded of how Dave put up with his lonely and frustrated bride?

Looking back on my introduction to life in Germany and to military marriage, I see a young woman on the run who did too much but never completely understood the world she stepped into. Dave was so busy and I was so preoccupied with my adjusting to military spouse life in this first year that his mother's advice back in her house between the twin beds became moot. The long days away from each other were followed by short nights.

As my German improved, stilted conversations with Frau Schauka continued to center on food and the possible invasion from the east. She showed me how her thumb and hand had been deformed by the work she had been forced to do during World War II—something related to large machinery and the weaving of heavy cloth or canvas. We formed a curious bond in which she represented the past for me and I probably held her hope for the future and continued safety from invasion.

Wildflecken continued to overflow with fresh, new recruits and young officers who were training in the forests of Germany for the jungles of Vietnam. Brigadier General Robert Montague, who served in Vietnam during the early 1960s, said in the aftermath of the war that a crucial mistake was to have pitched American troops, trained to repulse Russians on the plains of central Europe, into a tangle of mountain jungles and rice fields where enemy guerrillas could not be distinguished from local peasants.

Within six weeks Dave found an apartment in the village close to the post and I left the cramped attic with a handful of recipes and an indelible memory of the Schauka family's fear of the Russians.

I wrote in my journal that I needed self-discipline. Stagnation of the mind was my fear, according to a romantic note to myself about the importance of learning. There was still this question of acquiring German now that I was far from my teacher at the elementary school in Brüchenau. By *learning* I'm sure I meant *keeping busy*. When I read my words today I see my frantic self at work, trying to make the best of the situation; a classic trait in my family.

I had wanted to come here, or at least I went along with it—but what is this place? And what will become of me?

In our new apartment in downtown Wildflecken, above a clothing store, we had a view of rolling farm lands on one side and a bar frequented by U.S. Army GIs on the other. Multiple times each night, the sounds of the American country western song, "I Wanna go Home," wafted up to our window. I didn't drink alcohol in those days or I might have joined them.

To live off post in a foreign country is called "living on the economy," the *economy* being the local foreign community with whom the military has set up their enterprise. I began to grow weary of being the foreigner in their economy. I felt drawn to other Americans, especially when I learned that we were now close enough to the post to hear all the alarms that warned of an *alert*. During an alert we were supposed to grab a box of survival materials always kept ready with C-rations, flashlights, blankets, candles, matches in metal containers, water purification tablets, and go *somewhere*—probably not east.

The "alert box" sat in the closet ready to go. We would be informed by a siren and each day at 5:00pm the siren was tested. There were echoes of the old "desk drills" in school but these were more annoyingly persistent. Sometimes I wondered how I would know if it was a real emergency and would I just jump in the car and follow the Germans, wherever they were going? Would the invaders come by trucks and armored vehicles rumbling over the landscape? Would soldiers with rifles barge into my building and break down the door? Would I meet the Schauka family in some mountain cave? I don't remember fear, but I do recall studying the alert box in the hall closet and wondering if the flashlight would work and where the first meal of C-rations would be eaten and what it would taste like.

My mother sent me flannel nightgowns decorated with edelweiss flowers for Christmas. She didn't write letters—perhaps one in the entire two years I was away—but her gifts expressed her concerns. I wrote back that the nightgowns were much appreciated because winter weather was predicted to last until late spring. Our new apartment was again small with sloped ceilings but with all the modern conveniences; there was a large bathroom with a bathtub and hand shower, and a separate WC. Electrical appliances made in the States had to be used with large, heavy transformers to convert the electrical current. I was soon cooking and cleaning with all the gadgets we had shipped over in our household goods baggage that arrived nine weeks after we did.

I bonded with my neighbor across the hall, Kathy, from Dallas, Texas. She introduced me to the floor wax section of the commissary and we competed against each other for mirror shine finishes in our kitchens. By the end of 1966 Dave and I had moved five times in six months, and without news from the outside world, I was oblivious to the fact that American troop strength in Vietnam had reached almost 400,000 soldiers within a little more than one year.

Included in our baggage when it finally arrived were my art supplies: a paint box, brushes and canvases. But, as much as I loved painting and drawing, they were solitary activities and I had plenty of those already. It had been easier to paint in the midst of a busy family at home in Connecticut. I usually drew and painted right in the middle of the living room with my brothers playing piano or building model cars and airplanes and my grandmother in her chair by the fireplace talking about food or the latest gossip.

In Germany, I hungered for activities with people. I became the consummate volunteer, joining and organizing everything in my path. Keeping the floors shined in our apartment became a challenge after I was elected president of the Officers' Wives' Club, girl scout leader, children's ballet teacher, project director for the Protestant Women of the Chapel, organist and choir director. I don't think there was a dearth of talent in Wildflecken, only that I was one of the few young women who did not have children or wasn't pregnant. My strongest recollection of this frenzied array of activities was a moment with my small troop of girl scouts, trying to come up with an outside activity. I decided we would clean the weathered and neglected cemetery that was filled with named and unnamed displaced persons, and plant flowers there. I remember the little girls, daughters of American soldiers, laughing and playing among the rusted icons and plaiting daisies for their hair.

But what was my life with Dave? He loved camping and mountain climbing and preferred to both work and play outside. When there was time to get away together, it was usually an overnight camping trip to test a new tent or piece of equipment, even in the winter. He seemed happiest in woods and on mountainsides. I remember his smile, outside. The social aspects of military life, the Officer's Club activities and cocktail parties, were less enjoyable for him. In many ways this "hardship post" put Dave in his element and he excelled. His next assignment before Vietnam, as aide-de-camp to the commanding general of the third division, would be his torture.

Dave wrote often to his parents. His father was then commander of the New York State National Guard after returning from Vietnam. In spite of his military record and accomplishments, Dave's father was passed over for promotion to Brigadier General, presumably because of his criticisms of the conduct of the war after seeing it for himself. This disparity between the Pentagon and those on the ground was borne out in all accounts of the war, including McNamara's own admissions in his memoir. But in the throes of the war, anyone willing to speak up about the reality of the situation likely defused their own careers.

On November 4, 1967, Dave wrote:

Dear Mom and Dad,

It's been almost exactly a year that we've been over in Wildflecken—don't know how much longer we'll be here now that the time to Captain has been changed. Actually I would not be surprised to get my orders for Vietnam within one or two months from now.

David

His goal now was to get his time in Vietnam over with, but his orders would not come for another eight months. Before the escalation in Vietnam and the troop surge, moving in rank from 2nd Lieutenant to Captain took at least four years. Now it was reduced to two. Young officers were becoming cannon fodder in the jungle.

News about life in the United States and the progress of the war was limited in Europe. Only the *Stars and Stripes* newspaper was readily available. I heard little about domestic protests against the war in Vietnam. It's probable that Dave knew much more than I did. And, while we wives spoke around our coffee tables about when our husbands' next orders would arrive, any discussion concerning Vietnam felt taboo—even bad luck. Perhaps it was superstition, but the subject could stop a conversation and quiet a room, and what did we wives know anyway? We would not have heard that Martin Luther King, Jr., had taken the risk to condemn the Vietnam War in his speech at Riverside Church in Manhattan in April of 1967. He said that the United States had increased its commitment of troops in Vietnam "...in support of governments which were singularly corrupt, inept and without popular support."

In January 1968, Dave was promoted to First Lieutenant and we left Wildflecken for his assignment to serve as aide-de-camp to General Shanahan at 3rd Division headquarters in Würzburg, Germany, a larger post and a bigger town. Before we left Wildflecken, I received a commendation from the Post

Commander in our departure ceremony for my *outstanding community service*. My intention had been just to do, to keep moving. I was surprised to realize that other people noticed what I did and called it community service. I called it self-service, self-survival.

What Dave loved best was the *working life* of an infantryman, if one can call combat training in the field a regular working day. Now we would live in larger quarters on a big, bustling military post in the midst of an elegant and quaint city that had come through the Second World War largely unscathed. However, Dave was no longer doing the job he preferred in the field. Ultimately, this was the necessary order of events that would allow him to be sent back to the field again—the next time into a real war. When we arrived in Würzburg we were invited for lunch with the General and his wife and several of his nine children. I remember Dave's face having a serious expression as he sat across from me at the elegantly appointed table. I don't think it was the cream of leek soup in front of him that caused his consternation. It was more likely the disparaging remarks of the General about everything and everyone.

Dave didn't gossip or criticize anyone, but he did share with me that the General, during one of their helicopter rides surveying 3rd Division activities, invited him to jump out of the aircraft for asking a challenging question. I don't think Dave was wearing a parachute.

Dave's parents received the following letter written in February, 1968. He never complained about his work situation, but the move to what he called a desk job made clear what he loved to do and within nine months he would be in back in the role he loved best—but in Vietnam:

Dear Family,
  The job so far is interesting but not nearly as rewarding

as Company Commander. I don't believe I would like to be a General. I have, though, done much flying and seen many new things. General Shanahan is ADC for support, hence I visit the artillery, engineer, signal and maintenance units with him. You might guess that I saw little in the way of company or battalion size operation by these types of units in Wildflecken.

There are a great many officers here now—most even younger than me, believe it or not. Since August of 1967 they have been coming in regularly and rapidly. Most, of course, are very inexperienced and I was hard pressed to find an officer who I felt willing to turn A Company over to. None of the infantry officers were ready for command...

It's difficult to believe that he was only twenty-four. Later he wrote to his parents about what was important to him during his experience in Wildflecken:

...I had a very fine thing happen just prior to leaving A Company in January. A Major contacted the commanding general, and told him that A Co 2/15 was the best company in the Division after he observed and graded us. This was due to absolutely outstanding noncommissioned officers ... and the fact that the men in the company trusted and were willing to try hard and do their best with me. When they walked—I walked, when they were cold and tired—I was; I hit the dirt, mud or snow with them when we were fired at. I walked the line at night in a blizzard and talked with them—many other little insignificant things. Many other Company Commanders rode their jeeps, sat and ate chow in a nice warm tent, stood "observing" as their men advanced or were fired on. Nothing very important maybe—but my men saw me and knew I was with them and they were with me. It was a good company—high morale. I think too, the best in the Division and probably one of the most rewarding experiences of my life.

I had little knowledge of what he did in the field but I have a photograph of his promotion on our second wedding anniversary, June 9, 1968. We gathered in General Shanahan's office in front of a bevy of flags. The General stood between us and turned to a smiling Dave to present him with the silver captain's bars. Dave looked relaxed, even proud, in this official photo and was probably relieved to know that this meant he would soon be released from General Shanahan and desk duty.

Würzburg was an easier place to breathe, with music, art classes, a theater and a tennis court. Dave and I visited castles and prowled through antique shops in town. In the commemorative photograph of the promotion scene, I am peering around the General at Dave like a wood nymph who might dart back into the forest at any moment, if the wind changed, with my long, blonde hair falling over one shoulder.

Three weeks earlier Dave had told me that Howie Pontuck, a classmate at West Point and member of our wedding party, had been killed in Vietnam. Dave didn't share details, if he knew them. Just the words, "Howie's been killed." We stood in numbed silence, neither of us able to speak, in the living room of our Würzburg apartment and then continued preparing to go to a parade or a reception or some other military obligation. Dave changed quietly into his dress greens and I hunted for a hat to wear.

I thought of Howie, five foot two and solid muscle from gymnastics training, smiling like the Cheshire cat when he presented us with our wedding gifts two years before, Chanel perfume for me and soap and aftershave for Dave.

Howie died trying to defuse a bomb. A posting by a comrade on the virtual wall in the 1990s described his remarkable courage to volunteer to work with bombs and landmines; they said he was a happy, gregarious leader who would surprise his buddies by shaking hands, taking a step backwards, and doing a back flip somersault, landing on his feet—still smiling.

Howie had undergone circumcision in his last year at West Point when he embraced Judaism. On one of my weekend visits, Dave told me about it in hushed amazement at his friend's courage. It's ironic to think about the experiences we endure because we believe there is a future. Inventor, futurist and author Ray Kurzwell speculates that realizing there is a future is the special quality of the human mind that has contributed to our survival. He speculates that a Stone Age hunter, observing a tiger from a safe distance, could calculate with great accuracy which action might preserve his life. War, and the materials of battle, alters the relationship between what we think we can do and the odds of survival and yet we continue to believe in war as a method of resolution and carry on with hope. We are a remarkable and confusing species.

When Dave finally received his orders for Vietnam in early August 1968, he decided it was time to take part of his many days of accumulated leave to go with me to Switzerland before we returned to the States. He wanted to camp and hike in the heart of the Alps in the village of Grindelwald and show me the north face of the Eiger—a treacherous climb he dreamed about. He created a dream book with pictures, maps and lists of equipment he would need for the ascent.

But that climb would be *someday*, he said. Not on this trip in which he wanted to introduce me to the beauty of the area. On our small hikes up and down the mountains, every view upward was of magnificent peaks or slashes of blue-white ice in crevasses. The pristine valley below was dotted with wooden chalets amid fields of blue, pink and yellow wildflowers. Cow bells clanged near and distant, and from somewhere there was the long, languid moan of an alpenhorn. I walked gingerly over the solid ice bridges covering mountain streams. Once I took off all my clothes to Dave's delight to dip briefly in the frigid water of an icy glacier stream while he took photographs.

He said we would do "easy stuff" on this trip. On the third day of hiking and modest climbing, we narrowly escaped being swept off a rock face by a small avalanche as we approached the west side of the Eiger. It started with a trickle of stones just above us as we moved from foothold to foothold. There was a grumbling, grinding sound of rock against rock and I felt the surreal vibration of standing on a mountain that was in motion under my body. I tried to keep my balance. Shale and stone slid away around us. Dave held back a chunk of rock with his leg so that I could jump to a stable spot out of the stream of coursing stones.

"Don't look down, look up!" he yelled as he flew around the crumbling rock behind me, grabbed my hand and we leapt together over a narrow slot to a nearby ledge. Like two airborne mountain goats, we flew to safety just as a chunk of hillside the size of a refrigerator gave way behind us. I had focused on following his directions for the past few seconds but now I felt the airlessness of the moment. We flopped to the ground and clung to each other, still at a steep angle to the valley below.

"You're bleeding!" There was gash below his right knee.

"It's nothing," he said, taking off his T-shirt to bind around his wound. On the five-hour climb down to our camp, blood soaked through the makeshift bandage before we reached the bottom.

"We're safe—things happen," he said later as he cleaned and bandaged the wound. I was useless as a nurse. Bloody bandages were one of the aspects of growing up among nurses that I did not miss.

From our campsite that evening at sunset, I stared up at the mountain we had descended. The spot which had almost claimed us was a speck in the distance just to the left of the infamous concave swath that is the Eiger North Face. Dave was tightening the ropes on our two-person tent and putting order in the knapsacks we had carried up and down that day. He opened the canvas map case he had sewn weeks before on my sewing machine and unfolded a panoramic map showing the entire range of the Swiss Alps. He ran his finger across the tops of the ancient sentries and stopped on the Eiger.

"Some day I'll do the north face," he said. "That's my far-off dream."

I had no premonitions about my future with the Eiger and no present desire to go back up the mountain anytime soon. When I crawled into our double sleeping bag, my muscles were still tense and resisting gravity at first. As I closed my eyes, panic suddenly rippled through my body and prickled my skin. I was back on the mountain, flying, willing my body upwards, and then hurtling down, down, down, pressing into the earth. I locked my arms around Dave and tried to speak through panicked sobs. He stroked my hair, holding me close and said: "You did everything right up there."

On this trip we were magically a couple again after eighteen months of mostly separate lives. Now we were sleeping in a two-person tent in a double sleeping bag, eating fresh baguettes and cheese, looking up at the light from the window in the center of the north face at night. In twelve months we would be back here again. But not as either of us could have ever imagined.

PART FIVE

HOME TO BROKEN HEARTS

———⟨∞∞⟩———

I cannot sleep—great joy is as restless as sorrow.
—Fanny Burney, *Evelina (1778)*

The homebound plane was a chartered affair with propellers that roared from our departure at Rheine-Main Air Force Base in Frankfurt to our arrival at McGuire Air Force Base in New Jersey. It was 1968 and jets were not yet ubiquitous. I thought I was accustomed to the engine drone until my ears would pop periodically and the roar resumed. Around me was the now-familiar sea of my military milieu; army officers and enlisted men in green dress uniforms or olive drab fatigues punctuated by the occasional pastels worn by wives and children. The flight attendants served cardboard box lunches with ham and cheese sandwiches and eight-ounce cartons of milk and orange juice during the tedious ten hours. I pretended sleep to avoid the unease in my stomach and to hasten our arrival in the U.S.

I yearned for this trip to be over and to step back into the familiar landscape of New England to see road signs with distances in miles rather than kilometers. I wanted to get off this plane and head for Bayonne, New Jersey, where the Jaguar had already been hoisted off a cargo ship. I wanted to get on the New Jersey Turnpike and look for the "Welcome to New York State" sign. "Connecticut Welcomes You" would not be long after that. I wanted to go home. Two years was a long time to be away after never having been away.

Dave slept next to me on the plane. He liked to wear civilian clothes at every opportunity and today he wore tan chinos and a blue polo shirt. This was his privilege since he was officially on leave. Salutes would come only from those who knew he was a military officer. Now he rested incognito, his compact body curved in the seat with his head resting against the window. Just before we'd departed from Germany, he'd come home with a buzz haircut and, in spite of it, he was still handsome. The lack of hair made his eyes bluer and his eyelashes and eyebrows darker. I studied him as he dozed. I remember thinking that, even with the roar of the engine, we were in a rare time of quiet togetherness, as if we were in chairs in front of a fire, resting, before being hurtled into the unknown. His tanned arm stretched over the armrest between us and rested across my body. He held my hand with a reassuring grip. He seemed always alert even in sleep.

One odd but titillating pleasure about returning home was the feeling that I had become independent of my parents even if I would be living with them for the next year. I had gotten used to the idea of being married and away from the family compound. I wasn't severed from them but felt individuated. I didn't feel as susceptible to their influence, but I liked the idea that I was still a member of the clan. Now I could live with them for the coming months and be a grownup at the same time. Art school was a possibility.

The family glue that held us together was the unanimous and industrious goal to get ahead in the world. My parents and grandparents started businesses and kept them going against all odds: restaurants, nursing homes, trailer parks, fuel oil delivery, boarding houses. Whenever they saw an opportunity that even vaguely matched their abilities, they jumped in with both feet and kids, too. There was always a lot to *do* in my house growing up and I jumped at any chance to chime in and help in all the family enterprises. That's how one *belonged* to the tribe—by pitching in with whatever had to be done. It was probably this unflappable gumption trickling up from generations of Swamp Yankees behind me that buoyed me in the years after I received the shock that would eventually follow our return home. The message from the gene pool was not, "You can do it," it was, "You *will* do it if you want to."

Possibly this explained why I fell in step with Dave's interests in extreme sports like rock climbing even in ice and snow. During our stint in Germany we had camped in blizzards to test winter survival equipment and hiked through forests swarming with horse flies. I was not a total wimp and he never rebuked me at any time, but there were moments when I yearned for a cup of hot chocolate in my hand and a small campfire in front of me, but instead just kept walking or climbing—whatever we were doing. Perhaps he did perceive my facial expression as less than enthusiastic as he looked down at me scrambling at the end of a rappelling rope, but he never let on. He was always there with a patient voice saying "good job, keep climbing." So, I did.

He was completely an outdoorsman. Indoor amenities like kitchens, beds and living rooms were not as interesting to him as freeze dried food, ultralight tents and the latest version of a truly portable Porta-Potty. He used my sewing machine to create canvas bags and tarps for all occasions. Outside, in nature, on rocks, over mountainsides, through forests, he thrived and he wanted to share it all with me. Under his spell of enthusiasm for everything physical and challenging, I traversed, rappelled and developed strong fingertip strength.

I'm sure we held hands as our plane landed at McGuire Air Force Base in New Jersey. I probably grabbed his arm in utter glee. We were greeted beyond the tarmac by immense blue skies and flat coastal landscape tinged with the bright red and gold of early fall. Every truck, every license plate, every stop sign, looked good to me. On the drive to Connecticut I inhaled the view over the Atlantic to the horizon, the jaunty music of gulls. Seaweed perfumed the air. The verticality of forests and fir trees and the dense green of Germany receded from my mind as I feasted on this long-lost view of endless flatness. We stopped at a rest stop shortly after crossing the Connecticut state line and I contemplated kneeling down to kiss the ground in the parking lot, but I didn't.

My enthusiasm to be home pulled me as if I were a small mound of iron filings and a giant magnet stood at the door in Mystic. I ached for the sight of my parents, my grandmother and brothers, the prospect of rubbing the necks of the family cat and dog, the house, my old bedroom with shelves of paperback books probably untouched in the past two years. But these treasured images were lined up alongside the dreaded departure of Dave for Vietnam. I felt light and heavy at the same time. It was as if joy and sorrow came from the same well. Our life was an unraveling ball of twine bouncing down the stairs out of reach. The persistence of the war in spite of talk about peace meetings and strategies was the weight that underlay everything we did. There was no sense in charting our own course in life until next year, thirteen months from now, with Vietnam behind us.

The world to which we returned was even deeper in chaos than it had been two years before. 1968 had been, so far, a busy year for violence, protest and war mongering in the United

States. On April 4th, Martin Luther King, Jr., was assassinated in Memphis. On June 5th, Robert F. Kennedy had been assassinated in Los Angeles, less than three months after announcing his candidacy for president. These events were far-away murmurs in the cloistered life of American military bases in Europe. Our principle news source, the *Stars and Stripes,* something akin to the old *Grit* "good news" tabloid, delivered the party line to soldiers and their families throughout the world. Letters from home didn't mention murder and mayhem and I had not heard the voices of friends and family in two years. Except for a visit by my younger brother, Sam, during the summer of 1967, I had lived in a bubble, with little information about the outside world.

The re-entry plan after we landed in New Jersey was to drive to Connecticut first and see my family and then drive up to Schenectady, New York, to see Dave's parents. Within hours, we were turning into the driveway of my parents' home where the lanky yellow pines planted too close together lined the entrance from the main road. Here, hidden by weeping willows and overgrown evergreens, was the frenetic time capsule that was home. I suspected that my mother would be baking a turkey in anticipation of our arrival. It was one of her most predictable qualities; a turkey dinner with all the trimmings was always the top menu choice for special events in my family.

The two years of absence evaporated as we entered to the mingling aromas of roast turkey, sage dressing, squash pie and baked apples. There was a scramble to the door as everyone tried to greet us at once and we hugged each one: mother, father, grandmother, brothers, dog and cats. We carried in suitcases and bags of gifts. The phone rang with friends who asked if we had arrived yet. In my mother's embrace, the scent of her signature Devon Violet Cologne brought her back completely. My father, tanned and robust from a summer of outside work at the nursing home and his mobile home park, stood grinning in silence, pumping Dave's hand and clapping him on the shoulder. My parents were both in their late forties, still young in spite of my odyssey.

There were no discernible changes in the furniture or the décor of the living room. The grandfather clock featured in many of my interior sketches looked back at me from its same spot next to the entrance to the dining room. I was delighted to sit in the same old familiar, overstuffed chairs, then to run up the stairs to my former bedroom, sliding my hand along the wall to feel each bump and crackle in the wallpaper. The cat eyed me with attentive caution. *I will never feel tired in my hyper-happy state*, I thought, but as we settled onto the nubby cushions of the couch to talk, fatigue came like velvet mist. We were safe, for now.

We slept in the three-quarter size bed in my old room and filled the drawers and closets with our foreign life brought back from Germany. My room had been left intact in my absence. The blonde, rock maple bedroom set stood in the same arrangement, the bathroom off the hall smelled of my brother's Old Spice aftershave, the woods outside the windows were denser with oak and pine trees. The barn behind the house had fallen down a bit further. I set the correct time on my blue Baby Ben alarm clock on the bed side table and relished the familiar clicking sound of the winding key.

The next morning, Tiny, a mixture of spaniel, spitz and collie, sniffed my legs with lingering curiosity. She was fatter than I remembered but her doggy smell brought back our long car rides together and how she sat in the back seat and rested her chin on an open window with her eyes closed against the wind. Each moment felt as if I was turning the pages of a beloved picture book as Tiny and I walked through the village of Old Mystic. She stopped to re-introduce me to everything at her nose level. We had forty-seven days before Dave would get on another plane. Meanwhile we basked in idleness and I tried to discern the filmy web of life that had formed in our absence.

As I spoke with my parents and grandmother and brothers, I examined them, perhaps looking for the reflection of my own changes. I felt different but I couldn't figure out if *they* were different. I was out of synch with them. I had managed without them through loneliness, physical illness, language barriers, creating a new home. I wanted to account for everything that could happen with the passing of time. Had I been changed by my experience of trying to find my place as an army wife? How would I connect with other students if I went to back to school while Dave was in Vietnam? I had lived on fairy tales in my childhood and now I was Sleeping Beauty. Perhaps this is how prisoners feel when they return to the outside world.

Except for my father, when he went off to the China seas in WWII, and my grandfather's confinement in a tuberculosis sanitarium, no one in my family had left for such a long time. I'm amazed today when I hear someone say that they haven't seen their sister (or brother) for years (if they are still living). Is it the result of trauma, finances, physical distance, psychological distance? Do they choose to be separated? I knew only solid enmeshment in family life and yet I had been gone for two years.

The reunion with Dave's family was different than the one with mine. I barely knew the Crocker family before we left and they were not strangers to the absence and distance of living away in a foreign country for years at a time. Now I knew them mainly through the many letters they had written to us. They had lived a military life since their marriage at West Point during World War II. They knew the places we'd been. This homecoming was more a resumption of reverie. Rather than,

"What was it like to ..." they asked, "Did you see ..., and how was..." and "Did you get a chance to see the Smiths and the Sutherlands when they passed through Würzburg?"

They seemed more like loving colleagues than parents. Dave and his father spoke quietly out of earshot about Vietnam. After his term there as a division commander two years before, he had returned bitter and disillusioned with the conduct of the war. Dave's mother asked me questions about wives' club activities in Germany. It was curious to think that my parents knew nothing of what our life had been, except for what we could describe. With my family, I felt like an anthropologist reporting back about the natives of an uncharted territory. Dave's parents knew a lot about where we had lived, the people, the architecture, the scenery, the exchange rate between dollars and Deutsch Marks. Their inquiry was more a checking in about what might have changed since they were there.

As the days ticked by before Dave's departure, we engaged in the small talk of preparation, how to get things done, pay bills, paperwork, where things are, what I'll need, what he'll need. How I should take care of his baby, the Jaguar XK-E, in his absence. He took me to a gun shop and tried to convince me that I might need a gun for self-protection. I refused to touch them when they were taken out of the display case.

We had had the dreaded discussion of his "Last Will and Testament" while we were in Germany. I know that his purpose was only to inform me that it existed and where I could find it if I needed to. It's a normal procedure for one going off to war. I see him standing in front of me as if he were telling a serious story to a small child, speaking in a quiet, gentle manner and ignoring the fact that I was staring at the ground, trying not to hear him.

He was organized and had sent copies of his Will, life insurance, service record, birth certificates and our marriage certificate to the Army Mutual Aid Society, a repository of vital records for the benefit of army officers and their dependents. Evidence mounted that his departure was imminent and, as if I were following him up a mountain trail, I watched and mostly listened. My apprenticeship as waiting wife had progressed to the final test, what to do while he goes to war? Would I go to school? Would I work with my parents? Our common goal was just to get through the next year.

Every detail of his departure was under control except for a last minute case of poison ivy which covered his entire body including his penis. He and his brother who was also severely allergic to the plant had taken a hike in the woods a month before he was to leave for Vietnam. It was a very effective method of birth control.

We made plans for the first time that we would see each other after six months during his R & R (Rest and Recreation) in Hawaii. Each time he kissed me in the final days, he said something like: "And you'll get one hundred more in Hawaii to make up for the next six months."

He spoke of his time in Vietnam as unavoidable, a river to cross, an obstacle to remove. Once the orders are issued, he said he would face court martial if he didn't go.

"There's no other choice," he said. "I have to go even if Dad says the war is a mess right now." What his father had said was that there was a disconnect between what was happening on the ground, in the jungles, and what politicians and the Pentagon perceived the war to be and expected it to be, a reality which would not be unraveled from the fundamental untruths and hyperbole of the war until years later. But, I understood nothing about what he was about to step into.

"We'll survive—I'll be home by Christmas next year," he

said. "Then I have only one year before I can get out of the army completely."

I promised to write every day and prayed for the rash to go away.

"Letters—that's all we'll have over there," he said. "Where I'll be, there won't be any other communication except mail."

The anticipation of verbal silence, physical distance, had its own power. It began slowly with long silences and idle activities, constant unspoken preparation. We could drive for an hour together without a word between us. We unpacked and repacked, organized, cleaned, straightened, made lists. On our last night together on November 10, 1968 we barely spoke. We expressed our love for each other only with our bodies. The poison ivy scourge had finally resolved. I remember tenderness and pleasure and the sense that he was giving more than I could give back. It was the best and worst night of our marriage. Perhaps in our silences we were rehearsing; letters, slides and photographs would be our only connection for months.

The next morning—a Tuesday and by chance also Veteran's Day—at 5:00am, there was a quiet breakfast of his favorites, bacon and eggs. My father drove with us the ten-minute ride to a small local airport in Groton, Connecticut. Dave and I sat hand in hand in a corridor designated as the airport terminal with high windows casting frail shadows of the window frames around us in the gray, morning light. Every cough and footstep echoed off the drab, beige, industrial-looking, concrete block walls. We were the only customers.

Clouds and a light rain obliterated the transition from sunrise to daylight. A toy-sized prop plane waited in the mist on the tarmac. It would take him back to McGuire Air Force Base in New Jersey where he would find an army transport plane heading to another base in California. From there he would fly farther and farther west until it became east again, with brief stops in Hawaii, the Philippines, finally to arrive in Saigon. As we sat together on the metal bench it seemed that nothing more could be said. Words were too precious, too insignificant. We made small talk, small jokes. We spoke in fragments as if we were in a hospital waiting room anticipating news of the patient's condition.

"Watch yourself with strangers. I wish you'd let me buy that gun for you."

"I hate guns. I might shoot someone by accident."

"Time flies—you'll see—before you know it."

My fingers entwined in his, I glanced around the cinder block walls, not for the purpose of remembering this place, but for reassurance that we would be here again, we would meet next year in this spot. A door to the outside opened, someone looked in glancing left and right, and the whir of the engines outside filled the room.

He stood up to leave, "I'm going to find some pearls for you."

I remembered the string of pearls his father brought back from Vietnam for his mother two years before. What a clever, sweet way to say, "I'll be back," and suddenly he was leaving. My father and I watched him duck his head under the light rain as he strode across the runway and handed his bag up to a hand reaching down from the door of the plane. He smiled back at us and waved. He was wearing civilian clothes. The plane taxied into the rain and flew off over Long Island Sound. I looked away quickly from my father's sadness as he took out a handkerchief and wiped his face.

"Well—he's on his way—the sooner to come back," he said.

Now I could notice that it was rainy and cold. When we went back to my parents' house, I went up to my room and started to write a letter. I felt the crossover into the silence and the long wait. Evidence of the energy of our life together was everywhere in my old bedroom, his clothes with mine in the closet; books, music, souvenirs from Europe, furniture we'd bought together.

This pause without him gave these objects a quiet inanimate quality, as if they were resigned, like me, to my makeshift storage room. They matched my mood of suspended animation as I accustomed myself to waiting. I was not particularly organized in those days but superstition inspired me to create rituals, making order with letters, books and clothes at the end of each day, crossing the days off the calendar. I never figured out precisely the difference in time between Connecticut and Vietnam and puzzled over whether he was living the day before me or the day after. If we had spoken in real time at some point, he might have said what day and time he existed in, but we would never speak again and that possibility never entered my thoughts. My resistance against such ruminations and the urge to keep him under my sky, kept him closer, inviting hope to linger. Hope—that thing with feathers, according to Emily Dickinson.

Within a week of his departure I received a letter in his flowing script in a blue airmail envelope. A great reward for my first seventeen trips to the Old Mystic Post Office where I opened the small box and usually saw only Mrs. Williams in her cameo pose, sorting mail. Like me, Dave's first reflex had been to write. The letter was dated November 11th, the day of his departure. He described the land beneath the plane across the country and the colors of the sky. From the window of the plane he had seen the Southern Cross, a group of stars found in the southern region of the night sky. "A good sign," he said. "A good omen." Now he was under a different sky, finding the constellations of another hemisphere, looking for luck with a new heaven.

I wrote each day but would not know where to send the letters for at least two weeks. He would not be *in country* for some period of time. Before he left he said there would be first the arrival in Saigon, the receiving of orders at command headquarters, and the orientation to the country and the status of the war. Then he would depart to the front in the area of Pleiku where there would be the change-of-command ceremony to place him in charge of the one hundred and twenty men in Alpha Company of the 22nd Infantry.

There were few women in the area, he said in another letter, except Vietnamese civilians, especially "Coca-Cola girls," the small, young Vietnamese women in mandarin shirts who appeared out of nowhere from the jungle during periods of calm with beer and soda in a box strapped on the back of a bicycle.

Finally, after five weeks, a flood of letters arrived describing the country, the architecture, the trees, foliage, the Vietnamese people, the men in his company, his assumption of command, aspects of his job, and how much he missed me. As the letters continued into December, he wrote about the changing weather, the rainy season, the challenges of heat, humidity, mud and insects, and yearning for a shower, dry feet, a quiet night of sleep. I tried to picture his world but it was too frightening to dwell on.

I could not try to visualize his discomforts without increasing my sense of helplessness. I didn't want to imagine that he woke up to war each day and the same task of calculating how to stay alive and how to keep his men alive, the constant gauging of safe and unsafe. If the Coca-Cola girls emerged from the jungle with their wares, he learned it was a sign that the Viet Cong were not in their midst at that moment. I felt better about Coca-Cola.

One of the first photographs taken just after he arrived in Vietnam showed him in perfect form wearing crisp, clean, starched fatigues and spit-shined boots. I scrutinized the look of his body, his face. He appeared healthy, sharp, alert, perhaps even comfortable. I felt reassured—he really was okay. By his 25th birthday, on December 20, 1968, a photo in the jungle showed him thinner, shirtless, with a sheen of sweat that created a halo around his shoulders in the baking sun. I would learn months later that at the time the picture had been taken he had already received a Purple Heart and a Bronze Star. Did he tell me in his letters? Probably not. Or, if he did, he would have minimized the event. "Why create needless worry?" he would say.

I mailed package after package with cookies, magazines, pistachios, crackerjacks, camera film, ink cartridges for his pen. His letters and requests would arrive ten to fifteen days after he mailed them. Even if I fulfilled the request the very day his letter arrived, I knew that my response, my package, would not reach him for at least another two weeks. It took a month to six weeks, between asking for something, asking a question and receiving a response. It was a world controlled by the snail's pace of "airmail" and cargo ships. Mrs. Williams, the Postmistress, became my patron saint: *Our Lady of the Small Window at the Post Office.*

When his letters arrived I read them over and over. I worried them like a dog with a meaty bone. Even in the midst of war, he used his favorite Schaffer fountain pen with blue ink and wrote in bold flowing script, pages and pages on thin airmail paper. Sometimes he started with an apology for not writing sooner and explained the obstacle. At times the paper was smudged with dirt and I would hold the stain to my nose, hoping to touch something that had touched him, to find his scent in his world.

In January 1969, I returned to college. I had been accepted into the visual arts department of the Fine Arts School at the University of Connecticut and commuted one hour each way to the Storrs campus from my parents' home. At twenty-three, I was older than most of my classmates and an oddity because I was married. I wore the same paint-smeared jeans and baggy sweaters as other art students but I felt like a visitor from another planet. If people asked who I was and where I came from, I learned immediately to keep silent about the fact that Dave was a West Point officer in the army rather than a draftee.

The campus rumbled with rallies and protests. Privately, I shared the sentiment against the war, but I wasn't prepared for verbal assaults against me because I was the wife of a soldier. As I sat in an art class before the professor arrived I was prodded periodically by a classmate who asked, "What's it like to be married to a trained killer?" or "How is the wife of the killer today?" or "What does napalm smell like?"

Now I wanted to be invisible. Dave would ask about my college life in his letters and I had to say, "It's fine. It's great and I'm glad I live at home so I can get a lot of work done." I became too superstitious to share my situation with anyone. I couldn't protest the war and I couldn't support it. I lived in a state of suspended thought about the rest of the world. I didn't want to know that American troop strength in Vietnam had reached a peak of 540,000 in January of 1969. Make that 540,001. I didn't watch TV or read newspapers.

There was always a letter in flight from one to the other. They described places, people, living conditions, climate, weather and dreams about being together. They anticipated our meeting in Hawaii. The date was set for May 29, 1969. I yearned for him.

I bought a trousseau of new clothes. I went to school and did my homework. The letters at this stage were likely redundant with expressions of love and desire, probably sickening to the outside reader. But such is the nature of communication when one is only days from the arms of a lover after six months of separation. His letters were undoubtedly more newsworthy than mine. I avoided the "Waiting Wives' Club" organized on the nearby Naval Submarine Base. I didn't want to acknowledge that I had anything in common with them.

Dave Crocker, Vietnam, 1969

I drew and painted, studied art history and took a nutrition course to learn how to take care of myself. I jogged in the morning and walked at night. I sang in a chorus and conducted a small church choir. I helped my mother take care of my grandmother who had suffered another stroke. I drove my one-hour commute to school alone in silence, focusing my thoughts on what Dave might be doing or thinking at the same moment even if I didn't know which day was his—yesterday or tomorrow. I believed in the power of visualization.

Before Dave left for Vietnam, his long-held dream of a military career had faded. With his love of mountain climbing and wild places, he fancied the idea of moving out west—Colorado or Montana—and becoming a mountain guide. In his precise way he created journals outlining his dreams and ambitions with pictures, maps and poems. He created a commonplace book with quotations and photographs that inspired him. He was a good student and a master planner. We were a curious match. He built his dreams with the acquisition and organization of information and details, I built myself by intuition. Perhaps we were the same. I felt adored and I adored him.

It never occurred to me that anyone else might read my letters. My naïve fantasy was that they were for his eyes only. I fabricated that he could control things, that his discretion could prevent others from peering into our intimacy. He was the only person I could imagine making love with, the only person with whom I *had* made love. I reenacted our lovemaking in my letters with my own special code. I never thought of who might find and read my letters if he suddenly disappeared. But, someone did. Weeks after his death I started to receive letters from a stranger, a soldier I presumed by the postmark, who seemed to know me—too well. I tore them up and wondered if this person would arrive at my house. I continued to be glad that I didn't possess a gun.

When Dave's letters had arrived, I re-read them over and over to be sure I absorbed every detail and found every level of subtext. The prevailing concern among waiting spouses was that their loved one might return changed, damaged, or a stranger. I could not listen to that and I preferred to avoid situations where waiting wives expressed their worries. "They come home with nightmares and tempers out of control," they said.

But, they come home, I thought. *That's all I need to think about.* My focus was on the end of silence, the end of waiting. Whoever he was at the end of this we would find each other again. I did not imagine life without him. Winter and spring opened and closed in the tedium of waiting.

I remember the state of waiting, staring at the dizzying geometric pattern of the pink and black wallpaper in my old room, trying to empty my mind of fear. My parents had chosen the paper for me when I was eleven. They said I needed my own room away from my brothers. I was "growing up."

For the first ten years of my life I had slept in a room with my older brother, and when my younger brother was too old for his crib in our parents' room, they squeezed in another tiny twin bed and he joined us; we could barely walk between the beds. We lived together like a basket of puppies. I felt exiled, bereft of others when the time came to move to another room and become a solitary princess in a place that I would return to as an adult and in which I would eventually wait for Dave to return from war.

My brothers and I had devised a secret tapping code on the wall that separated us when I moved one room away. Nothing could thwart our maneuvers to communicate; we were so used to whispering in the darkness to each other with our blankets pulled up to our chins.

"Dad says he wants to buy a new car."

"I know. I heard Mama say we don't have enough money."

"Quiet, you guys, I hear someone coming up the stairs. We're supposed to be sleeping."

Now, I was back in this familiar place, surrounded by the fading wallpaper, back to the smell of coffee wafting upstairs at 6:00am, listening to the clink of my parents' breakfast dishes. Outside my bedroom window, I spot a black crow flying in a westerly direction, above the stand of pines, over the weathervane on the barn. I tap softly on the windowpane. Isn't Vietnam somewhere in that direction?

Friday, May 17, 1969. Six months have passed as if I'm in the back seat of a car on an endless ride. The waiting has devoured most of my attention in my old room, surrounded by elements of our life in hibernation: wedding presents, china, glassware, camping equipment, his clothes, my clothes, books, German nutcrackers, candles and beer steins. Still peeking from the shelves in this reunion site for my life *then* and our life today are the slumping dolls and petrified toys of my childhood. Nothing had been moved during my time away in Germany. The bookcase contains the arc of my reading life from *Anderson's Fairy Tales* to a first edition of *Silent Spring*. There is little evidence that Vietnam exists except for the mountain of love letters and photographs that Dave has sent. No map with pushpins marking his location. He couldn't tell me his exact location.

On this particular Friday, I'm distracted with a final project for an art class, my last exam in the visual arts school while I waited. In twelve days I will board a plane to meet him in Hawaii, paradise. This monastic life, and my yearning for him will be rewarded with a week in a hotel room next to Waikiki Beach.

I had fashioned a Japanese folding book of rice paper pages, a rendition of the moon passing behind cloud after cloud, painted in shades of black, white and gray. It was a small two-by-four-inch rectangle that opened like an accordion to reveal moon after moon on each page. They were droning, repetitive images meant to embody four thousand hours of waiting to see my love in the flesh.

At dusk, on this same Friday, the dog next door began to

howl in long unceasing tones. He continued until Sunday. I don't remember the moon. Perhaps he saw it.

As I painted my moons all weekend, my older brother paced back and forth nearby, trying to speak above the relentless baying of the hound. He was home to finalize his divorce after a brief marriage—less than three months from wedding to separation despite a previous five-year relationship. As I cut and pasted my moon book, we talked about the differences in our marital relationships. In my mind I summarized it this way:

Bob: *Suzanne is critical and won't take my word for anything.*

Me: *Dave is kind and considerate and always asks my opinion.*

I felt so lucky, almost too conspicuous in my happiness. But, superstition kept the lid on my exuberance. *Don't get too cocky.* Focused magical thinking—hope—will keep my beloved safe and bring him back to me.

In just two weeks I'll step out of a plane and enter paradise. My mental movie played over and over:

Scene one. He has arrived from Saigon the day before. I'm wearing a blue silk dress with bare arms and shoulders. My long blonde hair flies in the wind as I walk down the steps onto the tarmac. He is running towards me, bobbing through throngs of people, smiling and lifts me off my feet. He places a lei of tiny orchids around neck. We melt into each other right there, next to the plane.

Scene two. We're driving to our hotel to spend the next twenty-four hours in bed—maybe longer. I sit as close as I can next to him in the car, my hand stroking his leg. I might not see Hawaii on this trip.

Scene three. We're lounging together in a bubble bath. In his letters, he has said he really needs a long soak in soap and water—almost as much as he needs me. His skin is sun-browned, healthy and warm with no detectable scars. He seems okay, unchanged.

———◁◆▷———

Tuesday, May 21, 1969, I drive up to the university campus to deliver my moon project and speak with a professor about earlier work. His studio smells of chalk dust and linseed oil. He leans on the edge of a drawing table and cups his chin and small goatee in his hands. After a leaden silence, he waves his left hand toward the art work spread out before us—my artwork. "It's boring," he said. "Why don't you re-do it."

No. Sorry. I can't re-live anything of these previous months. How do I explain that I just want to move on? I want to get out of the back seat of this car.

"Make it more interesting," he said. "It's too controlled and calculated. There's no life in it."

On the hour-long drive back home with all the car windows open, no radio, and my hair flying out the window, I contemplated boredom in art and my difficulty to convey the experience of *waiting.* Perhaps I was too figurative. What if I'd just given him a blank canvas? I had wanted to do and not to think. Untranslatable suspense was my problem, not boredom. My life crackled with suspense. But there was also the element of superstition; that the wrong move, the wrong words could decay my waiting game and cause it to crumble. I had no words for the guy who sat next to me in art class and asked me over and over, "What's it like to be married to a trained killer?" And, "Do you know what Napalm smells like?" I couldn't explain who I was except that I was waiting.

It was not a boring day.

My parents' house had a long driveway that passed by the official front door and curved around to the back where we parked and entered the house through a side entrance. The front door opened into a parlor used on rare occasions for parties, bridal showers and funerals at which Uncle Albert invariably broke a Limoges teacup as he tried to hold the delicate china with his large, thick hands. He repaired cars and was more accustomed to handling carburetors and spark plugs.

Everyone who knew our house parked in the back, but as I entered the driveway, returning from school, I saw a red Volkswagen bug parked in an odd spot—on the grass—near the never-used front door. It sat right next to the apple tree with the groping, spiny branches. Three years earlier, the tree had grabbed my long, tulle bridal veil, whipped into its clutches by the wind, as I departed for my wedding.

About the red bug, I thought: *Someone who doesn't know us.* It disturbed me. I didn't want anything unusual to happen during this time when I felt the clock booming rather than ticking, as if the charm of normalcy, of sameness, could get both of us to Hawaii, unscathed. Perhaps avoiding risk was at the root of why my artwork was perceived as "boring." *Don't take any chances* was my mantra. Don't step on the cracks.

I passed the red bug and drove around the house. Even outside near the juniper tree next to the house there was a whiff of something and when I stepped in the side door, the atmosphere was thick and palpable. My brother stood with arms close to his body, hands in his pockets, head down like a marionette in repose. He looked up at me, put his hands to his face and started to heave with violent sobs. My father entered from the front room with the never-used door. He was silent, drenched with gray, his face slack and fallen. My mother came next, extending her arms as if to catch me. I was both drawn and repelled by the room from which they emerged and I thought, *Dave's been wounded.* My grandmother, who usually sat all day in the living room near the door, was tucked away in her room—perhaps the most ominous sign of all.

The house was jammed with sadness, packed solid with the smother of something terrible. I entered the room reserved for special events and the dropping of delicate porcelain and I saw them—two army personnel in dress greens—a colonel and a sergeant. They were sitting in our unused parlor drinking tea out of my grandmother's Limoges china.

I understood at that moment that they were waiting for me—the guest of honor. As I entered, there was a brief tinkling clatter of cup against plate as they set down their refreshments and jumped up to find their official stances. There might have been a greeting, a "how are you," an introduction. But I remember nothing except the words like swords that fell from their lips, excoriating my future, cutting me off from all that had been relevant for me up to that moment. The Colonel held a piece of paper, a telegram, and began to read. The Sergeant stood in a stiff *at ease* stance with his arms slack at his sides. I wanted to back away—to widen the space between me and them. *Don't get too close*, I told myself. *You haven't heard anything yet. Perhaps it's not too late.* And then the standard speech began.

The words ignited a vision of Dave standing in a raging fire. He wore no shirt and the flames licked up at him from below. How could words do this? They had not yet described a scene.

"On behalf of the President of the United States and the Department of the Army we regret to inform..." The Colonel continued to recite the unfathomable text and a litany of barbarous military expressions: bravery, heroism, killed in action. The sergeant muttered condolences that fluttered down to the carpet between us like small "amens." There was no comfort in anything they said. I suppose they didn't know what to expect each time they delivered their message. They had to be ready for anything, but there was nothing *to do* except try to stay upright as the room tilted down in their direction. The weight of their words sagged the floor. If I didn't take care, I would be sucked down too close to where they stood and we would all fall down into the cellar, through the cement floor and whoosh—down, down to the center of the earth to molten lava. *They're invaders, troublemakers, marauders who know nothing. This is impossible.* These were my private thoughts. They finished their tea and left.

Dave Crocker, Vietnam, 1969

I held the arm of the banister as if it could ground me and keep me from floating up through the ceiling. The image of Dave in flames played continuously behind my eyes. He was not fighting the fire that engulfed him. He simply stood still and glistened in the heat. *They've made a mistake*, I thought. *They came to the wrong house.*

But, after they left there was still the telegram lying on the coffee table. Why did they have to leave that? A curtain fell in my mind as I tried to block out the truth, but then it flared into flames, the same flames engulfing Dave. My mind was a logjam of splinters of thought. Mom approached me with a syringe of something. She was a nurse, but what an abhorrent idea. How could I think my way out of this if I was sedated? I escaped and went to my room.

Those who remained that day somehow survived the rest of the afternoon and the evening. Reality seeped in like water finding its way through any minuscule crack. According to the notifiers and their schedule of events, Dave had been dead since Friday. Or was it Thursday or Saturday in Vietnam? I never wanted to understand the time difference between us. I kept him in my time. But now exactitude became an obsession. I wanted to know how long he had been dead without my knowledge.

Perhaps I did know something. Perhaps he died when the dog started to bark on Friday. How do animals know these things? Those long mourning howls in the background while Bob described the dissolution of his marriage and I thought: *I'm so lucky.* I asked my brother recently what he remembered of that day, long ago when the notifiers arrived.

"It was cold." He said. "February."

"No, no," I said. "It was a warm, sunny day in May."

"It was cold," he repeated.

I thought I'd never sleep again, but that night of the day the news arrived I fell asleep as if I needed to be unconscious. At dawn, I was on the border between fiction and truth. *The sooner I can believe this, the sooner I will find a solution.*

What a difference a day makes. The furniture, books and clothes in my room had not moved in the night but their meaning was transformed. Yesterday they belonged to a young couple. Now they were the remnants of a marriage, the property of our former selves. Everything loved and useful was instantly useless, painful to behold. The closet bulged with orphaned uniforms, shoes, coats, shirts, and trousers still holding his scent.

I got out of bed and tried to think of what I used to do before yesterday. *I used to brush my teeth,* I thought, but now there's no point because I have no need to eat. Every action, every reaction, had changed. I went to the post office and found a letter from him. My eyes locked onto the familiar loops and swags of his handwriting. I imagined his tanned face and the heat of his skin as he wrote to me from the other side of the earth. Before. I tried to fantasize that this letter was evidence of a terrible mistake. The green men had notified the wrong family.

I could not open the letter. If he was really gone from the earth I had to stop imagining him alive now. I thought about Jacqueline Kennedy, sitting in the motorcade in Dallas, covered in her husband's blood. She knew how to behave, how to manage a horrible situation. I had never imagined myself in the same boat with her. Now we were sisters joined by disasters.

How to rescue meaning now? Do normal things. What *was* normal? I drove up to the University to pick up another final art project. It was easier alone in a car. The burden of others' grief annoyed me. I hated to hear, "I'm sorry. What can I do?"

Why not drive? On and on. Forever. Driving fast towards the horizon was comforting. It made space for my pounding heart and surging thoughts. Food wasn't interesting and seemed unnecessary now. The signals from my body to my brain had been short-circuited, preempted by an ache in my sternum. I imagined entering the art building, pretending to be normal, engaging in small talk, taking my work and driving away.

The teacher whose office was my destination was famously colorless, evidenced by his wardrobe of white clothes. He gave lectures and painting demonstrations in white shoes, white pants, white shirt and sometimes a white jacket. When I recall this last meeting with him, I'm not sure if it was his whiteness or his reaction that made me remember him. When I climbed the stairs to his office, I suddenly needed an echo. He sat at the far end of the office at a desk, relaxed in his chair, wearing his whites. I entered, stood in the doorway and blurted out, "My husband's been killed in Vietnam." It was all improvisation. My intention was lost to me. I did not know what I needed.

He said nothing. He appeared to change from white to translucent, shrinking even further into his seat. I crossed the blank space between us. He stared, then stood and handed me my project without a single word. Perhaps he didn't even know I *had* a husband in Vietnam. My words tinkled to the floor in front of me and evaporated. I took my drawings and left. What did I want from him? Perhaps just an echo so that I could get used to my own words making this new, incomprehensible speech, or maybe I wanted him to say, "That's impossible. You're mistaken."

Before the green men, the notifiers, departed, they said a "survivor's assistant" would arrive by Friday to help me with details of paperwork and funeral planning. I had two days to think—alone. I was blank, unprepared. I had worn the denial of death and danger like a heavy metal jacket. It lay in tatters now. There was nothing left *except to think*. What would Dave want? The daydream of him in flames continued. Did he want cremation? What would I do with everything else? What would I do with his ashes?

Dave's sister, Dottie, says that I sat for hours in front of the fireplace in my parents' living room and stared into it. The next morning I said: "This is what we have to do. Will you come with me?"

If she's right, I deserved to pat myself on the head and say: "Good job. Your brain, your heart is still working. You'll be okay." But I only remember that I was busy, thinking, thinking.

My brainstorm bubbled up from wherever one stores anger and righteous indignation in the body. I needed to *do something*—for both of us. Dave had been wrenched from his life at age twenty-five and I was obsessed with how to put things right for him—to extract him from a dubious war, free him. Nothing could give meaning to his death. Perhaps I wanted one last experience with him.

Dottie didn't hesitate when I asked her to go with me to take his ashes to the north face of the Eiger in Switzerland. She knew the spot from a family holiday growing up with her brother when they lived in Germany. I knew he needed to reach the North Face, somehow.

I also knew that he had always disliked ceremonial military pomp and circumstance. So I would help him skip his elaborate funeral. The coffin would be packed with things I could no longer bear to look at: his uniforms, my wedding dress and—yes—perhaps all the letters. I thought that I'd never be able to read them again. And if for some reason I was no longer able to guard them, they must be safe—forever. Now there was only the arrival of *the body* to see if this was really true, after all.

The mortician at the funeral home in town was Edward MacDougal, affectionately known as Mr. Ed. His son Eddy had been a quiet boy in my high school class. Mr. Ed was tall and thin with a long, serious face. He had the perfect look for the funeral profession: clean shaven, a tall slight frame and a charcoal gray suit. Smiles were rare. Hopefully he smiled at home. His clients were not always at their best but it was difficult to imagine him cavorting among the living. Calm, quiet, stillness was his specialty and I felt comfort under his steady, solemn expression.

We had met before under similar circumstances. He was a familiar sight with his hearse or black station wagon at the back door of the nursing home in front of our house. He buried my grandfather, and he came to our house to carry out my youngest brother Danny.

In 1962, when Danny died at age seven after a long illness, Mr. Ed picked up the small body in his arms from my parents' bed as if he had found a fragile, wounded bird, and carried him outside to the hearse. He wrapped him in a blanket against the February cold as if transporting him from one warm bed to another. Even at fourteen, I recognized the professional consideration of this man who seemed to own only one suit. Now, eight years later, I knew I could tell him what I wanted to do. He didn't blink an eye when I described my plan.

"Just remember you can't dig up the box later," he said. His words were stern but his manner kind. The bereaved need compassion, but also they need the facts. I appreciated working with an expert and there was never a moment when I felt patronized or treated like a child, even though I still looked like one.

"Don't worry," I said. Digging up the treasure was beyond my imagination. Sealed for eternity was the plan.

Soon, the most sensitive representations of my relationship with Dave would be safe and I wouldn't have to worry about where they were or who might find them. They would reside in my memory. These symbols—the wedding clothes, diaries and letters—would not make him more real to me. It pained me to look at his handwriting. I had to put them out of sight.

I was halfway there. I had Mr. Ed as my collaborator. He said "the remains" would arrive within two days. Dave was no longer a person. He was an envelope being mailed back, empty. The survivor's assistant arrived, a young Captain, like Dave, and a great comfort, especially with his candor that his wife was the same age as me and she could be in my shoes. Such a thought made me feel less alone, that I was not the only one in such a disaster. My parents invited him to stay in our house, but he chose a local hotel. "Army regulations," he said.

I looked forward to his arrival at our house after breakfast each morning. I wanted to jump into his arms, just to be held again by Dave, by proxy, but I didn't. He asked questions about Dave in a gentle, neutral way and listened intently. He explained what would happen from the military side of things: the choice of headstone, the funeral ceremony, the awarding of medals, widow's benefits. As he sat next to me on the sofa, leaning forward with his elbows on his knees and his hands clasped together, I was tempted to share my secret plan with him but I was afraid that I could be breaking some obscure military rule or regulation. My scheme for Dave's delivery to the Alps was my personal survival plan and I didn't want any roadblocks. I played with the idea of an exit strategy after that for myself, but resolved that it was a stupid, selfish idea, and certainly not something that Dave would do. My mantra now was: *What would Dave do?*

O n the following Sunday, May 26, Dave's father and I went together to identify the body. I had to be sure. I climbed the steps to the front porch of the funeral home and entered the small anteroom before the viewing area. People line up here to sign the guest book. I needed a breathing space before I could enter the door to the room holding the truth.

My legs wouldn't continue for a moment, but Dave's father kept walking and entered the room by himself. He disappeared into the space of flowery smells in which metal folding chairs stood in horizontal rows in front of the casket. I glimpsed around the corner to acclimate myself. I prayed that I would not recognize Dave and I could exclaim, "They made a mistake!"

Where would I find the courage to approach the coffin? Dead bodies frightened me. How could I see him like this? Inert, waxy, composed for eternity—if it *was* him. I had to know. And with small steps I moved closer and closer. Beneath the open, gray metal lid of the casket I recognized the high forehead, the straight nose, the small dime-sized indentation on the right side of his chin where he had been hit by a lacrosse stick at West Point.

Yes. It was him against the white satin pillow; ghoulish, silent, petrified, unable to appreciate his plush surroundings. I stood as close as I could tolerate, near the shoulder of his father who had folded down onto the kneeling bench. My feet were glued to the floor. I thought of who might have touched him last and closed the lid in Vietnam. I didn't see peace in his face. The air was too thick to breathe in this museum of death, even for the living.

He had been embalmed in the morgue in Vietnam as was the military custom, dressed in army dress greens and made-up to look still living. Imagine *that* occupation. The skin on his face was smooth and thickened with pancake makeup. Even the stubble of facial hair was obscured making him appear barely pubescent. The flesh looked hard like colored wax. On his neck, just above the collar, the skin appeared folded on itself, as if he had been repaired by a hurried seamstress or clothed by a busy dresser. I thought about the sketchy description on the telegram of the incident that killed him. The shrapnel had hit his neck, his chest and his right arm. I imagined the wounds hidden beneath his uniform. The hair was wrong. It was combed straight up like a crew cut rather than parted on the side and he was wearing the insignia of some unit other than his own. His preparer in Vietnam clearly didn't know who he was and what he looked like in life.

But, it *was* him. Next to me I heard the sound of his father's labored breathing as he touched his dead son, his namesake. Dad Crocker took a small comb from his pocket and combed Dave's hair, parting it on the left. His hands trembled as he replaced the incorrect insignia with his own. He laid his hand where his son's heart should have been beating.

These mistakes and inconsistencies, the bad hair and wrong

insignia, conveyed a message that people were anonymous in this war and were falling in such numbers that even the morgue was making mistakes. Except for the information on his dog tags, they *couldn't* know him in the place where corpses are gathered to be washed, shaved, dressed and sent home. This confirmed my decision that his body would not be desecrated any longer. He would *not* be buried in a hole with a military funeral conducting his send-off; he would go back to the Alps—with me.

The funeral ceremony took place on Memorial Day, the day I was to leave to meet him in Hawaii for R & R—Rest and Recreation. The date wasn't intentional, just a coincidence. I believe in rituals and their healing effects, but I would have preferred to miss this one. Fortunately, I had my secret. And the thought of it protected me from the rushing torrent of distasteful but perfunctory events required during this time which only served to leave Dave further and further in the past. We still had a thread stretching between us. I could not have survived the funeral if I thought he was a participant, if I thought that his body was going into the ground in front of me. As I stood next to the coffin in the cemetery, I gazed down at myself from a branch in the maple tree above. I saw a thin twenty-three year old girl/woman standing motionless in a dark blue A-line dress wearing sunglasses that hid her eyes from everyone as she accepted the ceremoniously folded American flag. She looked just like Jacqueline Kennedy, except for the hair.

When the coffin was buried in Mystic's Elm Grove Cemetery during a service befitting an American hero, only a select few knew that his remains were not there. It was my little conspiracy to save the intimacy of our couple. The coffin brimmed with the hundreds of letters spanning our brief four years together. They were packed in twenty, # 10 cardboard letter boxes and placed underneath my wedding dress and his dress uniforms. Even his spit-shined shoes went in. I held back only two letters and his commonplace book. I needed only those fragments to embody all the rest. The letters I kept back say little of significance—no missives of love—they are merely samples of his handwriting and his syntax. I put them in a tiny basket with a lid and left them in my old room in my parents' house.

By the time we stood under a baking sun at Elm Grove, I knew the cremation was complete even though the ashes would not return for another week from the crematorium in New Haven. It was a bizarre comfort to think that somehow Dave would be restored to himself with the contamination of war burned away; grains of sand and soil from Vietnam would be separated from his flesh and the thick makeup melted to oblivion. Perhaps it was this thought that enabled me to manage the endless funeral service on that blistering day in May with the thunder of rifle shot and the mourning sound of *Taps* from the bugle. The intense heat seemed appropriate; it was a record-breaking 100 degrees. As the sun bore down on us, my great-uncle Ephraim fainted in his dark suit and was quietly carried over to a shade tree and ministered to by our family doctor. When I was handed the folded flag that had covered the casket, I had a fleeting desire to open the lid and pop it in with all the rest. What would I do with this reminder otherwise?

A week later the funeral home called to say that the ashes had returned. I went on my last visit to Mr. Ed's establishment. We had not spoken about urns or other containers. I wanted the original receptacle into which he was poured after the burning. By chance, it was a small cardboard box with thick sides, big enough to hold a large cantaloupe or a bowling ball; manageable for travel. My next challenge was to live with the box and its contents until I could deliver it to Switzerland.

I was afraid to open the box at first. I thought I might see something recognizable like a tooth or a fragment of bone. I did not want to know him in this form as fragments of himself. I wanted what was left to be unmolested and liberated in its entirety in a place he had loved. Now, I was simply a courier connected to his body only through this last mission.

During the week that I received his ashes, more than one hundred U.S. combat deaths were reported and the drawdown of soldiers began. One week too late for Dave. American troop strength in Vietnam was reduced in 1969 by 60,000 from a peak of 540,000. Of the 58,195 killed during the war, approximately 15,000 were married. The average age was twenty-two. Seven were women.

At the cemetery after the ceremony, Dave's parents planted a tiny apple tree they had grown from a seed.

The box of ashes sat on a table near my bed waiting for our trip to the Alps. It was the first thing I saw in the morning and the last that I saw at night. It reminded me that this was true. This really happened. I now shared my room with a box that contained my beloved. The dream of our future was over except for my last hope—that I would be lucky enough to take him far away from this room, this country, this war.

Dottie couldn't go to Switzerland until August. She had a job as a nanny in London for most of the summer of 1969. Dave had written to his sister earlier in the year to encourage her to resolve her malaise and lack of direction in college by working and traveling in Europe. I wanted her to be able to honor her work commitment and I postponed our trip. Why not? Past, present and future had warped into a tangle of ideas like threads that go nowhere and fold back onto themselves. Going in August also meant that Dave and I would be back in Switzerland at the Eiger together, sort of, after having been there exactly one year before.

The postponement also meant that I had to deal with getting through June and July. These months, which are among the most beautiful times of the year in Southeastern Connecticut, were now unbearable with their beauty. The breezes too soft, the weather too fine, the river garish with sparkle, the sky too blue, too bright with a light that pierced every corner of my grief. Nature's loveliness pained me and exaggerated my loss. I wanted to share it with him. I remembered how much Dave loved being in nature, looking at nature. Is he dispersed in all this now? Is there some philosophy or religion that can help me escape this horrible realization that he is utterly gone? Evening and night brought relief from my jealousy of everyone whose loved ones survived. There is no escape in the first days and weeks of loss. It permeates the body like shrapnel and each day another fragment finds its way to the heart.

Strangers annoyed me. I watched them walk hand-in-hand as they window-shopped along Main Street in Mystic. Smiling, walking slowly with their heads tilted back to take in the smell of salt air, peering over the seawall at the sight of boats next to the docks along the river. They all behaved as if it was just another nice day in this slow coastal village. I was not interested in shoes or clothes or maritime knick-knacks in the store windows as I walked through town. Every object had lost its usefulness. No destination appealed to me, but forward movement was *essential*. I needed to keep moving without regard for the quaint eternity of nineteenth century clapboard buildings. A life-sized, cut-out display of Smoky Robinson stared out from the music store window singing, "Baby, Baby, Don't Cry."

I squinted into the sun as I turned a corner next to Kretzer's

News Stand and a hand shot out in front of me holding something bright. I stopped short. It was a red poppy made of crepe paper with a green wire stem held out to me by a veteran in a khaki uniform. He wore dark-framed Clark Kent style glasses and sat in a wheelchair parked on the sidewalk. He didn't smile. His body slumped into the chair, inert, but his arm had moved towards me like a missile. The poppy almost hit my nose. His other hand rested in his lap where he held a can for collecting change. Was he a giant puppet with a string controlling that rocket arm? I stared at him for a long moment. He rattled the can of change and broke my spell.

A horrid thought crossed my mind. *This could have been Dave.* Disabled, confined to a wheelchair. Perhaps he's better off after all—lost to the vapor rather than returning as a version of himself. He wouldn't want to live like this; his body dismantled. I captured this idea and crowded out the memory that he had once already survived a car wreck and, in spite of serious injury, recovered to perfect form. The image of the red poppy etched itself into my memory as a symbol of an unthinkable alternative to death. Permanent physical disability could have been worse for Dave with his love of athletics. This was long before the amazing robotic resources that are available for the wounded warriors of today. I could not see Dave languishing in a VA hospital.

I ntrinsic in the will to survive is the power to reason, to ratio-nalize, to make things useful and normal, to make sense of the insensible, or at least to cast around for *reasons to live* in spite of a broken heart. When Michel de Montaigne asked himself in the sixteenth century, *how to live?* His answer was, *survive love and loss.* This was now my full-time occu-pation. I examined every crevice of my mind for the logic of my situation. Fantasies that Dave could still read my letters helped for a moment but didn't last long. I played in my journal writing that perhaps I was dead and he was alive. *Just keep writing and tear it up*, chanted my inner child. The process of writing letters was so familiar in my "old" life that the act of sitting down and taking out a piece of paper or a notebook instantly transported me to a more comfortable place. *I'll write my way out of this*, and sometimes I wrote just single words over and over. My hand moving on the page was a comfort as I repeatedly copied "everything returns," a phrase I found in *Siddhartha* by Hermann Hesse.

Dave's parents managed grief in their own way. They were shocked that no further news was received from his superior officers in Vietnam about the circumstances surrounding his death. His father continued to reassure me that I should or would receive a letter giving more elaborate details of what happened. I couldn't speak my feelings; I didn't want to wound them any further, but I didn't care to have any more news from the army. I'd heard enough.

His father, however, understood better than I did that something was amiss when proper military procedures were not being followed. He was Commander of the New York State National Guard and busy with deployments of his own units to Vietnam and notifications of deaths to families. He left Mystic after the funeral saying that he had, unfortunately, many letters of condolence to write himself and he wrote to the Commanding General of Dave's division to express his disappointment.

4 June 1969

Sir:

My son, Captain David R. Crocker Jr., commanded Company A, 2nd Bn 22nd Infantry. This is an element of your division. On 17 May he was killed in action while commanding that Company.

As of the date of this letter his widow, Mrs. Ruth Crocker, has received form letters of condolence from President Nixon and General Westmoreland. She has not received the more personal and informative letter from one of Dave's superiors which I assured her she would. This sorry performance of the absolute minimum reflects on all of us in uniform and helps erode the reputation for compassion for which many of us have striven a lifetime.

The letter must be written. Beyond this there is the unessential 'nice touch.' There is a similarity between my own and my deceased son's name. Several members of your command and I have served together. It would have been appropriate under those circumstances, though surely not required, to have written also his mother and myself.

The callous and cavalier attitude which these failings reflect have deeply affected our attitude towards the Division, the present-day Army and the war in general. Considering that we have spent our lives in dedicated service, as have you, the failings have wrought a tremendous change. Imagine the effect, then, on others in this situation who are not hardened and disciplined to the vagaries of military life.

In the latter case the fact that I have had to write this letter, itself, renders any further action on your part ineffective. I, however, suggest that you have your procedures reviewed to ensure that you do not generate future letters in a similar vein.

Col. David R. Crocker, Sr

Two weeks later a letter arrived from Col. Robert Fair, Chief of Staff, who happened to be an acquaintance of Dave's father. Fair explained that letters were, in fact, prepared but then had to be, "hand-carried to Headquarters, USARV in Long Binh, where they undergo a final examination prior to approval and dispatch by that headquarters."

Even letters of condolence had to sit on a few desks along the way to the bereaved. Col. Fair continued saying that he knew of an outstanding young company commander in the 2/22 Infantry named Crocker—but had not known that he was David R. Crocker, Jr. until about thirty minutes after he was wounded.

He said: "I followed his evacuation back to the hospital and the desperate attempt by the medics to save him. Prior to the receipt of your letter, the Commander of the 3rd Brigade was making arrangements for the establishment of a patrol base to be named in honor of David. This base will be constructed when the tactical situation permits."

This may have been comforting news for Dave's parents but I don't recall any conversation with them about it, or any news of its eventual construction. Did Col. Fair imagine that one day we might visit this dubious "patrol base"—or would just the knowledge that it was there be enough? Could he imagine that a parent could be consoled by such an offer?

General Williamson eventually responded to the letter from Dave's father with a fatuous attempt to make amends. He apologized for the *administrative breakdown.*

He said, "It occurred in what we refer to as the higher headquarters administrative establishment. I wish I could say that this has never happened before but your experiences and my honesty tell us that it has and that some delays will occur in the future. I hope that the investigations that your letter prompted will help us to reduce this number to the absolute minimum. You and I have dedicated our lives to the military service. Your son has given his. I sincerely hope that this administrative breakdown, as painful as it is, will not dampen our dedication or lessen our endeavors toward accomplishing those missions that our country asks of us. Enclosed are a few mementos of the Division that I hope will be prized possessions. We are sending a similar packet to David's widow."

Prized possessions. I never opened the packet. It would not be the last in a stream of posthumous awards and medals. A Bronze Star arrived in the mail one day in a small, blue cardboard box followed by two Purple Hearts. Perhaps next they'll send a partridge in a pear tree. As I unwrapped them I thought, *who could be comforted by these?*

Everything went into a shoe box. On my visits to Schenectady to see Dave's parents I took the box along and they would pore through the contents in silence, examining the relics of their son's career. My trips to their house in upstate New York were important for them, I imagined, and I felt closer to Dave there, too, in their generous house full of treasures from Europe, Pakistan and Japan. There was one small room devoted to books and family photographs. I was glad that the door was closed when I arrived and I didn't stumble onto the picture of me and Dave embracing on the beach in front of the Black Sea, our wedding pictures and his West Point graduation photo.

I remember his parents silently playing cards at a small table next to the window; his mother wearing sunglasses day and night in case her eyes welled with tears; his father trying to recover the ability to tell funny stories about misdeeds at West Point and snake catchers in Karachi. They kept a steady, generous stream of kindness towards me.

In the last letter written by Dave's father to Col. Fair, there is again a generosity of spirit even in the midst of profound grief. He was determined to teach, to set the right tone, to represent the "grand old army" that his son thought he was entering.

Schenectady, NY 12306
26 June 1969

Dear Bob,

Thank you for your letter of 15 June and for the comments therein. I was deeply shocked that the over supervision which has characterized higher headquarters in Viet Nam has permeated to the extent of letters of condolence. If we can salvage some improvement out of my experience to expedite the procedure, we will have gained some.

My people throughout this state are heavily engaged in both notification and in survivor's assistance. So I have seen both sides of this problem. I should like to outline the procedure here, which might assist in coordinating the entire matter.

We get our assignments from CG First Army through delegation of authority to CG Ft. Hamilton. After personal notification is made, the notifier calls back to Hamilton. They in turn notify IAG Washington and an official telegram is released. Counting time lags and the International dateline if IAG notified the VN Headquarters as soon as they knew personal notification had been accomplished, this is when letters should be dispatched. Needless to say they should never get to the USARU level—except, perhaps, as info copies after dispatch.

From my personal point of view the lag caused great anguish to all of us. We buried Dave on the 29th of May. We viewed him on the 26th. Thousands of doubts and concerns afflicted us. Was it an accident with a U.S. Claymore? Was he in his track? I can't possibly enumerate all the things that assailed us. The letters do not answer all these and never could—but they provide details which help all adjust through the stress. The letters should beat the body home. Had you been allowed to mail yours when they were written (and when our notification was confirmed) this would have come to pass. I'm sure from my contact with others who have gone through this that the need for information is universal and immediate.

I hope that this material may assist you and the boss in getting this one aspect of the war straightened out.

We have progressed to the point where we pray that fewer and fewer people must go through what we have, and that we may with honor disentangle ourselves from the morass.

Our very best wishes to you and the Division for bloodless successes.

Sincerely,

Dave Crocker, Sr

Early morning was the best and worst time of day. When I first awoke I felt it was all a dream and then reality seeped in. By the time I was fully awake the pain behind my sternum had returned, rejuvenated for another day. It seems a miracle that I slept at night without benefit of alcohol, medication or illegal drugs but I had no experience with them. In Schenectady, I would wake up at dawn and go downstairs to the kitchen where Dave's father had made coffee and then in silence we went out together to weed and tend his large organic garden before he headed to his office at the National Guard Headquarters. It was in this garden, days after the funeral that I told him of my decision to take Dave's ashes to the Eiger. "That's good news," he said, his eyes filling with tears. "Both his mother and I prefer the idea of cremation. You did the right thing."

It is possible that Dave's sister had already told them. I had waited for fear that even they might try to stop me from doing the only important thing I could imagine. I still didn't know them as well as I would, eventually. My audacity in *not* telling them what I had done with their son's remains until two weeks after the funeral is as puzzling as my charmed ability to sleep at night. I was treading a thin line between being clear that I was doing the right, the best thing, and the fear that someone would get in my way—even his loving parents. My fears were ridiculous though. It would have been impossible to stop me.

Weeks later, Dave's parents received a portion of what they needed, but would never hear in their lifetimes a first person report about what really happened on the day of their son's death.

Dear Colonel Crocker,

This is what I've been able to reconstruct concerning David's death.

His company was engaged in a reconnaissance in force when an enemy bunker was located by the scouts. The bunker was unoccupied and the scouts continued to move. David got off his M113A1 and, accompanied by an artillery reconnaissance sergeant, a Vietnamese interpreter and his radio operator, approached the bunker.

The radio operator's antenna probably hit a trip wire and a booby trapped 82mm or 60mm shell was detonated. The shell was located in or next to a tree. At any rate it was suspended higher than the bunker. The artillery sergeant and interpreter were killed immediately. The Dust-off ship for David arrived in just a matter of minutes.

The medics on the ground reported that David's chances were slight. We received this report when the chopper was enroute to Cu Chi.

I am certain that the letters to the next of kin are more timely as a result of your letters. I hope life for you and Ruth has returned to some degree of normalcy. David was known as one of the most outstanding Company Commanders in the division with an unlimited potential for the future. We were all proud of him.

Col Robert Fair, Chief of Staff

Reflecting on this time, and trying to understand why I was so dispassionate about hearing the *real* story back then, I believe that I had concentrated so deeply on our relationship and our communication and devotion to each other that the possibility of his death, in its swift, violent fashion, was incomprehensible. This is why the letters had to be buried. *They were the dream.* The dream was denied. I could not hold both his death and the dream in my consciousness. My former self, the one who orchestrated the cremation and the burial of the letters, was a fragile being with good ideas, formless in other ways.

I was so lost for weeks after his death that I went to my former college and asked the guidance department if I could take a personality test. I didn't know who I was or what I wanted to be. They obliged me with the administration of the Minnesota Multiphasic Personality Inventory test (MMPI) during the completion of which I could only think of answers that Dave might give. The results said I should be a physical therapist or sports coach—perfect jobs for him.

There was nothing on my agenda beyond my mission to the Alps. I was mostly not present or available to all the caring from family and friends. The long stream of consciousness letters I wrote to Dave's friends from West Point were furtive attempts to communicate with men who I felt were in league with him. I imagined he would have approved of my being in a relationship with any of these men, if one had developed. One needs human contact at these times but the propensity to behave like a pathetic re-bounder is unavoidable.

I acquiesced to attend the college graduation of Dave's brother Tom in Pennsylvania at Dickinson College and his commissioning as an ROTC officer. The drive down from Connecticut with my father and brother was interminable; six hours of torture for one who needed to keep moving. I sat silently in the back seat and stared out the window at the landscape. Even contented cows were intolerable, standing so oblivious in their idyllic scenery and pastoral farmland.

People at the graduation were too animated and cheerfully solicitous. Graceful granite architecture, chatty people and efforts to pull me into conversation were all a fuzzy irritation. *Let me think in peace.* Gossip was especially annoying. It smacked of people with lives and relationships. *Don't you realize there's a war on? People are getting killed as you prattle on.*

On June 8, 1969, my father wrote to Dave's father, a letter that Dave's mother shared with me years later. It was written the evening before what would have been our third wedding anniversary. My father was largely silent for weeks after the funeral. He and Dave had worked together on the construction of the nursing home building during the summer after our wedding. It was Dave's first experience pouring concrete and using heavy equipment. He loved it. I had never seen my father get along with someone so well and for such a length of time—almost two months. I was sure that Dad's unpredictable anger would surface, that he would fly off the handle about something, but it never happened. They worked side by side without incident.

When my father spoke about Dave's death it was usually indirectly, describing the progress and condition of the tiny apple tree in the cemetery that had been planted by Dave and Ruth, Sr. Dad attended prayer services at a small Pentecostal Bible Chapel several times a week to which he had migrated after the pastor of the Quakertown church, Cousin Fred, died. I sensed how hard my father tried to contain himself in this letter and, at the same time, reach out to Dave's parents. He grieved quietly here but I understood that he was grappling for answers from his God:

Dear Ruth and Dave,

Today I went down to the cemetery several times—I took the glass cover off the little tree for a few hours to let it get some direct sunlight, then I put the cover back to make sure the seedling was protected during the night.

I would never wish that the reminders of our Dave were not here around me, for that would mean that somehow I failed to appreciate the wonder of what he gave of himself to us and to his country, but I do earnestly yearn for something or some way to keep his presence alive among us. I admired him so much and loved dearly his gentle, unassuming ways as he sought to express that great capacity for kindness which he possessed.

These last few weeks I have had a great struggle with my own personal faith as it relates to our heavenly Father because I did make it a point of frequent, earnest prayer that the Holy Spirit would be with Dave in his hours of trial and grief. I wanted above all else that there would be peace and comfort for him in the assurance of a close and loving presence of our Lord during those terrible days.

I do believe that Dave knew the strength and joy of the enfolding love of God and that we too can find rest in the assurance that he rewards our faith and prayers and "doeth all things well."

Bob Whipple

Was there irony in this ending that sounds like, "God knows best?" My father appeared to be shaken and shattered even as he tried to keep his faith intact. He didn't try to convince me with insipid platitudes that there was some greater good to be understood. We grew closer, even without words, as if he knew that grief must be simply allowed to exist and would eventually yield to strength and courage.

My mother loved maxims. I don't recall advice—only warnings and sayings. She repeated: "time heals all wounds," but I didn't want time. That combined with "good things come to those who wait" just added insult to injury. There was nothing to wait for except my trip to the Alps. My Protestant religious education about death and the possibility of life in the hereafter was already in the reject bin before this happened. On the occasion of my brother's death when I was fourteen, I preferred the vision of one being *released* from the limitations of the flesh. I didn't like the notion of his little, crippled body having to navigate around in heaven. *I hope he's finally free*, I remember thinking.

Perhaps my failure to buy into the idea of life after death was simply the hodge-podge combination of church affiliations that I grew up with. My mother had been a member of the Episcopal church, the "frozen chosen" as they like to say; my father was raised in a Protestant fundamentalist household where his mother relied daily on a "message from God" and received it by flipping through the Bible and letting her finger land on a random passage.

Mom became too busy running the nursing home and tending to sick family members to attend church as we grew up, but Dad hopped from church to church once he left Quakertown, leaving each one as soon as he detected any disagreement with his personal beliefs about God and scripture. I followed him around and substituted the quality of the music for religious tenets. I wasn't concerned with what they believed as long as they were pleasant people having a good time, making good music. I transcribed their hymns into five-part harmony and sang first alto with a church vocal group I called "The Simple Tones."

There had always been death lurking in my childhood but I remember it as a slow, stealth process. The nursing home residents who we lived among usually walked about the place at first when they arrived. Gradually they slipped into chairs and then into beds—and then disappeared. Their daytime clothes turned into nightgowns and pajamas; their bodies withered and contracted. Death took time as if one had to practice and rehearse the stillness.

Illness, bed sores, difficult patients and problems with employees were the usual table talk conversation at our house. Death seemed to just *happen* in the normal progression of things. I heard simple pronouncements at mealtimes like, "Miss Johnson passed away this morning." Death was a lingering process surrounded by an attitude of superstition and fatalism. As soon as someone died in the nursing home, an expectancy permeated the atmosphere about who would be the next to die because common knowledge and superstition among the staff was that *death happens in threes*. The nurses on their smoking break out by the back door might speculate that Mrs. Smith looks more peaked than yesterday or Miss Sadie had another bad night.

One exception at the extremes of this range of "normal" death was something I witnessed at age eight or nine. It was the old man with a shock of white hair and a flannel nightshirt who tumbled from the second-story window above the kitchen, across the yard from my bedroom window. Did I see his plunge? Or was it invoked so often that I acquired an image of what it looked like? Did he leap or fall? I do remember Mrs. Ballastrassi, the day nurse, with her white support stockings, her starched white uniform and nurse's cap standing close to my mother. They were out of earshot next to the yellow hollyhocks by the back door, talking about the incident. As I watched them from my window, she looked down at the ground and held her hand over her mouth as she spoke. I knew they spoke about him because frequently she or my mother would look up at the window with their eyes following his presumed trajectory to the ground.

As a child living amongst very old people, I remember a feeling of being with people who were benign, harmless and helpless for the most part. Nurses were in charge and directed them toward their destinies. Many patients stared vacantly or chattered nonsensical phrases or didn't speak at all. The old man who leapt—or fell—was one of the non-speakers who usually sat in a chair by the window with a length of fabric around his waist tied to the chair. The nurses repeated that these restraints "kept him safe." Children didn't voice opinions in this setting but I was left with a small voice questioning if it was his will, his confusion, or his knowledge that carried him out the window.

In spite of all the departures for eternity around me, my grandfather was the first person I remember seeing in a coffin when I was eight. He was taken one day in a car from his tiny basement apartment in the nursing home next door, and he died of cancer and tuberculosis in a sanatorium two years later. When he lived next door, we grandchildren used to see him every day. We would deliver his afternoon tea and stayed to watch the *Howdy Doody Show* on TV. But after he left his apartment we saw him *only once* from a distance during his twenty-four month slide towards death. He looked like a tiny head on a postage stamp as he waved to us from a high window in the plain, brick building at Uncas Hospital. It was late September 1954, and my youngest brother, Danny, had been born on August 20th, four weeks earlier. We held him up in our arms in the parking lot for Grandpa to see.

My son, Noah, would be born on Danny's birthday twenty-four years later.

At Grandpa's funeral I received the message that I should not get too close, even though he appeared to be only resting—but very pale—from my view among the rows of chairs lined up in front of his coffin at Mr. Ed's funeral home. My mother feared that tuberculosis was contagious, even in death.

The death I became acquainted with as I grew up respected the voracity of the body. Death took time. It didn't simply pluck one from the earth in a single gulp, especially those who were vibrant and healthy with an appetite for living—like Dave.

Traces of Dave's life in Vietnam came back via the mail for weeks after his body returned, but not the first-person accounts that his father wished for. My father-in-law wanted someone to come forward and say, "I was there. I saw what happened." Periodically a box or crate or envelope would arrive. One sweltering day in July 1969, a tractor trailer pulled into my parents' driveway. The driver backed up onto the lawn and used a crane to lift a huge wooden crate, half the size of a piano, labeled "Property of Captain D.R. Crocker." He deposited it next to the infamous apple tree that had snagged my wedding veil.

The crate contained a stone rice grinder and the accompanying paperwork explaining that Dave had purchased it in Vietnam. The grinder consisted of two pieces of carved gray granite, about fifty pounds each, one fitting inside the other with a hole in the top piece for pouring in the grain. A stick could be inserted in another hole on the side to push the top piece in a circle and separate the chaff from the rice in between. Dave liked rocks and stones and I could see him admiring the compact symmetry and functional design of this piece—now a sculpture, a souvenir of Vietnam. *But, how would they grind their rice? Should I send it back?*

My relationship with the post office had changed. Mrs.

Williams looked sad when I came in to check our mailbox. The arriving mail now informed me mainly of life insurance benefits, sympathy, widow's compensation and Dave's acts of heroism. A letter arrived from Major General Wickham in which he said he was "... honored to inform you that your husband has been awarded posthumously the Bronze Star Medal (First Oak Leaf Cluster), Purple Heart and the Combat Infantryman Badge."

He continued on, saying that "Prior to death, David had been awarded the Bronze Star Medal for heroism, Good Conduct Medal, National Defense Service Medal, Vietnam Service Medal, Vietnam Campaign Ribbon, Parachutist Badge and Ranger Tab. Arrangements are being made to have these awards presented to you in the near future by a representative of the Commanding General, First United States Army."

With any luck, by the time they looked for me for this presentation, I would be somewhere else—hopefully Switzerland.

When I read descriptions of Dave's "acts of heroism" today, I am confronted by my denial of the danger that he faced, that he put himself in. I had somehow adopted his attitude that it was his job and that he was good at it. He didn't hesitate to put his life in danger for the "greater good." I presumed that he disliked pomp and circumstance, the ceremonial, frilly aspects of military life. He was thrilled that we didn't have a military wedding, for example, in uniform with swords drawn. He did not express himself in the traditional forms of patriotism, the decorating of daily life with flags and bunting and wearing uniforms any more than necessary. But, judging by these medals, he hadn't spared himself life-threatening situations. He hadn't hesitated to jump in a disabled vehicle containing vital communication equipment while under rocket attack and save the rest of his unit from destruction. This single event took place four months before his death, according to a letter accompanying one of his Bronze Star awards.

My thoughts are wandering again to the contents of those buried letters because I'm not sure now what I was reading in them then. Did he reveal more to me than I was ready to understand at that time? Was I so blinded by the desire to hold my breath until he came home safely that I ignored the reality of his situation?

One package from Vietnam that arrived after the funeral contained a notebook in which he had written:

> *To Think.*
> *Wonder if, when, where,*
> *I go to do;*
> *It takes the thinking fear,*
> *All inside becomes you*
> *And you become whole*
> *To like the finding.*
> *Time passes—*
> *And if it stops to pass*
> *It won't hurt or bother*
> *Except those who remain*
> *To think.*

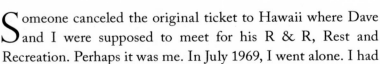

Someone canceled the original ticket to Hawaii where Dave and I were supposed to meet for his R & R, Rest and Recreation. Perhaps it was me. In July 1969, I went alone. I had to go. I needed to live through the fantasy of going to paradise and I had to do *something* while I waited to go to Switzerland. Dave had described the translucent turquoise water and the soft air in a letter when he stopped on his way to Vietnam. It will be "like paradise," he said, in a letter.

I needed to escape from well-intended sympathy. I had become an object of interest to some young men in my small town who thought I needed the comfort of male companionship. Now that Dave was gone, I couldn't say, "sorry, I'm married." Maybe it was the Jaguar I was still driving around in. I started driving the Land Rover Jeep that Dave had bought just before he left for Vietnam, to throw them off my scent. I couldn't imagine why these men could be interested in a widow. I yearned to be touched and loved but not with these guys. They weren't him and I wasn't myself.

"They're after blood money," my grandmother said. "They think the government pays you a settlement when someone is killed over there."

She spoke as if we were back in the Civil War. What did I know? Maybe she was right. Or perhaps they were prompted by their mothers just to be kind. It was a small town.

I flew to Oahu on a non-stop flight from New York. The plane was almost empty and I had three seats to sleep on for the twelve-hour flight. I comforted myself with the thought of flying through the same air in which Dave had traveled. I recalled his descriptions of the clouds and sky. I looked out the window for the Southern Cross: his good luck sign. I considered taking his ashes, but I didn't want to take him back in the direction of Vietnam. From this point, he would only go east with me until we reached the Alps. I wrote in my journal that the world was easier to accept at thirty thousand feet.

I imagined a Hawaiian lei placed around my neck when we landed. Perhaps those tiny white orchids attached to a string of pearls. That's what I would have wanted for that thin, pale girl under the maple tree in the cemetery, but at least she got herself to paradise and found a room on the top floor of a hotel on Waikiki Beach.

I refused to go to the military recreation area hotel where Dave and I would have stayed, even though it was inexpensive. Happy couples were there, ecstatic to be reunited. No point in torturing myself. The distractions of this new place were soothing. It *was* paradise. On the beach the birds screeched in a deafening chorus at dawn to get up and get moving. Right after the birds, the pile drivers took over the sound waves, announcing the over-building of new hotels. I carried Dave's Leica camera as if it were an extension of him and clicked away, capturing the Pacific and the sky—for him.

At the hotel coffee shop I ordered man-sized breakfasts of oatmeal, eggs, bacon, toast and pancakes while the waitress stared at my size-two body. I intended to eat but, finally, only a few bites of oatmeal appealed to me as I sat in front of meals that I had probably unconsciously ordered for Dave. I wandered the streets and white beaches. The vastness of the island sky and the endless horizon comforted me. It was a relief to be away from the continuous condolences of friends and to appreciate beauty rather than resent it.

I took hundreds of pictures, mostly clouds, as if I could capture this place for him. Or perhaps I was capturing him up there. I visited the parents of John, a classmate of Dave's from West Point who had been a groomsman in our wedding. I knew that John was in Vietnam but he had written to me saying that his parents would welcome me if I visited Hawaii. They had recently returned from Pakistan with loads of handcrafts and were opening a gift shop called "The Satin Bull." I painted a sign for the store with a red, raging bull pawing the ground. John's father climbed with me to the top of an ancient, extinct volcano.

A young man my age, a student from Pakistan, was staying with them. He took me around the island but never intruded on me with questions or sympathy. I felt a great, steady kindness in his big brown eyes. He didn't cajole me to eat or to do anything.

He simply drove me around and showed me the island: the rain forest, the Polynesian Cultural Center. On July 21, I sat in a car with John's parents and the gentle student in view of a volcano and listened on the car radio as Neil Armstrong described his first step on the moon. How could life continue like this and leave Dave stuck in time?

Returning home to Connecticut meant facing the possessions that had lost their relevance and necessity, those that couldn't be buried. What would I do with the Jaguar XK-E— Dave's pride and joy? What about the vintage Land Rover jeep? Would I pack away his eclectic collection of books—everything from *The Marquis de Sade* to a first edition of *The Old Man and the Sea*? Except for the vehicles, I hesitated to do anything. These objects said little about our intimacy and it was normal to *keep things* in my family. As the daughter of a mother and grandmother who saved everything, I knew that they would be happy for me to join the program.

Everything stayed in my old room: teak furniture from Denmark, china and glassware from Germany, barely used wedding gifts, even the top of our wedding cake still in the freezer in the basement after three years. These possessions were transformed in their meaning and usefulness, becoming the traces of the dead: clothes, pictures, a wallet, a toothbrush. They lay about like beach glass, objects separated from their original meaning. They were commonplace things, shoes or a shirt of his, but all embossed with a new category.

The time finally arrived to go to Europe for Dave's liberation. In early August, my father drove me to Ft. Dix, New Jersey, to board a military transport plane to meet Dottie in England. She was two years younger, but both of us had grown up with three brothers and we each loved the novelty of finally having a sister. We could have been twins, the same height and weight with similar long blonde hair, blue eyes and nice teeth. Our sisterhood has continued since then in spite of how much she had to tolerate on that trip. The grief process never follows a straight line and there we were together, a sister and her brother's widow, consoling each other but each experiencing a separate sadness. I still see Dave in her face when we meet today and talk about children and grandchildren and this distant adventure in Europe that summer.

When I departed for England from New Jersey, there were few security measures at the airport. No one asked what was in the eight-pound package I kept with me at all times. I had taped the box of ashes shut and placed it in a carrying bag with handles. I don't think I anticipated any questions about my carry-on, but I could say I was a professional bowler and traveled with own personal ball. There were no scanners or x-rays back then. But even so, I can still feel my great sense of relief as I took my seat on the plane. We were finally going to Switzerland together and no one knew my secret companion. The flight took fourteen hours and the box remained at my feet like a sentry.

I don't remember saying anything to other passengers about who I was or what I was doing, but, strangely enough, I made friends. Perhaps I said I was going to meet my sister and we would tour around Europe. Probably some of the facts bubbled out of me. They had to go somewhere. I sat next to two women who were teachers in an American school just south of London. They were returning from summer vacation for the fall term. During the flight I developed a fever—possibly sympathetic malaria—and could barely move out of my seat.

Almost three months of rumination and little food was the likely cause. Months of hyper-vigilance, staring at the sky in disbelief, takes a toll on the body. But I was almost there—I can't stop *now*.

I'm sure that my fear about being thwarted in my project made me discreet about revealing my plans but I recall a strong comfort with these two women—a safe haven. And I must have looked and seemed in a horrible state because after we landed, they brought me to their home and took care of me for almost a week. I have no memory or knowledge of my illness. Perhaps they found a doctor and provided medicine. I remember waking up in a small bed next to a window. The sun that poured in through the leaded glass panes was the purest and most enjoyable sparkling light I'd seen in months. They said that I'd slept almost continually for the first three days in the tiny room decorated with chintz and lacey curtains in their English row house.

They brought trays with coddled eggs, toast and tea to my bedside until I could stand and walk, and they located Dottie in London. Perhaps I told them my mission in my delirium. When I became fully aware of where I was and what had happened, my bowling ball box was there next to the bed—untouched.

I was restored by their kindness but my mission pulled at me. Dottie arrived—smiling, soft-spoken, happy to be free of the "crazy" children she had nannied for two months in London.

"Never become a nanny to the children of a psychiatrist," she warned us all. I could laugh again although laughter still felt like a foreign, unnatural experience. Sustained happiness requires trust and relaxation. For a long time I would continue to feel that I was immersed in a private world of unremitting sorrow.

It was as if I had been dropped into the first act of a tragic play and I had no script for the second and third acts, and no way to leave the theater.

Dottie and I set off from this nest of compassionate care in a rented car to make our way to Calais, France via the ferry from Dover, England. We lived simply, camping and eating bread, cheese and fruit, because it didn't occur to either of us to do anything else, especially to cook. Dottie remembers that I was not happy with her map-reading skills, but she tolerated my impatience. She was generous towards me and we figured things out as we went. There was no set plan to be anywhere at any particular time.

Somewhere in Normandy the car broke down and, once again, a stranger came to our aid—even in driving rain. He recognized my American accent immediately as I spoke in halting French and he began a profusion of thanks in French for the allied landing on D-day and for saving him from the Germans.

"Ah les Américains! Vous êtes magnifiques; nous les Français vous sommes si reconnaissants! Merci beaucoup!" he beamed at us as he pulled a bucket of tools from his car and worked on the engine until it started. I have returned to Normandy in recent years and the French are still thankful to Americans. They speak with heartfelt gratitude and ask me if my father or grandfather landed here on the beaches during the war.

Back in 1969 the countryside of France was still recovering from the war. Dottie and I passed through towns with broken houses and people working with tools and cement, pushing wheelbarrows full of rubble. We saw walls still laced with bullet holes. Water was undrinkable as it had been in Germany the year before, and neither of us were adventurous about food. We continued to live on our Spartan diet and added Muesli cereal and milk for nutritional balance.

There was no clear plan of when we should get to Switzerland except that Dottie had to be back in the States before September 1st to go back to college in Oneonta, New York. I had no limits on my time, no interest in the future. Dave's death occurred in the midst of my final exams so I had a list of "incompletes" on my college transcript and I wasn't sure I'd ever go back and complete them.

Dottie and I only began to plan our trip in earnest as we drove. We finally hatched the idea that we would take the ashes for a visit all around Europe to the places Dottie recalled from Crocker family travels, especially the spots that she remembered as a child with her big brother. Switzerland would be our last stop. It was too painful to go to the places in Europe where Dave and I had been together as recently as last year—except for the Eiger.

Was this trip, this quest, fun? I think so—as difficult as it is to recall pleasure during that time. We had a purpose and Dottie was the perfect companion: calm, smiling, joking, tolerant, ready to do things. I see myself with my hands gripping the steering wheel, looking out at endless vistas with foreign traffic signs, relieved just to drive and drive and drive. In this part of the world I had lived *as an adult* for the first time and in a marriage, in my own home with a man I loved deeply; this was the place where I had ultimately *grown up* in a relationship to which I could never return.

In Frankfurt, Germany, we found the house where the Crocker family had lived in the 1950s and visited Rapunzel's Tower, a favorite of Dave's according to Dottie. We avoided Wildflecken and headed north on the autobahn to Copenhagen to see *The Little Mermaid*. Dave had a framed, black and white photograph of this diminutive statue that hung in every place we had lived. It hangs in my son's apartment in New York City now.

As we drove from country to country I became tired more quickly and flashes of anger welled up within me at times. We were now a group in the car, Dottie, me, and my internal rampaging demons, meandering together over the countryside. I didn't know what post-traumatic stress was and wondered if I was finally becoming like my father—prone to intense feelings of rage. I felt tired of being an American and convinced Dottie that we should only speak in French and German to people we met, ignoring the fact that they would recognize our accents anyway. It was as if I wanted to disguise or re-invent myself like Sherlock Holmes solving a mystery. And Dottie kept on beside me like a faithful Dr. Watson.

We slept in campgrounds in my small, two-person tent and met other travelers to whom we wouldn't tell about the purpose of our journey, but became friends. As in that hackneyed phrase, we lived in the moment. We sat up in front of our tent at night to watch the stars if it wasn't raining, we foraged for milk and bread in the mornings at the campground kiosk. I see that trip as a continuous ethereal panorama in Technicolor with fields and farms flashing by and my eyes on the road up ahead.

I'm sure I made our travel harder than it had to be. We conducted ourselves like two dawdling special agents on an indefinite mission. I remember a peculiar feeling that nothing was real or meant anything except our eventual destination but I wanted this trip to last as long as possible. Dottie went along with all my off-beat ideas in the intrepid spirit of the Crocker clan. One night, rather than camp in the rain we attempted to find a room in a military base hotel somewhere in the middle of Germany. The country was still teeming with Americans stationed there to resist Russia or to deploy to Vietnam. The hotel manager said that only one dormitory-style room was available with three beds and there was one woman checked in already. "Not a problem," I said. But, as we stood rain-soaked in the doorway, we discovered our room was already more than full with two women and two men—and they were not happy to see us.

I flung the key into the room and we left. We slept in the car on the side of the autobahn. Dottie didn't complain but I was disappointed that I had given up the room with barely a whimper, by some standards. My father would have gotten physical and thrown them out. My mother would have stood her ground with her hands on her hips and said, "Say there. What are you doing in our room? It's time for you to leave." Perhaps I was afraid to unleash the grief-related anger that was beginning to bubble up inside.

We made our way down through Germany to the border of Switzerland and finally the Alps were in front of us. These grand peaks do not visibly change except for the seasonal shift from less snow to all snow. They rise up like sleeping elders with glacier streams linking river hands in the valleys below. They are as close to the embodiment of permanence as the earth can offer.

The question of what I would do *after* our quest for the rest of my eternity murmured in the back of my mind. I decided that when we finished here, and Dave was with his beloved mountain, and Dottie had left from an airport in Germany, I would go back to Bremerhaven on the North Sea to visit a young German man we had met along the way in Denmark. He worked as a typesetter for a newspaper and our conversation in Tivoli Garden in Copenhagen had been about education and the differences between German and American schools—not about death or the Vietnam War. Before I became a widow I enjoyed the mystery of the unforeseeable future, but I was convinced I'd lost my appreciation for romantic sentiment. I hoped for nothing but I craved companionship. His job seemed interesting as well as his hazel eyes and he was a great conversationalist. It was research, somewhere to go, a way to postpone going back to Connecticut.

It took the mountain top ...to give me the sensation of independence. It seems to me now that the very element in my character that took possession of me there on top of the mountain, the fierce independence ...to remain ... no matter how it scared me when I tumbled, was an inheritance.

—Eudora Welty *One Writer's Beginnings* (1983*)*

As Dottie and I drove through Interlaken, Switzerland, to the village of Grindelwald, the sky was clear and blue; the same weather as exactly one year earlier when Dave and I arrived there. The Alps rose up around us, dabbed with snow at the top, and wildflowers sprayed over the mountainsides. We found the same campground from the year before with the same view looking up to the north face of the Eiger. I rediscovered the good bread and cheese in the same small kiosk—a shed open on one side with a counter—where Dave and I had bought lunches for our hikes the year before. We pitched our tiny two-person tent under the single, bright eye of the Eiger, the lighted window in the middle of the rock face. I was greeted by a fresh, reassuring echo of sameness. Nothing had changed: the blur of pink, blue and yellow flowers, the massive dark wooden beams of the chalets, the busyness of other campers milling about, the glacier river with cold, rushing water the color of translucent stone.

We took the last cog train of the day up to the first station at Kleine Sheidegg, a restaurant and hotel high above the valley, to get our bearings for the next day. From here, exactly twelve months ago, Dave and I had taken the second cog train up through the tunnel that was drilled diagonally through the Eiger, arriving at the Jungfrauhoch in the heart of the Alps: a vast white landscape of frozen rivers of snow and mountain peaks with clouds beneath us. Skiers clomped about in their ski boots through the restaurant and into an ice replica of a house—complete with electricity and ice furniture—carved into the glacier. How odd to think that we were back here again—so soon—but he was not himself. Now he had to be carried. He had crossed over without me into a form only suitable to stay permanently in this place.

Back at the campground that evening, after our reconnoiter for the next day, Dottie and I sat in front of our tent, watching the sun glance down the North Face. Tomorrow we would be parted from Dave. It was ten thousand feet up to the spot where we would deliver the ashes. My memory was vivid from the climb with Dave last year but now I scanned the view over and over to estimate the distance we would have to hike in order to arrive at the right place for our ceremony. Dave taught me about scale—that studying an approach to a point far away, miniaturized by distance, is important in order to understand where you are when you get there. And I wanted to plant in my mind the exact place we would leave him, even if I knew that everything on the surface of the mountain is eventually washed down to the valley below and into rivers.

He might reach the Mediterranean Sea some day.

From the alpine hotel and restaurant at Kleine Scheidegg, before the train enters the mountain tunnel, it is a twenty-minute hike to the edge of the base of the vast, concave face of the Eiger. From there, we would work our way over beneath the face to the spot I had memorized from below.

On the morning of the second day, there we were, all together for our last climb, Dottie and I on foot and Dave in the backpack. We inhaled the fresh icy smell of glacial air and hiked across the stone and scree, the bits of rock and gravel constantly washing down from the face. Miles of wildflowers stretched out below us. It is the scree slipping down the face that makes the Eiger such a treacherous climb in warmer weather. Ice climbing in the winter months is preferred for an ascent because the face is frozen except for the occasional avalanche. I wanted to place the ashes at the spot from which a climb up the face would begin.

Early snow dusted some spots around us and at that moment I realized that we had not even thought to bring climbing boots. We were both wearing sneakers, oblivious to rocks and snow; we were unprepared for anything beyond walking. Looking back, this fact of not bringing equipment and proper

boots is one of the obvious signs of my deteriorated mental state. I was the one with *knowledge,* supposedly. In hindsight, it was careless and ditzy. But, at this time, it didn't deter us or even seem to matter. In "mountain weather," things can change from clear skies to clouds to rain to snow to

Ruth at the Eiger, August 1969

blizzard in no time and the North Face is famous for its quick changes. Perhaps I put my trust in nature, the place where I believed Dave to be.

We kept moving and Dottie never complained or lagged behind, even though the slope and scree made for slippery hiking. Those who come to this spot are usually scouting out or beginning a climb up the north face, but there were no tents or signs of activity, neither above or below. We were alone and I was thankful to have the whole area to ourselves. Once again, I felt that what I had decided to do was precisely right. We were bringing Dave as far as possible from an unspeakable end to a better place. Clouds were moving in as we found a spot directly in the center beneath the face.

With the great concave monument of the Eiger scooping up behind us and the valley sweeping far below, we improvised our ceremony. Dottie stood next to me facing the valley, speaking to the wind as I poured the ashes. They didn't hesitate at the surface, but mingled quickly with the other fine, gray, rocky silt and disappeared before our eyes. One of us had the foresight to bring matches and we burned the cardboard box right on the spot. How quickly he evaporated as if he had been absorbed into the mountain.

Mission accomplished. We had turned a tragedy into a mountaintop experience. I hugged Dottie and we hiked down, laughing at our frozen feet. That evening we ate Swiss Raclette, melted cheese and boiled potatoes, in a small restaurant next to the campground and met a group of British college students. We sat on long benches in the crackling light of a wood fire and listened to them sing American folksongs. "Puff, The Magic Dragon" was a favorite, repeated over and over.

Dave would be proud of us. I had learned what to do from how he lived, not from how he died. One of the books he had introduced me to was *The Prophet* by Kahlil Gibran. That night, crouched in our tent by candlelight, I re-read Gibran's words on death and yearned to approach understanding.

You would know the secret of death.

But how shall you find it unless you seek it in the heart of life?

The owl whose night-bound eyes are blind unto the day cannot unveil the mystery of light.

If you would indeed behold the spirit of death, open your heart wide unto the body of life...

Trust the dreams, for in them is hidden the gate to eternity...

For what is it to die but to stand naked in the wind and to melt into the sun?

And when you have reached the mountain top, then you shall begin to climb.

And when the earth shall claim your limbs, then shall you truly dance.

PART SIX
RECOLLECTIONS AND RECONNECTIONS

———— ⌒⌒⌒ ————

The events in our lives happen in a sequence in time,
but in their significance to ourselves they find their own order,
a time-table not necessarily ... chronological.

—Eudora Welty, *One Writer's Beginnings (1983)*

The year is 1998. Most people don't know my earlier life. They know nothing about Dave or my three years of marriage or the tragic end that resulted in the burial of our letters and my trip to the Eiger with his ashes. They don't realize that I kept his name. Some assume that Crocker is my maiden name. A few may know that I went to Boston for graduate school where I lived in a house with seventeen people, and that I met Noah's dad there in 1976. No one could know that I often imagined a young woman standing on a beach reading a letter to the sea.

The image in my imagination became so continuous that I decided to write a play. Her name would be Julie. *The Letter* became a play in one act about a girl/woman who loses her love in the Vietnam War. She creates stories about his life in battle and his relationships with his comrades. It ends with the reading of a letter in which she asks if she could have done anything differently to prevent his death.

This was my first attempt to purge my mind, or perhaps to open my heart, about the past. I had never studied playwriting, but I had read, seen and performed plays. I liked the idea of bringing characters to life onstage, but I never would have guessed the outcome of trying to fictionalize my experience. On the first night of rehearsals for a staged reading, I began to have doubts.

The stage was empty of props and scenery. The harsh, bright houselights exposed the common world—the mechanical life—of the theater. Dust, ropes, chairs, and dull painted walls decorated the giant interior cube of the black box performance space. The actors stood in groups waiting to begin. The director and I sat on folding chairs in a darkened area about twenty feet downstage, facing the area in which the actors would perform.

"Okay. Let's start with the first scene," said Brian, mid-forties, an elementary school teacher by day, a fledgling theater director by night.

The play was to be part of a workshop performance of several short plays with limited sets, props and costumes presented at the Eugene O'Neill Theater Center in Waterford, Connecticut. With only one week of rehearsals, it was an opportunity for playwrights to try out new works with actors. In this small theater festival in which my play was to be presented, Brian had been assigned as director by a board of advisors.

Why not? I thought.

A youngish man who had been a toddler during the height of the war could bring an objective perspective to this work-in-progress which was laced with anger, irony and anti-war sentiment, but was, supposedly, *not about me*. The play was about someone who tries to transport herself back into the war so she can understand why her lover died in the midst of it.

Murmuring ceased as the lights dimmed into blackness and a spotlight beamed down. A woman stepped out of a cluster of actors and into the lighted circle on the floor at center stage. I liked her tall, slim figure and the long dark hair framing her face. She didn't have exactly the right body for this role (she didn't look like me) but I liked her appearance. She seemed earnest and wistful as she clasped her hands in front of her and gazed out into the darkness. She inhaled and then appeared to hold the inhalation, beginning her monologue in a tight, pinched voice.

Why is she holding her breath? Why isn't she speaking on the exhale of that big breath she took? She will never make it to the end of her speech; an important monologue in which Julia questions every-thing she thinks she understands. I turned sideways to glance at Brian. He continued to stare straight ahead at her. The actor went on in a small, unsupported, high voice—airless. When she finished she looked in our direction, hunting with her eyes for our faces out beyond the light surrounding her.

"Thank you, Iris," said Brian. "Let's take a five minute break."

Iris and the other actors moved away out of earshot.

"Listen, Brian, we can't do this," I said in a loud whisper. "Something's wrong. She's all wrong!"

"She'll be fine," said Brian, shuffling through the script "A little more rehearsal and she'll get into it. Why don't you call her and talk to her. Tell her what you want. It's your play."

I wanted to say, "Dammit, you idiot, you're the director!"

Instead I said, "Okay—but this is scary. She's crucial in this piece. If she's not believable, to me, the whole thing is a farce."

Brian stared blankly at me. He was excellent at staring with-out revealing emotion—or even thought. "We can't put another actor in this role. It's too late. We have a performance in three days," he said.

The play presents an evening in the imaginative life of Julia and her fantasy of what her beloved experienced in the war. Her thoughts are enacted in scenes behind her on stage. In the final moments, the imagined soldiers, her lost love and Julia become a chorus together, chanting the poem, "History Lesson," written by poet and Vietnam veteran, Kevin Bowen.

I didn't say to anyone involved that the play was based on my life. It was my story but I wasn't ready to own it—to claim it—as my story. What was I thinking? Perhaps that I was tough, objective even, that I could put something personal out in front of people and say—"it's fiction." It was also the first piece of writing that emerged when I began to have the desire to write in 1997 about my experience twenty years prior. I had never tested myself like this in public. Silence about my experience with the war had felt safe until now. But now with my words rapidly becoming a farce, I rationalized further. I thought that I had only two problems: an inexperienced actor who clung to a notion that her character was passive and inert, and a director who did not seem to care about my play. Never had I imagined that my words might land in *dispassionate territory*, in the hands and mouths of people so far from the spirit of the historical time of the Vietnam War.

I also had assumed that I could write as if this had happened to someone else, not to me. How could I be so naïve? I was being exposed—to myself. I was discovering that I had responded to a nagging desire to drop my silence about Vietnam and speak about how the war affected fictional people—not me in particular. But as I created, I remembered. And the more I remembered, the more I needed it to be a true story about real people. Perhaps, even after almost twenty years, I was still not far enough along in my own reflection about my experience. But I had to start somewhere. This was my leap of faith. "Just begin," I had said to myself when I started writing.

Iris was thrilled when I called her.

"Oh, Ruth, I love this play. I love this part. Julia is so perfect for me. She's so strong. I'm going through a tough time right now trying to leave my husband. I am getting so fired up about my life through this play," she said.

"Really? How so?" I was incredulous that she spoke with such passion and energy in light of what I had seen in rehearsal.

"Yeah—it's connecting all the dots for me. It makes me want to get on with my life. When she reads that letter at the end to her dead husband—whew—that is so powerful," she said.

"Can you imagine losing someone in war?"

"Not really. I've met some veterans but they've never talked about Vietnam."

The next day her rendition of Julia had the same flatness as the previous rehearsal. Other scenes with other actors worked. There were not enough male actors available so all of the soldiers in the scenes set in Vietnam were played by women (an unusual circumstance since this was long before women gained the right to participate in combat on the battlefield). The women actors brought a different spirit to these lines that I had written with male soldiers in mind. The women were stronger characters, more nuanced, more interesting, I thought.

But—in the middle of it all—the character who was actually "me" was lifeless, a hunk of driftwood. I didn't believe her. She could not tell the story—my story. Was it the story or the story-teller? When do stories tell and when do they conceal?

I loved the synergy with the other actors as we rehearsed. I rewrote scenes, happy to have their suggestions, but I secretly wanted to rip off the heads of Brian and Iris. I wanted to declare war. They became the focus of my fulminating frustration. I was surprised to find my anger like this—accidentally—when I thought I was managing my feelings just fine. It was horrible and innervating at the same time. Iris saw her character as a victim who was *intending* to acquire a backbone—someday.

"I see her as a sad person in a state of shock," said Iris.

"Well, what does one *do* in a state of shock?" I asked.

"I don't know. She's hypnotized by it all," said Iris.

"She can't be hypnotized for an entire play. Not this play. Can't you see that she's *not* passive? Would a wimp be saying these things? Try imagining what your life will be like after you get the courage to leave your husband." I ranted at her. We had reached a curious impasse. She continued her droning, life-less delivery of lines. Brian worked on dramatic lighting changes. He wanted the play to look snappy. If only I was working with professionals, I thought.

At the single performance of my play, the theater was filled to capacity with many Vietnam veterans in the audience. One audience member told me afterwards that this was the first time he had been able to cry since he came back from Vietnam in 1970. People liked the play—they even seemed to like the character of Julia, played by the dead Iris. But, even with positive responses, with people describing it as moving, provocative and non-sentimental, I was unconvinced about my creation. Faking isn't easy. I thought I could stay behind the curtain and tell my story from the wings. I can't blame Iris and Brian for my deeper problems with the play, my buried history, and with my reluctance to say what had happened to me.

What is the truth here? Was I hiding from my own story? Maybe this wasn't meant to be a play. Perhaps Iris in her dogged stubbornness against giving life to the character was onto something. The character of Julia *could* be construed as a shadow; a passive imposter embodying my silence. But why did I need to invent Julia, anyway?

I had learned a basic truth: *no one else can tell my story*, at least not in this mode. So far I had not convinced even myself. Had I not studied the character of Julia enough? Did I not understand enough about what I had lived through?

Finally, playing between fiction and non-fiction was dissatisfying—possibly even dangerous. I could end up in the police reports: "Small town playwright murders director and actress before burning down historic theater barn."

The play was presented the next year in Boston at another festival and this time I read the part of Julia. Ed Bullins was the director, but my desire to stay incognito still thwarted any satisfaction with the presentation. I still felt like a trickster unto myself. The thought of retrieving the letters from the cemetery had not yet entered my consciousness and I would not meet my "band of brothers" at a reunion of Dave's unit for another seven years. Writing this play and seeing it performed was an initial swipe at reconnecting with the past. When I eventually met the men of Alpha Company in 2006 and heard their stories, I felt myself unfolding at last. Not falling apart, but peeling away layers. Dave was finally emerging from the fog of war and becoming vivid again.

At that first reunion in 2006 I met others who understood, without saying, why I had not yet gone to visit the Vietnam Memorial. They understood what it might feel like to experience the blunt force trauma of seeing the names of thousands of war dead and knowing that someone you love is among them. They understood a prolonged need for silence—and they remembered Dave.

PART SEVEN

OF MONUMENTS AND MEMORY

—————⬥⬥⬥—————

*From 1964 to 1972, the wealthiest and most powerful
nation in the history of the world made a maximum military
effort, with everything short of atomic bombs, to defeat a
nationalist revolutionary movement in a tiny, peasant
country—and failed. When the United States fought in
Vietnam, it was organized modern technology versus
organized human beings, and the human beings won.*

—Howard Zinn *(2005)*

May 2008. It is a quiet Thursday morning at the Amtrak
train station in New London, Connecticut. Three other
passengers stand in the sun on the platform, reading newspapers, organizing their bags and sipping from paper cups of
coffee. They are strangers and I quell my urge to blurt out, "Hey!
I'm going to Washington to see the Wall for the first time. I
always said I would never do this!" I even booked a business
class ticket to exaggerate the importance of my decision.

But, I stand here like everyone else and don't say a word.
The dry air smells of dust and diesel. A train whistles from some
indeterminate distance with the sound coming closer and closer

until suddenly the whole place snaps into action. People emerge from inside the station house, barricades go down, lights flash and the mammoth metal train gleams into sight from around the bend in the track. A conductor pops out from a shiny portal like a cuckoo from a clock door and we passengers become a group, coalesce into a line, and step up to board and disappear into the canal of seats behind the windows.

As I find my seat, I feel a tug in my chest. I never thought I'd make this trip to see the Vietnam War Memorial. I've never thought that the sight of this monument would provide any meaning to my experience of losing Dave in Vietnam. Rather, I fear that being in the presence of more than 58,000 names of the dead in this egregious war could pull all my sublimated feelings to the surface. Ranting and raving, moaning and crying in public has never been my style, but perhaps I'd enjoy some of this behavior. I tell myself that I'm doing this for *them*, the guys in Dave's unit whom I'll meet in Washington.

"We're all going to The Wall together," they said.

Yet, I'm not convinced of my decision, even though I'm on my way. I choose a window facing southeast to watch the coastline for as long as possible. The carpeted plush seat is just soft enough to persuade me that I can sit here for eight hours.

I recognize that I still need to resist this old, distant war and keep my feelings tamped down in place at the same time.

A rising screech of metal wheels against the track confirms that the lumbering weight of our train is moving now, lurching ahead and picking up speed, until the squeals become a melody line above the whooshing, grating, grinding chorus of our fickle departure. We're only ten minutes behind schedule. I remember train travel in France and Switzerland where schedules and time-tables are serious business. European trains leave stations on time in an atmosphere of purpose and direction. They move out with a consistent acceleration. American trains seem to depart stations as if they're not sure if they should go or stay—just like me. We rumble from the station and I stare out the window in my muddled ambivalence heading south to a reunion, a reunion with the remnants of Dave's unit in Vietnam.

My resistance to the seductive power of monuments has helped to sustain me over the years against irrational sentimentality, that state of mind that could seduce me into thinking that Dave's fate was acceptable, that my loved one died for a good cause. Going to the Wall will not help me to remember him. I understand war memorials more as *political statements* or political necessities, not as an impetus for memory. A name on a war memorial is like a bookmark placed in that page of a life. We know nothing else about the person except that this war took his or her life.

My train car is almost empty. I see just two or three heads rising above the high seat backs. Either most of my travel companions are very short or it's too early in the schedule that started from Boston's South Station before daybreak and will continue on to New Haven, New York, New Jersey, Maryland and Washington. How could I have been so clear about *not* going and now—I'm going. I surprise myself and yet I'm not surprised. I recognize me, intent on forward motion, accommodating the past, ready to try a new idea.

If I drove down to D.C., I would have flexibility, but I also could change my mind and decide to take a side trip, avoiding Washington altogether. With a getaway car, I might convince myself to veer off-course to Williamsburg, Virginia—and be a tourist instead of a war widow. This train limits my choices; it will deliver me right to the spot. I will inevitably see the monument and Dave's name. After almost four decades, I'll go to the memorial with some of the men—just boys back then—who were with him and still cherish his memory.

I met the soldiers in Dave's unit by chance in 2006, thirty-six years after his death. They had started to have reunions in the late 1990s. Part of their reconnection process was reminiscing about my husband, their Company Commander. Eventually, following the reunions, they began to write tributes to him on the internet via the *virtual Vietnam Memorial Wall*. Dave's brother Tom discovered their writings and forwarded them to me. When we were introduced by email, they embraced me as if

Members of A Company 2/22, 1969

I was the long-lost, even though we were total strangers. And they invited me to join them at the next reunion of the 22nd Infantry Regiment Society in Omaha in 2006.

"We have stories to tell you," they said. "We remember seeing pictures of you." And for the first time, I met the people who witnessed his death. I had never heard a first-person account until then.

"The next reunion in 2008 should be at the Wall in Washington," they said in Omaha. It seems there were others like me who had said that they could not or would not go. But now, as reluctant as I was, I was also fortunate. They said to me, "If you go, we'll be there." These are the same guys who were there back in 1969 when the unthinkable happened.

Grief is narcissistic. It feeds on an emotional state that sounds a lot like the old song: *Nobody knows the trouble I've seen.* When I met the guys from Dave's unit, I realized that they had also grieved his loss, acutely, along with all the other deaths and injuries they saw. I needed to get over myself and accept their invitation. To share this experience with them would be the closest I could come to sharing something with *him* again. It hadn't occurred to me until I met these men that grief was a gift that could be shared because it represents a memory.

As my train travels south parallel to Interstate-95, I'm reminded of another trip long ago when I was heading for a different reunion. I drove down the east coast on I-95 to Ft. Benning, Georgia in August 1966, to meet Dave at the end of his six weeks in a swamp. We were two months married when he departed for Ranger School, an infantry officer training that was a jungle war simulation with heat, humidity, insects and poisonous snakes. My role was to wait.

After he left, I'd taken a job selling tickets at Mystic Seaport in Connecticut and was given a name tag that said "Mrs. Crocker," but I often did a double-take when people addressed me that way. The name sounded matronly and I was still a teenager, working until it was time to take the long drive south in Dave's dream car, the Jaguar XK-E. It was the longest road trip I'd experienced by myself in my life and I have little memory of it except my hair flying out the window as I drove hour after hour. There were some looks and stares when I stopped for gas and food, but a slim, nineteen-year-old girl with long blonde hair alone in a dark blue Jaguar XK-E with out-of-state plates attracts attention.

I didn't know then that more than half of what was to be a

213

three-year marriage—I would spend without him. I waited for him in military housing, German apartments, airports, officers' clubs, at the kitchen stove, in our bed. Any location could be a potential waiting area. I would learn that, for military wives, waiting is a designated occupation. During his first duty assignment as a platoon leader in Germany, he worked fourteen to sixteen hours per day, six to seven days per week. He was frequently sent away for military field training. Each time we were to meet again after a two- to three-week separation, I would primp for hours. I wanted to look good, but I don't know what it was like for him to wait for me. Perhaps he told me in his letters. Did he fantasize how I might be reinventing myself each time we would meet again?

At one point, while waiting in Germany, I auditioned for a USO show and became a lead singer in a group of six entertainers called *The Blue Berets*. My strategy to see Dave paid off when we were sent to his remote training site in the forest hinterland. We were a troupe of two women and four guys performing excerpts from current Broadway shows like *The Fantasticks, My Fair Lady, South Pacific,* along with Pop and folk songs. Onstage I could see Dave beaming at me from the audience. And after the show he managed to sneak me into his quarters where women—even wives—were strictly not allowed. We had a memorable night on a mattress on the floor in the middle of his room and I snuck out before dawn.

Back in 1966, preparing to meet him in Georgia after his six weeks of Ranger School (three months after our wedding), I gathered my wardrobe like a bride. I changed my hairstyle and makeup. While Dave slogged around in a swamp, I shopped for false eyelashes. As in all aspects of military life, there was an underlying order or ceremony to even the smallest details. Dresses or suits were permissible but no "slacks." If I had a question, I could consult the handbook given to all prospective brides at West Point: *How to be an Officer's Wife*. There I learned from the illustrated pages the fine art of eating a chicken leg without using my fingers as well as how and when to leave calling cards on visits to the homes of superior officers. Was there a section on the proper etiquette for meeting your husband as he emerges from a swamp? The pages are a blur now except for that chicken leg.

On arrival at Ft. Benning I was expected to join other wives who were all there for the same purpose. No housing was available and those of us newly arrived were invited by women already living in quarters on the post to stay in their spare rooms. I ended up with Debra, also a wife of a 2nd Lieutenant. She was small and friendly with a soft southern accent. Almost everyone in the military eventually develops a southern twang or at least the addition of "y'all" to their vocabulary.

"Y'all must be so excited to be here," she said. "I miss Bill *so much* I can hardly stand it. Just think ... only three more days."

When it was time for bed, Debra said, "You shouldn't sleep all by yourself in the guest room. You can sleep with me and we'll keep each other company."

I was surprised but I couldn't think of a protest and I was new at being an officer's wife. I had never slept in the same bed with anyone except Dave and—as far back as I could remember—my grandmother on nights when I had nightmares as a child. Maybe this is something they do for protection when the men are away, I thought. Her invitation seemed unusual but what did *I* know. Maybe it's in the Handbook.

That night I woke to moans of "Bill, *Bill...*" and Debra flinging arms and legs over me. I lay like a corpse as far as I could on my side of her double bed and waited for morning when I politely escaped to find a motel room and eventually an apartment. For the next two nights I ate dinner by myself at a Howard Johnson's restaurant where the apple pie with vanilla ice cream tasted almost as creamy and brown-sugary as the one my mother made. I came back to join up with the waiting wives on the day we were scheduled to meet our husbands.

"Where have you been?" they asked in unison.

"Wasn't I supposed to find a place to live?" I said.

We drove out together to an obscure place where we would meet our young Rangers as they emerged for the first time in six weeks from an area considered by normal people to be uninhabitable. It was hot and humid, the kind of southern afternoon that conjures up plantation house porches with languid ladies in gauzy, white party dresses fanning themselves.

My anticipation mounted as we turned down one dirt road after another and finally arrived at the meeting spot—a clearing surrounded by scrub brush and trees dripping with Spanish moss. There were no road signs, and no plantations in sight. We parked on an area of flat, hard Georgia red clay and got out of the car to stand and wait. My heart pounded as the sultry air pushed against my face. My legs burned from standing in the sun and dampness pressed through my nylons and into my tight skirt. We were a gaggle of young women all dressed up in new shoes, stockings, white gloves, smart A-line dresses, and bouffant hairstyles like lacquered beehives—perfectly secured with lots of hairspray. We balanced on spike heels piercing into the clay as we swatted bugs that were attracted to our makeup and perfume in that shade-less remote spot—and waited.

There was nothing to do except stand, chatting and giggling, surrounded by the click-click-click of insect sounds. Someone in our group said she knew the men would emerge from the woods and present us with lists of foods they craved. *That's ridiculous*, I thought. *Don't they feed them out there?*

"They've been living on snakes, rabbits and bark," she said, as if she knew everything. "Catchin' things with their bare hands. They have to brush their teeth with leaves and twigs."

I couldn't imagine what I was about to see. How did the others know so much?

And me—*nothing*. Maybe I shouldn't have taken off so fast from Debra's apartment. In fact, it was just the excuse I needed to avoid socializing with the other wives. I still was not adept at chatting and making conversation with people. I felt awkward with other Army wives, even the ones who were my age, and especially those who were focused on getting pregnant and having children. I felt like I was still a kid, too young to be married.

Within the hour, ragtag soldiers in dirty, dusty fatigues began to emerge in ones and twos from the surrounding brush like a group of boys who had finished a game of hide and seek. Was it them? Would they simply straggle out of the swamp? Fear flashed through me that perhaps I wouldn't recognize Dave. Their faces all looked the same, smeared with taupe colored dirt, smudged, grimy and unshaven. I glanced around with a tiny burst of panic welling up inside as people recognized each other and ran into each others' arms. What if something had happened? What if? And then, there he was, in front of me, smiling! It was *him*, skinnier, but whole and in touching distance with his tender, concentrated way of looking down into my eyes. He was a revelation of all that I had been missing. And, as he apologized for his rank, sweaty smell, he took me in his arms and pressed a shopping list into my hand. I didn't recognize his smell: something like soil and plant life. It made him seem foreign and familiar at the same time. But, it was his face, his hands, his skin against mine as he kissed me, his dusty olive drab fatigues pressed against my pink sheath dress and white gloves.

He was caked with dirt, but I didn't care if his mud and dust rubbed off onto my Barbie-esque outfit. It would still be hours

before we would be alone together, before I could take him to
see the nest I had created in our new apartment with trails of
white boric acid everywhere to ward off roaches, before our real
reunion. I could live with cockroaches if it meant I could live
with him. The smudge of dirt on my dress was evidence that we
were together again. But we were only in the first phase of this
peculiar reunion ritual. After our welcome, the men still had to
go back somewhere for a debriefing and a shower.

Was there some other purpose for us waiting wives behind
this snapshot meeting in the woods? Was this part of learning
our roles in the spectacle of military circumstance? We could
know and see some things, but not all. Only parts of the story
were revealed step by step, ceremoniously. A censor, a program, a
filled-out dance card seemed to lurk everywhere. Perhaps it was
my youth and lack of experience; I allowed myself to be led from
one event to the next. My education was ahead for me, I thought,
and I would learn more, eventually, about confidentiality levels,
security clearances and what one was permitted to tell the *wife*. I
would almost know what was going on.

After the Kodak moment at the edge of the swamp, we waiting wives got into our cars and drove back to the post. We were
to wait for the next event when they emerged clean, laughing
and relaxed from Company Headquarters. We would accom-
pany them later to the steak house famous for first meals after
Ranger School. But before that there would be the reception at
the Officers' Club and the balancing of purse and punch cups
and dribs and drabs of conversation with strangers from all parts
of the country.

"And where are you from?"

"You drove down all by yourself?"

"I didn't realize Connecticut was a state."

At least there was finally the warmth of his body within reach.
I wanted to touch his arm but I knew from some instruction,

somewhere, that it was not good form; no public displays of affection, please. He smiled and smiled and threw glances in my direction from wherever he was in the room.

Later that evening at the restaurant, platters of giant 24-oz steaks came in endless succession out of the swinging doors of the kitchen, hefted on the shoulders of waiters who snaked through the throng of hungry diners, mostly soldiers. Dave said that this was the meal they had talked about for six weeks in the swamp. We sat at large round tables with condiments, bread baskets, baked potatoes and steaks arriving as soon as we sat down. It was "all you can eat" and family style—almost Roman style—with some guys bolting from the tables and running outside to retch up their meal after weeks of near starvation. The room was a sea of ravenous, ebullient soldiers who needed to eat first before anything else. Dave stopped after his second steak. When we left the restaurant we had twelve hours alone before his Airborne training started the next day. I don't remember if I told him about my night with Debra.

On this train to Washington, staring out the window at the panorama of the east coast flying by, I yearn for it to be that old trip with *him* at the end, not just his name on a memorial. What a luxury to reach a time in which it's okay to desire him and acknowledge his loss at the same time. This is progress. Memory can be a true and comfortable friend of grief.

We pass a small house on an island no bigger than the house itself, like a playhouse on a tiny tray, floating in Long Island Sound—an inaccessible honeymoon cottage. The landscape films past my window. Were these places here years ago? Why does it matter? This time my progress south is marked by the burgeoning of spring. White dogwoods announce themselves and weeping willows cascade with yellow green streamers. I remember when it was too painful to take in beauty. When I first realized I could never share another thing with him again, the sight and sound of everything beautiful was unbearable. How did I survive that? Perhaps my intuition had suggested what to do next, and next, and next, until it was comfortable to live in my body once again.

A woman with smooth bobbed hair in a fashionable pantsuit outfit and a Hermes scarf passes by in the direction of the café car. She might be sixty and reminds me of some friends who are in search of a relationship. They tell me how lucky I am now to have a thoughtful, interesting man in my life today, an artist from Switzerland whom I married aboard a sailboat in 2007. "Does he have a brother?" they ask.

"Maybe I'm just lucky in love."

I have been lucky, in spite of loss. Beloved people are not replaced. Their love is indelible and unique. I've made room for more love.

As we pass by the train station in Stamford, Connecticut, the plum trees are blooming. So much of spring is pink and yellow in the northeast. In the south I'll find the redbud tree that sings out from among stands of gray bark and wispy green pines. Dave was born in Macon, Georgia, in redbud country. But he was not *from* anywhere—he lived everywhere as an army brat. He was a Southerner by birthplace, but had a growing desire for more defined roots.

Before he left for Vietnam, he said, "From now on, I'm from Old Mystic."

This was my hometown and where we last lived together. But on the Memorial in Washington, D.C., the town listed under his name is Schenectady, New York, the place where his parents were stationed at the time of his death.

Dave's name was left off the stone memorial bench erected in Old Mystic in 1986 to commemorate their Vietnam War dead; the committee organizing the tribute decided he was not really *from* the town. This is the hard reality in New England. Boundaries are clear and severe. One needs generations of family presence under your belt to be "from" the town. And don't think you can sneak in by marrying someone who's part of the in-crowd in the area with a lineage going back two hundred years.

An Asian couple arrives across the aisle from me on the train. Perhaps they are Thai or Vietnamese. The man's mauve gray suit appears oversized for his slight frame. He murmurs in a measured, soft, polite tone into his cell phone and then hands the phone to the woman next to him. She's younger and speaks with more energy and animation to the same caller, her voice silky and musical.

The man seems wearied, perhaps by age or illness, as if each movement requires mental propulsion, a strained intention. He is a fragile comma in the seat. His hands move in slow, tethered gestures as he picks at a muffin on his tray table. These people are comfortable traveling companions for me because they seem so generous with each other. I enjoy watching them. Where did they come from? What have they lived? For years I avoided any images that reminded me of Vietnam. Now I'm in a writing group with a Vietnamese woman. She is a window into myself in my museum of thoughts about grief and response to tragedy.

Not long before this trip, I spoke with the mother of a young Marine who had been killed in Iraq. She told me that one day, eight months after her son's death, she heard herself laugh. "I was surprised at myself," she said. "I never imagined I would laugh again."

How do we allow grief to enter and leave? We simply *do*. I don't remember a conscious decision to exist in a state of mind. Maybe the act of surviving is as Erica Jong described in *Fear of Flying*, we are being born over and over again.

The skin color on the Asian man's face and hands is a flat yellow gray. I watch as his partner opens a box of juice for him and he takes a long slow sucking drink, barely moving his head. She gently wipes his mouth after and dabs at the front of his shirt and jacket with a napkin. I approve of her style of caregiving. Her gestures are empathic, slow and sensitive. He is withered, almost helpless. They are graceful towards each other.

She places some large white tablets in his hand. He stares at them for a moment and then his hand moves to his mouth. He tries to eat from a plastic cup of chopped fruit but he holds the spoon so long over the cup under his gaze that juice dribbles onto his jacket again. She wipes his face and jacket front. When she looks in my direction I glance down and study the age spots on my hands.

Dave would be sixty-five this year.

I watch New York zip by my window. Row houses and apartment buildings line the sides of the tracks. The occasional bursts of forsythia are fading, the pert maize color softening to a ragged ochre with sprigs of green. Pink cherry blossoms and ruby-rust Chinese maples sparkle like jewelry in small yards as we zip by. We pass a public swimming pool. I wonder if the guys in Dave's unit knew what a swimmer and diver he was—like an

Olympic sea bird, sailing off the high dive. I glimpse him twisting through the air, slicing into the water, emerging long seconds later from beneath the surface with his assured smile, tossing his head to shake the water away. I see him relaxed and exhilarated, glistening in youth at night after days of swimming or gymnastic competitions.

He had been a deep, quiet sleeper before our stint in Georgia, but his nights changed for a time after Ranger school. His sleep became restless, full of ghosts from the swamp. I was awakened by yells and calls to, "get down!" "get away from there!" "watch out!"—his arms and legs lurching and thrashing as if he ran to or from something. He never spoke about it the next day. Didn't remember, he said. Other more experienced wives said the shouting out and jumping up during the night was normal after weeks in the mock battles of infantry training. I hoped that he didn't mistake me for the enemy.

After sleeping on the ground and practicing for war in the swamp during Ranger training, he also needed a knife nearby. During his Airborne training at Ft. Benning, I discovered it under the mattress one day while making the bed, a hunting knife with a thick, black hand grip and a broad shiny six-inch blade. It scared me. I knew that he handled guns and other weaponry all the time, but I didn't think about it. I didn't connect him with *using* weapons—especially to kill. Target practice was the limit of my imagined gun world. With a knife like this you could fillet a big fish or even dig a trench around a tent. As mild and gentle as Dave was, this blade under the mattress was a jarring reminder that his life was a daily courtship with aggression and violence. I was a long way from the reality of war and the training of soldiers. Weapons were a *concept* for me. I had never touched a gun other than an air rifle. But here was a big sharp knife in my bed and I needed to move it out of such close range. When Dave came home that night I joked that we could use it to nail some of the giant palmetto bugs that terrorized me in our apartment. I suggested that we keep it in the kitchen.

On the train, people get on and off at every station, except for the Asian couple, my anonymous travel mates. Their past becomes my invention. I imagine a life for them in China, Vietnam or Washington. I invent an escape from Cambodia. I create their destination and a family reunion of children, grandchildren, nieces and nephews wearing tee shirts and silk, talking on cell phones and playing violins. I ponder if Dave and I would have had children. He thought it was too soon when we first married. "Let's get Vietnam out of the way first," he said, and I agreed with relief. I was terrified of childbirth.

The Asian man pauses in the midst of sitting back in his seat as if he's not sure whether to go forward or back. The train slows. A plane soars overhead. Time stops for a second and we are suspended in the moment; the plane, the train, me, and the man. He suddenly sits forward in his seat and shutters our dream, his eyes closed. He is a curved, seated statue: a vision of peace. Moments later, they depart the train at Penn Station and melt into the crowd.

Newark, New Jersey, and I'm surrounded by new people on board. This trip reminds me of the coming and going in military life, constant change in the midst of sameness.

A woman startles me as she plops down in the seat next to me. It had seemed part of my living room after being so long empty. She arranges shopping bags at her feet. I move my belongings to accommodate her and shrink closer to the window. She is so suddenly close with her musky cologne and the tinkle of her bangle bracelets. I feel territorial, jealous of my space and my peace for contemplation. Doesn't she realize she's sitting on Dave's lap?

She is magnified by her loud cell phone conversation: "Just mix a little chicken in with the rice. He'll eat it eventually. Don't let him manipulate you. No one is good with Fonzie like you. Oh yeah ... my mother. She hates the other residents at the assisted living. I don't know what I'm going to do with her.. "

I keep my gaze out the window even in the tunnels.

The Vietnam war will not be over until it ends for everyone.
Over four hundred thousand U.S. veterans are still recovering
from wounds inflicted on their bodies and their spirit. Sixty-three
million souls in Vietnam are still suffering from their 'victory'.

—Le Ly Hayslip with Jay Wurts,
When Heaven and Earth Changed Places (1989)

At a previous reunion in Omaha in 2006, one of the men in Dave's former unit told me that he was about to be divorced after thirty-five years and four children. He said he had never told his wife of his experiences in Vietnam and now he knew he never would. "She would never understand," he said, "and I couldn't begin to find the right words, anyway. You had to be there. You had to see it."

What would Dave have told me about war if he had returned? We were still learning about each other before he left. There were the situations he *did* write about, like the letter describing the death of one of his platoon leaders—whose wife had just given birth to their first child. Dave asked me to write to her and send condolences.

He wrote to me about his First Sergeant's dilemma in which, in a peculiar lapse, he had placed letters to his wife and his Hawaiian girlfriend in the wrong envelopes. There was the soldier who shot himself in the groin. Dave called it the "fireball" incident. The letters are so close by—less than a mile away from my home—but so inaccessible six feet under the earth.

There is a taboo in our culture about unearthing things—especially graves. In other countries where land is precious, like Switzerland, every buried person is dug up after thirty years and carted to the bone yard. It's a small country and every inch of space is carefully utilized and re-used unless it's occupied by an Alp. Here in the U.S. we have lots of space and bury for eternity. It was this promise of permanence that appealed to me when I buried the letters instead of him; it was my permanent time capsule.

A different urgency about those letters is stalking me now. The letters will tell me the plans we made and remind me how we understood our life together then. But will this reconstruction carry me back into the land of longing? And what if I had been able to meet him in Hawaii as we planned? What if he had come back and left the army as he said he wanted? What if he did become a nature photographer and trail guide in the Rocky Mountains as he dreamed? And, will I be reminded that he spent too long in field combat duty in Vietnam because the normal transition out of battle was delayed? The plan had been to meet in Hawaii for his R & R as soon as I finished my final exams. Was his R & R request related to my schedule? Did that delay his transition by those two weeks during which he was killed? Was I somehow culpable with all the rest—for the single reason that I was oblivious, outside the information loop? Can I disinter answers or will I create more questions?

Now I know that long before Dave went to Vietnam there were scores of witnesses who understood that the war was perpetuated by a series of missteps and escalating blunders on the part of many. Perhaps the letters will have clues as to how I understood the world back then. Perhaps I'll be reminded that my hope was based on an unconscious belief that the best, the brightest, and the best intentioned would be spared. How else could I let him go, otherwise?

At a conference on women and war in 2009, I spoke with the mother of a soldier killed in Afghanistan sixteen months earlier. "How could this happen?" she sobbed. "He signed up for the Army because he needed health insurance for his daughter who was born with a congenital heart defect. He was just trying to do his best for his family." I recognized her belief that somehow those who have good intentions are—or should be—protected against all odds. This kind of faith deludes us, but also sustains us through the unforeseen. War memorials, besides being a focal point for grief for some, are also a reminder of the risks of going to war. Is it because I kept myself oblivious to the risks in Dave's life that it is so difficult to visit the memorial today?

But, I'm on my way, regardless of my reservations and confusions. I won't turn back now.

Dave's parents visited the Vietnam War Memorial almost as soon as it opened to the public on November 11, 1982. They sent me a rubbing of his name. I remember my shocked sadness when I opened the envelope and pulled out the light gray impression of his name on rice paper—a grave rubbing that bracketed his short life.

We are approaching Union Station in Washington, DC and I'm not ready even after seven hours. Tomorrow, May 3rd, would be my mother's eighty-seventh birthday, but she died on January 1st of this year. I haven't missed celebrating with her in years, even in her dementia when she thought she was perpetually twelve years old. What would she say about this trip? She'd probably deliver a warning like, "Watch out for strange people and dirty hotel rooms."

I remember from childhood the story of how my parents had a brief reunion in Washington, D.C., just before my father was shipped out to China on an oil freighter, the *Marmee*, in World War II. During his stint in the U.S. Navy he spent two years in the engine room alternately feeding a coal furnace and reading the Bible. My mother said that his many trips through the scriptures by the flickering light of the furnace on board ship had ruined his eyesight. But the meeting between my parents in Washington in 1944 was a romantic legend. She had left my older brother Bobby, three months old, in the care of her mother.

"Oh, it was something! The long trip from Connecticut. The train going down packed with troops. Your father found me at the station. I never felt so in love," my mother would describe, over and over. "Washington was full of soldiers. There were no rooms in hotels." She said they finally found a pitiful place in a boarding house where the matron demanded evidence that they were married. My mother, in her turn-the-tables style, demanded to know if there were bedbugs in the room. But their dream time was cut short by an emergency telegram from my grandmother saying that Bobby had a fever and was crying non-stop back in Connecticut. My mother made the excruciating choice between love and mother-love and got on the next train back home. When the war ended one year later, my father returned and they created me.

The train is underground now, winding down to a lugubrious pace, giving me a last chance to dwell on my reversals of decision—doing things I never imagined I would do. We slow to a stop and I crank up my energy to enter the mob of people popping up from their seats, organizing, grabbing luggage and moving on. It's rush hour at Union Station. People stream out of arriving trains and swarm at the heavy glass doors leading up to the marble floors and soaring white and gold archways of the main hall.

The interior of Union Station is an American baroque palace and at the time it was built in 1907 it covered more ground than any other building in the United States. This grand ceremonial place designed to be the entrance to the nation's capital now contains smart shops with impeccable window displays lining the wide hallways of black marble leading to the streets. Cafes and restaurants open out under the central sanctuary of the interior dome. Confident wait staff in black clothing and clean, white butcher's aprons bustle about as they place gleaming crystal and silver on brilliant white linen tablecloths. It is the accustomed elegance of a fashionable military officers' club in Europe or an Embassy dining room or a dinner party at the Superintendent's home at West Point: the sunny sides of war and military life.

Amid this exuberant decadence of beaux-arts style I know I must keep moving. Out of the hypnotic expanse and timelessness of the main hall, doors lead to connecting areas that feel like dark high school hallways in contrast. Rivers of travelers stare straight ahead and brush by with purposeful expressions. They seem to know where they're going. I panic briefly in the rip-tide of the rushing crowd before I find the escalator to the metro. The hotel—the site of the reunion—is somewhere outside the city. I'm lost, but I have time to be lost and my condition feels justified next to my ambivalence. The momentum of people moving keeps me going and the names of metro destinations sound exotic. I'm still perseverating: *What am I doing? Where am I going?*

"Head for Vienna," says a beefy black man with an unrecognizable dialect in the information booth when I give the hotel address. I board the metro and, entranced by other station names like Foggy Bottom, I miss my station. I'm lost, again. I spot a young soldier wearing desert camouflage. He's young, perhaps twenty, completely outfitted in military field dress—from short-cropped hair, to hat, shirt, pants and combat boots and wearing the insignia of a sergeant. He's part of a new war with new colors, desert tones for a place with sand instead of foliage—muted browns and beige—not the green olive drab of former wars. He has the soldier's gaze—looking just to the left of my ear or over my shoulder. He's watching something else, ready. Perhaps he knows where we are now.

"Sorry, Ma'am. I'm not from this place," he says.

Who *are* the natives here? I stop a young man with scuffed topsiders, a tie and messenger bag who tells me I'm at the wrong stop, that I went too far. "Take two stops back to West Falls Church."

Dave knew this place. He lived in Falls Church and attended high school nearby when his father was stationed at the Pentagon in the late 1950s. When the rest of the family moved on to Pakistan for the next duty station, Dave stayed with a family friend so he could finish high school and apply to West Point. He didn't get a congressional appointment in his first application and spent one year as an enlisted soldier at Fort Belvoir while he waited to be accepted. By chance, I'm in the very place where Dave left civilian life and started his brief military career.

As soon as I climb into the first cab in a column of taxis outside the metro station, my taxi driver launches into a monologue. He's worried about the increase in the price of rice from $40 per 100-lb bag to $76.

"I have to eat a certain type of rice—sticky rice—for my digestion," he says.

Rice. I remember dozens of pictures of rice paddies. The stone rice grinder Dave sent back from Vietnam still sits in my backyard. *What about the people who might need this?* I had wondered, when I received it two months after his death.

We are five minutes into the trip when the cab driver migrates from the price of rice and food to life in his homeland, Sierra Leone. I've heard about the atrocities of the eleven years of civil war but I'm not ready for the detailed account of my driver's hero and mentor back home:

"He was tied up to a tree and had to watch his mother being raped! My hero yelled, *kill me, kill me.*" The cab driver is weeping at this point. "Finally they killed him—they just killed him!"

We are suspended in three directions: my cab driver is in Africa, I am in Vietnam and we both are in Washington. His shocking story pulls me away from my anticipation of the reunion. I focus on him and ask questions and hope that he can see the road through his tears and that the ride will be over soon.

"The drugs are destroying my country," he says. "They're coming from Nigeria! No one wants to farm anymore in my country. They are leaving the land and going to towns—but they have no skills."

In a long wail, he pours out the atrocities and injustices against his people. He is ranting, perspiring and glancing in a staccato rhythm from the road to my reflection in his rear view mirror. As we near the hotel, he summarizes the plight of Sierra Leone and his efforts to send money back to his people.

I give him a big tip as if it will make a difference—for one of us.

Any pangs or uncertainties I had about this trip were suspended for the ten minutes it took to travel from West Falls

Church metro station to the hotel. The taxi driver needed, actually demanded, an audience. His story grabbed me by the throat as if these moments with a stranger had been planned as my own personal desensitization process against any details of war I might hear over the next three days. Did he understand the healing that comes from speaking our grief? Or is the collective consciousness of humans so great that we continually look for connections, soul by soul. Or—do I just look like a sympathetic listener?

I have come here because of kindred souls.

The prospect of being at this reunion brings Dave closer, almost back to life. I could be jealous of those who lived with him the daily life, the camaraderie, and even the horror of his last six months while I sat thousands of miles away in my bubble of safety—waiting. Some of these guys saw him every day in Vietnam and possibly spent more time with him, in total, than he and I did during our entire three-year marriage. They were the last to see him alive. They were the last to be in front of his eyes as he was loaded onto the helicopter in which he died of his wounds.

Would I have had their courage to endure what they saw?

The hotel lobby is cavernous: The Radisson—a red plush and gold version of Union Station. Uniformed staff in burgundy jackets and white collars set a tone of competence and civility. A magnificent elevated bar floats in the center of the space with shimmering mirrors and glasses and patrons sitting on display as they drink and converse. The lobby is filling with Indian women in saris and men in shiny suits who have arrived for a wedding. They spill out through glass doors into garden and pool areas. They laugh and speak with animated, quick movements and hand gestures as they gather friends and family members around them.

This is another world from the gentle hospitality of the midwestern hotel in Omaha where the last reunion was held. Can I find my connection again in this urbane palace with my "brothers" from Missouri, Montana, Iowa, Nebraska, Virginia, California, and parts unknown? They have treated me like a sister, a royal sibling, since we met. Their adoration rekindled an ancient memory of being the Captain's wife. I was something special merely by association. After his death, I wanted to dissociate myself from the military and all of its offspring organizations. It was only in the company of Dave that I felt I had a place in the army, so I cast myself out. It's a curious feeling now to step back into the other half of a relationship again; to be *Mrs. Crocker the wife of,* again, with a bunch of soldiers.

I remember trying to appear grown up long ago. The *I* that is now is looking back to comfort the *I* that was then—my young, overwhelmed and confused self—and bring her along on this trip.

And suddenly here's Dick next to me, a platoon leader in Dave's unit, his beard whiter than the last reunion. Other recognizable faces approach. I glimpse the flash of crimson that signifies members of the "Order of the Red Ant Society." I see clusters of middle-aged men, wearing jeans and suspenders, paunchy, balding, bearded; all wearing around their neck a wide red ribbon that carries a gold medallion etched with a cartoon ant.

At some point after the war, the noxious Red Ant, endemic to Vietnam, became a metaphor for the worst of daily life in the jungle. Swarms of biting, stinging red ants could engulf any unwary person on foot, or in a tank or track. The only escape was to roll in the dust. Induction by friends into the fictitious "Order" became a "Medal of Honor" ceremony for the enduring ordinary soldier. They made me an honorary member at the last reunion in Omaha.

The hospitality suite reserved for our group is full of veterans and family members clustered around tables. Several guys from Dave's unit work with snippets of red, white and blue like a patriotic Santa's workshop. Hundreds of tiny American flags on small posts, six inches high, are being attached to gold pedestals and each labeled with the name of someone lost in Vietnam. The flags are broken down by company and then by platoon and squad to smaller and smaller groups until people are once again with the names of those whom they knew, forty plus years ago. Eight hundred and twenty tiny flags will be distributed among surviving comrades, carried to the Wall and placed on the granite slab under the panels that bear their names. It is touching to see all these people (mostly men) working on this huge craft project; preparing a small present for each of their lost buddies.

I spot a circle of familiar faces from the last reunion. Do I belong here? Am I a welcome sight or a sad reminder? How ridiculous I am. It's me who carries the ambivalence about my relationship with the memorial. They are welcoming—they embrace me and say how happy they are to see me.

I meet Phil, Dave's track driver. He bears a striking resemblance to Dustin Hoffman—a softer, smiling, friendly version. Over the past year, Phil broke his silence about the war. He found the detailed letters he had written to his parents and has been recounting his memories of Vietnam to all of us in a stream of emails ever since.

His stories range from horrific to humorous. He described using Rhome plows—huge blades attached to tracks—in Vietnam to peel away the jungle for easier access to "Charlie," the enemy. He recounted how sometimes the plows would unearth the corpses of the Viet Cong who had been dragged away and buried in shallow graves by their compatriots. Phil said that, when this happened, they would dig up the corpses and rebury them deeper in a mass grave site. Such an image would have been intolerable years ago, but now I was even able to look at the graphic photos Phil brought along with his story. What's changed? It's not strictly the passage of time. I've made myself look at things. I can almost deal with the sight of blood, as long as it's not in the midst of an act of violence, and I can control my urge to run out of a room containing a dead body thanks to working in a nursing home. But how did they learn to cope with what they saw?

Joe enters the room and hugs me. He decoded classified messages and carried the code book around on the heels of Dave. Today, in his early sixties, he is lean and youthful. He fights back tears when he speaks about "the Captain," as he refers to Dave. Once again I'm plunged into a bath of fierce, friendly admiration and loyalty, and love—in fact—for the young man who they still are reluctant to call by his first name. It's a matter of respect, they say.

Ken, white-haired and seventy-two, has come to a reunion for the first time. He had also been a captain back in 1969, an intelligence officer, older than most—age twenty-nine at the time—and with a wife and two children. He says he knew Dave better than others did.

"He was one of the calmest guys over there," Ken said. "I was in charge of radar and was only over there about seven or eight days when one of my guys woke me up in the middle of the night to tell me there was activity just outside our perimeter. I went out and found Dave and several of his guys quietly observing a reconnaissance unit of the North Vietnamese army. I was spooked. I wanted to shoot flares and call in an air strike but

Dave kept telling me I was making too much racket and going to create a worse problem. He was so damned calm. It really helped me."

More men slip into the room and recognize each other and me. Those attending a reunion for the first time are easy to spot. They stand at the edge of the room just inside the door and search to find and remember faces not seen in forty years. As I stand next to Phil, a man comes up and asks him if he was the guy whose leg was cut off when his track was blown up. A strange abrupt question, but I heard this kind of conversation opener at the last gathering. This is part of the reconnection experience. People bring the disconnected fragments of memories that they carried home from Vietnam. There is a broad latitude of memories that simply bubble out of people and the listeners respond with patience and decorum. Many of these men said that it was scary to attend a reunion for the first time, as much as they wanted to come.

Phil's glance rests on the man's face for a moment. Then he quietly says: "No, that must have been someone else." The man smiles and nods his head, backs away and moves on to another group. Phil turns to me and without hesitation starts to tell the story of the day he refused to go on a mission because he knew that the road they would take was loaded with landmines. "My time in-country was almost finished—Dave understood," he says. "He didn't make me go."

"Doc" arrives with his wife. He was the medic who tried to save Dave at the scene of the explosion. Some of the others have said that he still can't speak about those moments. He tries now, but tears come to his eyes. At the last reunion he said he wanted to tell me everything. But he's not ready yet.

"It's okay," I say. "I can wait." Even though now I yearn for details.

The atmosphere of these reunions reminds me of the days

Command track, A company, 1969

and months following 9/11, when no one was a stranger. To be another human being was enough to initiate contact and conversation.

That evening we make our way to a banquet along with the other two hundred and fifty people from the regiment. Seventeen of the original one hundred and twenty members of Alpha Company are present at this reunion. They make sure that I will be at the same tables with them. They jockey to pull out my chair. They are doting and caring. Everyone offers me kind words and a glass of wine. As soon as we're seated the stories begin as if we surround a campfire. Not raucous with one story piled on another but quietly—like a poker game. Joe, next to me, recounts the night he and another soldier were on patrol with a young lieutenant whose brother had recently been killed in another area of Vietnam. Joe's voice lowers almost to a whisper. He speaks in small bursts, glancing at me between sentences:

"It was pitch black—and we could smell the enemy. They had a smell like fish. Maybe all the dried fish they ate. We knew they were close by when we smelled them. We heard a rifle click. The Lieutenant was crazed by his brother's death. He wanted revenge. He wanted us to open fire. He knew it was suicide. 'Go on, blast the gooks,' he kept saying." Joe continued hunched over the place setting in front of him, hands clasped in his lap, his upper arms clamped against his chest.

"We froze. We knew it would be sure death for us. We refused! It's kind of a big deal to refuse a direct order. Next morning the Captain came to me and asked what happened the night before. I broke down. The words poured out of me. I knew he wanted the real story and later that day, the avenger, that's what we called him, that suicidal Lieutenant, was gone. Poof. Just like that. The Captain—Dave—took care of us. He knew what was war and what was just crazy."

His story had poured out as if a dam had broken. He looked at me and then down at his hands.

How do I find words to respond? I thought.

"Thanks for telling me this, Joe. It really helps me to understand what it was like over there." My words feel frugal and pitiful. I need to share something back, about Dave.

"He had a big respect for you guys—I remember from his letters."

I ask Joe if he knew that Dave also wrote poetry. He shakes his head "no." I see his brow furrow. His glance drops to the plate in front of him on the table.

"I hope you don't mind all this," he says.

I feel like I want to spend every minute with these special people who had known my beloved, but, for some reason, I can't or don't. I'm not really "one of the guys." I'm a guest and, strangely enough, I feel remnants of the old form, the military decorum. Even if I have an urge to jump the fence, I feel my obedience to some social convention. I tell myself that I need to let them have just each other sometimes, to talk among themselves, to unravel the knots of years.

Except for the trip to the Wall and the banquets each evening, the whole reunion weekend consists of the gathering of small groups of those who knew each other 'back then' and always with a gentle murmur of telling and retelling the stories. I see them talking in their small groups, constantly. I don't always join them. When I do, they are always welcoming.

Many people bring slides or old photographs that have been morphed into digital presentations. At the first reunion, in 2006, I brought some slides of Switzerland and showed them the place where I had placed Dave's ashes at the north face of the Eiger. I showed other slides of Dave relaxed and smiling, at the same spot, taken during our last trip together the year before in 1968. But those pictures of him, from his other life, seemed to create silence. Perhaps it made him more real, young and innocent—as they all were back then before they experienced war.

The utter seriousness of our endeavor also pulls me back from constant interaction with people. They all seem like mentally healthy, cheerful people, but this impending trip to the Wall feels like a funeral or memorial service and bears down on me. They boost me up with their condolences and now I can accept them, willingly. I don't want to miss any gesture or offering of words and good will. We haven't even had a chance to know each other's sense of humor yet. Perhaps we're all afraid of irreverence. But I am baptized in details about Dave's life that I never would have known if I had not met them, if I had not been willing to make this trip.

Finally, we gather in the hotel to take the buses to the

memorial site. The group meets on a large patio next to the pool, aged soldiers wearing shorts and plaid shirts, jeans and denim and always the ubiquitous red ribbons. There is a briefing about how we will board the buses and disembark and how to assist those with various handicaps or disabilities. There are veterans here of the regiment from all wars going back to WWII. Those who were formerly leaders resume their old roles and bark out orders. There is a playful resistance, a jocular dissent. People mill about and refuse to stay in orderly groups.

"You see, Sarge, we haven't changed a bit!" a member shouts out amid nervous laughter.

Canvas sacks containing the tiny flags are handed out to each unit representative. People are warned that they must get back on the buses at the end of the day or risk spending the night camped on the grass of the Mall.

"We better bring C-rations for Gonzo, he always got lost in 'Nam," chimes someone. Nervous laughter bubbles within the crowd. We all yearn to laugh.

The bus is too cold, too big, too touristy. We ride above the streets of Washington immune to the sounds and sights outside. We take our seats at random and Phil chooses the seat next to me. We sit in silence for the first few moments watching the city roll by through the tinted glass. I'm without words. There is something anesthetizing about this conveyance. We could be going anywhere.

Phil suddenly turns to me and begins to relate yet another version of what might have happened "that day." This abrupt movement into a story is a characteristic of the group—as if an invisible story stick is passed and that person begins, sometimes out of complete silence, like now with Phil. They continually ruminate about what happened to Dave and how and why, as if it happened yesterday. And the *freshness* of these stories makes sense because the guys tell me that this is something new. These moments haven't been spoken of before and certainly not like this with the people among whom it all happened.

Phil continues. "We were talking last night. Maybe it was a blast set off by a remote device. We thought maybe someone was targeting specific people. Why wasn't I there? What was I doing that took me out of the field that day? I don't know why I wasn't driving for him that day."

What can I add to this? I'm grateful for these utterances. Dave is real again after all these years thanks to these generous men and their recollections.

"Phil, I'm really glad to be going to the memorial with you and the rest of the guys. I can't imagine doing this any other way," I say.

"We're here," someone yells. We stream from the buses out onto the expanse of lush spring grass between the Lincoln Memorial and the Washington Monument off in the distance. Our small entourage of Alpha Company is shepherded by our resurrected leaders to a stand of shade trees. Pictures are taken of former platoons and units in every possible combination and formation, with and without flags. Flags wave everywhere, the gold thread of insignias flash in the sun, wheel chairs are maneuvered over the uneven sod. We are a motley band in plain clothes like a volunteer brigade as we mingle under the cooling shade of spreading maple trees, waiting for the command to embark in the direction of the memorial.

Dick, Dave's platoon leader, asks me to lead Alpha Company. Am I channeling their lost leader? This is a new challenge because I'm not even sure where the memorial is or which way we would march. I rely on him. He'll nudge me in the right direction. He hands me the little flag with Dave's name on it.

Hundreds of tiny flags flutter as they are passed out. Without choreography we "fall in" and create a semblance of a formation and the march begins. We are Alpha, so we are first, and somehow I lead them to the right place, parting a sea of curious sightseers.

"Okay. This is it. We're here," someone says. Our little march took less than five minutes. I'm light-headed and disoriented. It's too fast, too soon. The sun broils directly above us.

The monument begins on our right and as we approach I realize that we are experiencing the end of the war first. We are walking into the tide, and the height of plaques bearing names begins to surge as we count down the years. This is the power of the image—the fact that names are placed in the order in which

Dave Crocker, center, Vietnam 1969

they died over the entire chronology of the war. The memorial grows as we walk. We are moving from 1975 back in time towards the highest peak from 1969 to 1968. Faces squint up into the sun, scanning the surface as they look for the names of comrades. I feel the intensity of the vast number of the dead as I read hundreds, thousands of names on the wall beside me; a roster of the worst order. No one name stands out. They are endless up and down and across the black stone.

Dick is always near me, guiding me. The wall surges up at this point in its procession through time. Names flow into each other. They seem only millimeters apart. Without a guide I would be completely lost. I'm glad for the starkness and severity of this place even when blasted with sunlight. If I felt grace and softness it would be too much. Dick is my shepherd in my task of placing Dave's flag.

"There he is," he says, close behind me, pointing upwards. I glimpse the embossed print of Dave's name two feet above my head in a sea of names. Position by date of death imposes a semblance of order on this terrible list but highlights the magnitude of the war dead. As soon as I look away from the wall I lose him in the names around him. Even here, especially here, etched in stone, he is swallowed by the war.

Tears stream down on the faces around me. I hear the murmur of names as the others stroke the wall as if it is braille. I am relieved that Dave's name is too high for me to touch. I did not plan my composure, but I keep it. It is all I have in this sea of sobering facts. As we step back from the memorial face—the vast legion of names—the tiny flags clustering beneath them create a bright meager contrast on the flat rock at the base. They look so small, so timidly heroic.

After all the words are spoken, the names are said and we leave, I imagine the hundreds of flags left in front of the panels like an encampment of abandoned toys. They will be wet with dew if they survive until tomorrow morning. I see them spirited away as souvenirs in the pockets of children.

That evening at the reunion banquet we experience two traditions. The first is a recollection and symbolic reenactment of the relationship between the writer Ernest Hemingway and the 22nd Infantry Regiment. The legend goes that Hemingway spent time with members of the 22nd in Paris in World War II. And when they moved out to a battlefield position just before

Thanksgiving, Hemingway sent smoked turkeys from Paris to the troops for the holiday. At the reunion, a distinguished member of the 22nd Regiment Society carves up a twenty-five pound turkey in front of the entire group. The honor at this reunion goes to Awb Norris, now a retired colonel, who entered the Georgia State Guard at age fourteen in 1944.

The second tradition is the "Table for One." Next to the podium, in front of the entire group, a small table about three feet in diameter is set with a black tablecloth, a single place setting, an overturned wine glass and a single red rose. A speaker describes the scene:

"A slice of lemon on the bread plate symbolizes the bitterness of loss, a small dish of salt represents the tears shed, and the overturned glass reminds us of the toasting and conviviality that can never happen again. The rose represents the love of those left behind."

Silence fills the room before the chaplain begins a prayer. The metaphor of the table evokes the loss on both sides of the question, those lucky to remain and those departed. The murmurs of "it could have been me," or "I don't know why I made it back and they didn't" and "we don't want to forget" are continuous. It is sobering for me to be reminded again that those who gathered at the reunion want to face their memories. They pursue them now. There are no speeches about or glorification of war, just the occasional "war is hell." As sentimental as this scene could be construed with the turkey, the lonely table and the prayers, it feels right in this setting; elements of remembrance to mark an indescribable memory.

At our table for ten there are nine people. Once again I am with the guys of Alpha Company, these men who have lovingly brought me along like a sister since our first meeting in 2006. The tenth chair—beside me—remains empty even after inviting people to sit with us. Everyone at the table notes this and when the waiter comes, he places a dinner at the empty spot. My table mates joke that someone is obviously sitting there. Finally we have something to laugh about. They nod in affirmation to each other and say they're glad he ordered steak.

This is the power of reunion when people can connect not only with each other but also *with everyone missing*, including the selves that they were in the past. Here, in this rarified atmosphere, kindness reigns. "We're here to take care of each other," is the oft-repeated phrase. The invisible story stick never stops moving. It is as if the forty years in between then and now is only a blip on the historical landscape.

As stories flare up again, the people at our table frequently lapse into conspiratorial tones about "what happened that day to the Captain." The speculation of a remote controlled device surfaces and spreads around the table as if only the right answer, the why, the how, can put things straight about *that day* for which they all feel responsible to understand and remember. "If he just waited another five minutes for me to go with him," said Ken.

If only—if only.

I'm happy to be privy to this talk. As individuals, this has been their rumination for years. Now they have the luxury to be reunited with the only other people with whom they can converse about it with depth and meaning. And I can listen. I can *see* the dust, mud, the ants, the jungle and the bunker. I can learn *what happened*.

They speak about the pleasure of working with Dave, his friendliness, leadership and humor, and then the discussion rolls forward to the final scene in Cu Chi province; a deepening sketch of the last days, the last moments. The chance events of May 17th: a last minute inspection of a bunker that had already been checked, a new-comer (a conscientious objector) to the unit who was handed by Dave the radio instead of a gun, the trip wire to the booby trap that everyone said they would have seen if *they* had gone in. The radio antennae snagging the trip wire as it entered the doorway, the explosion, three people blown to bits, others maimed by pieces of junk metal in the bomb, Dave's cry: "I'm hit!" And then the chaos, the medic's attempt to stop the bleeding. Doc's helplessness to keep Dave alive, and the Dust-off helicopter trying to land amid swirling debris, and the tears, silence and despair when his fate was known.

Dick said the entire company completely fell apart for two days following Dave's death. "People just sat around and cried," he said. "Another unit was sent in to stabilize and comfort the men. I still think of him every day of my life."

The table is cleared and we return to the hospitality room where we look at old photos of Vietnam. Several people had scanned them onto DVDs. Pictures of their scrawny youth, caked in dust, playing with monkeys, holding guns that looked too big for them, smiling from the top of tanks and tracks, standing in mess lines, holding onto their childhoods with teenage horseplay in the midst of war. This is the real feast, assembled after forty years, seeing each other again from the safety of a far mountain. "Yes, we survived that, but how?" they say shaking their heads, as they pass the cup of kindness among themselves—and to me.

Now we are bonded by the sharing of stories together and I tell them about my desire to dig up the letters. But we would have another reunion before the decision was finally made and carried out on November 1st, 2011.

PART EIGHT
MY BUDDY'S HAT

There is no glory in battle worth the blood it costs.

—Dwight David Eisenhower

It's late April 2011, and already broiling hot at the entrance to the National Infantry Museum and Soldier Center in Columbus, Georgia. This outing is part of the planned program of events during my fourth reunion since 2006 with the veterans of Alpha Company. Once again, we're part of a motley crew of former GIs who served in the 22nd U.S. Army Infantry Regiment in various wars, a few spouses, and me, the only Vietnam War widow in the group. In spite of the fact that we are here among about two hundred veterans of all ages, our section of the bus—those connected in some way to Dave's Company back in 1969—behaves like a merry band of war buddies, joking and teasing, ribbing each other about things that happened long ago in the region of Tay Ninh. Now they include me in their repartee, as if I had been there, too.

Our bus driver, Ike, a thin, talkative man with a striking resemblance to Morgan Freeman, lightens the atmosphere further when he chimes in over the loud speaker in his melodious

Georgia drawl throughout the two-hour bus ride from Atlanta with quips like: "Whatever you folks do back there behind me, don't wake me up while I'm drivin'."

How amazing to be on a road trip with these guys who were with Dave forty-two years ago in the jungles of Vietnam.

Each time I'm with these men at a reunion I'm flooded with the feeling that Dave is present among us, that he is smiling at me from somewhere in the room.

Joe, who carried the code book on the heels of Dave back in '69, sits next to me. Quiet moments are rare in this group and when they occur I know that a memory has been retrieved, wrapped in words like a gift and is about to be presented to me. I'm like a visiting dignitary in these gatherings, beloved and honored, and served morsels of their long ago experience as if they know that I need to be nourished on these trips. This time it's a mouthful.

"I want you to know that I would have died for him. We all loved Captain Crocker," said Joe, staring straight ahead at the back of Ike's driver seat in front of us.

Such strong, spontaneous utterances are normal among these men, but it's hard to know what to say back except, *thank you.*

I'm ambivalent about this particular journey—not about the pleasure of being along with this special group and being *almost* one of the guys—but, once again, dubious about visiting military tributes and war memorials even though I survived the trip to the Vietnam Memorial very well in their company.

I try to participate in activities like visiting military posts and memorials by keeping a look out for inconsistencies, irregularities, the little flaws in the whole cloth of the dramatic, cinematic re-telling of war such as we are about to experience at the Infantry Museum. My vigilance is evidence of the compromise I always feel at these reunions; I want to be with these people and hear their stories but I can't condone military proliferation and dismiss unjustifiable wars. I manage this mixture of feelings by interviewing my younger self and reflecting on my early brush with military life. *What did you enjoy back then? Were you proud? Were you afraid? What did you understand about war and militarism? Who was I?*

The museum sits all by itself about a mile outside the heavily guarded gates of Fort Benning and rises up abruptly like the Pantheon in Rome, a monolithic, granite structure in the center of a manicured plateau bordered by Georgia pines. Ike tells us to remember our bus number or risk spending the night on the grass under a tree as we pour out onto the sidewalk like dutiful ants marching to a picnic. This is reminiscent of the instructions we received before we boarded the buses to the Vietnam Wall Memorial in Washington, as if it is the nature of our group to become lost and forgetful children when we travel together. I like this sentiment and I'm glad that someone is watching out for us.

The wide concrete walkway, the huge glass doors, the stone façade in front of us are all grand, solid, modern and sturdy—impervious against tornadoes, hurricanes, and possibly humans. The brochure said it was built with funds from a private foundation and they supposedly cut no corners.

Out back behind the museum are the remnants of the original "temporary" wooden buildings salvaged from Fort Benning. Seven were saved from a recent tear down and sit clustered in two neat rows with a tiny marching area between them; it's an "authentically recreated World War II Company Street." These last remaining seven are simple structures thrown up overnight during the troop surge in World War II and were never meant to last. Now they're considered quaint and nostalgic of the old days, the 1940s, when soldiers lived like toughening boy scouts at summer camp and ate from sectional tin plates on long wooden picnic tables in a mess hall resembling a rustic nineteenth century polka dance palace. Even *I* felt a twinge of historic satisfaction when I saw the old buildings—as if I were viewing an enclave of endangered shacks at Plymouth Plantation or visiting the Alamo—recalling these simple, square, mustard-yellow constructions that were still in use when I lived as an army wife at Fort Benning for one month in 1966, while Dave completed Ranger and Airborne training.

They're a lot smaller than I remember. They look like playhouses.

Just before the grand entrance to the museum, our greeter stands ten feet above us on a granite pedestal. He is a bronze statue of a single infantryman, a giant fifteen-foot Gulliver, lunging forward in vintage World War II fatigues and helmet, glistening under the southern sun with a bayonet rifle in the ready position. We gather beneath him and snap photos of each other.

Walking into the vestibule behind him, we are dwarfed again by the domed ceiling three stories above and the broad expanse of cavernous, empty space surrounding us. This is our launch pad, the spot where we must breathe and suck in extra oxygen and take note of the shiny gift shop, the Soldier Store, tucked in the corner on the far left, and inhale the aroma of roast beef from the restaurant on the mezzanine to our right, because—we are about to go to war. Supplies and sustenance might be needed soon. Exuberance is building in the group. My companions are possibly recollecting their experiences as young infantrymen forty-plus years ago as we crane our necks back to absorb this magnification of space.

"There's supposed to be a room in here that simulates being

in Vietnam," Ken says, his eyes darting around the space. He was a captain, an intelligence officer, back in 1969. The others nod in affirmation with serious expressions, glancing at me, at one another, and then up to the soaring ceiling. Did the architect intend to make us feel so small in this place?

No one expresses nostalgia for the old days. Bill aka "Lumpy" is emphatic that visiting the country of Vietnam is not on his bucket list, but the chance to visit a simulation of war as a tourist with old comrades has an appeal. Since the late 1990s the long tide of trying to forget the war has turned. They are working to recall situations and find people from their days in Vietnam. I sense temperatures rising and hear voices lifting among them. Could they be as nervous and ambivalent as I am about visiting this place?

This is only a museum, I remind myself, but anticipation is building almost as if we *are* going to war. The folks checking our tickets and stamping our hands for re-entry tell us that we are about to be part of the "Last 100 Yards," the phrase that symbolizes the job location and duties of the infantry. "And don't miss the I-Max movie about battle," they shout after us. Up ahead, over the heads of the crowd, a darkened tunnel beckons. We make our suggested donation (this is a non-profit organization) and become a troupe of Pinocchios, drawn towards that darkness in front of us, the entrance to the "Last 100 Yards Ramp."

We enter into a filmy half-light after the swinging doors slam shut behind us and glimpse a cartoonish battle-worn landscape lit by artificial candles and campfires. We move along en masse as if we were packed together, row after row, in an amusement park tour boat. I'm reminded of the *Pirates of the Caribbean* ride at Disney World where pirates and their victims droop from the windows and balconies of elaborate stage sets except that we are walking through the front lines of a Revolutionary War battle.

Simulated flares career overhead; life-like soldiers on both sides of us are shooting, being shot at, shouting out to each other, and eventually descending from above with parachutes as we make our way to the World Wars. We creep forward up a small incline as one battle flows into the next and the background sounds change to match the ping, pop and boom of the weapon du jour, from flintlocks to mortars and submachine guns. Each war has its own musical score from Yankee Doodle to Toby Keith. Wherever U.S. infantrymen have fought since the American Revolution, we are among them, watching them portrayed by mannequins with strong but haggard faces, slim, muscular bodies, and tattered uniforms.

The movie recommended by our ticket taker features newsreel clips of men in actual battle, shoulder to shoulder, preparing to jump from airplanes, slogging through mud, landing on the beaches of Normandy. Face after face of young men flash by with determined looks and unfathomable thoughts. The camera lingers so close that their young, acned faces become a topographic map of Everyman—so close that I thought I could see their hair grow; these young men barely out of high school still maturing, carrying bayonets and tossing grenades. There is little text or discernable words amidst the cacophony of moving, jumping, shooting and explosions. The seminal message was that the greatest gift you can give your buddy is protection and courage. *You're not alone; we're all here to take care of each other. We're here to die for each other.*

Ironically, I'm watching clips of Vietnam with people of Dave's Company. We passively observe the chaos, the unpredictability, the adrenaline, the testosterone and the waste of war from cushioned seats in air-conditioned comfort.

"What did you think of the movie?" I ask them as we file out. Those who answer are unanimous. "It was great," they said. "That's how it is in war. You rely on each other. You need each other."

I'm sure they're right. How could one go to war without accepting the standard: "All for one and one for all!" It was when they returned that they had to face being alone with their dreams and memories, but that aspect of war is not so easy to represent and codify. Perhaps that's why we're here in this place, this *museum*, trying to get a handle on what was and what happened.

Four of us enter the Vietnam jungle simulation room. It's too dark and real for some of the guys. They back away from bamboo encroaching on all sides from floor to ceiling, the Punji stake pit exhibit, and sounds of explosions and drenching rain. Lumpy says, "Let's get out of here." We slip out a side door back into the Cold War.

Sandwiched between areas titled "Securing our Freedom" and "The Sole Superpower" and graphic representations of the Revolutionary War, the World Wars, the Korean War, Vietnam, and finally, getting right up to date, the Global War on Terror, there is a small circular enclosure called the "family gallery." Photographs and drawings cover the walls inside and depict decades of soldiers departing from or returning to parents, sweethearts, spouses, and children at home. Scores of pictures show women (presumably wives or girlfriends) waving heroically at train stations, clutching letters to their breast, or sitting surrounded by children arranged next to a portrait of a soldier. Young couples jump into each other's arms on tarmacs next to airplanes and cars. In the center, enclosed by these scenes of parting and reunion, a folded flag sits on a pedestal under a glass case. A shaft of light from above shines down on the triangle of red, white and blue. The dedication plaque reads "to those who don't return from the last one hundred yards."

Dick arrives at the display and stands next to me. "I was hoping you wouldn't see this part," he says.

I wanted to say that it is the only part of all this that I can really understand. How could I miss this? I have one of these triangles at home. But I know that Dick, with his kindness and persistent compassion, understands everything.

The folded flag *is* a powerful image, wrapped tight, full of mute compressed energy. It could be a tri-cornered mandala for some; a symbol in a dream representing the search for completeness, self-unity. It holds mystery. I find the silence of this flag at the center of this exhibit baffling and scary, like a "danger" sign on a back road lit up by car headlights. It's the surrounding photographs that touch my grief spot and stir my sorrow. I would have liked to have been one of those young women in the happy reunion photos, jumping into my husband's arms after his return. This gaudy triangle in front of me, the representation of sacrifice, the consolation prize, reminds me of something plunged into hibernation.

Even for me—a recipient of the flag—there is an ambiguity about the meaning of this *gift*. What do the folders and presenters intend to convey when it is handed to the bereaved? Is it a souvenir, a soft, huggable transitional object? What transaction have I entered into by accepting it?

The National Association of Uniformed Soldiers prints a summary of "flag etiquette" on the back page of the small notepad they send out to members. Based on my observations of American flags flapping in my neighborhood, these are little known guidelines. For example "display the flag outdoors only between sunrise and sunset, unless illuminated by a spotlight." And, "When displaying the flag indoors, always position it to the speaker's right." And, "Never allow the flag to touch the ground or any other object while on display."

There seems to be a world built up around our relationship to the flag, and even those who have had an intimate and direct experience as a recipient may be unaware of the cultural life surrounding the flag.

I remember standing under a tree in the cemetery and watching six, crisp and spit-shined soldiers in dress uniforms folding the flag with mechanical precision. I was close enough to catch a whiff of their aftershave lotion as the flag was about to be presented to me. One could imagine that there is a script that accompanies this oft repeated act of an honor guard folding, pressing, compressing the cloth exactly thirteen times into a triangular period to punctuate the end of a life.

In fact no official text exists that explains the folding and the folds. There is, however, a generally known script underlying the folding process (supposedly known by those who do the folding). But the U.S. Flag Code (Public Law 94-344) states that there is a prohibition against the acknowledgement of the words and they cannot be mentioned in official ceremonies. To do so would be a violation of the First Amendment which requires that verbal expression not create the reasonable impression that the government is "sponsoring, endorsing, or inhibiting religion generally, or favoring or disfavoring a particular religion."

The following is the *unofficial* script represented in all flag folding ceremonies and can be found in many governmental and military manuals even with the above prohibition of public disclosure. The origin of the script is unknown. Some speculate that it may have been written by an unknown chaplain considering the Judeo-Christian overtones. It seems that decoding this experience may not be appreciated by some non-Christians who also consider themselves patriots and who may have received a folded flag on behalf of a deceased veteran. Here is the script from the U.S. Flag Code:

1. *The first fold of our flag is a symbol of life.*

2. *The second fold is a symbol of our belief in the eternal life.*

3. *The third fold is made in honor and remembrance of the veteran departing our ranks who gave a portion of life for the defense of our country to attain a peace throughout the world.*

4. *The fourth fold represents our weaker nature, for as American citizens trusting in God, it is to Him we turn in times of peace as well as in times of war for His divine guidance.*

5. *The fifth fold is a tribute to our country, for in the words of Stephen Decatur, "Our country, in dealing with other countries, may she always be right; but it is still our country, right or wrong."*

6. *The sixth fold is for where our hearts lie. It is with our heart that we pledge allegiance to the flag of the United States of America, and to the republic for which it stands, one nation under God, indivisible, with liberty and justice for all.*

7. *The seventh fold is a tribute to our Armed Forces, for it is through the Armed Forces that we protect our country and our flag against all her enemies, whether they be found within or without the boundaries of our republic.*

8. *The eighth fold is a tribute to the one who entered in to the*

valley of the shadow of death, that we might see the light of day, and to honor mother, for whom it flies on Mother's Day.

9. *The ninth fold is a tribute to womanhood; for it has been through their faith, love, loyalty and devotion that the character of the men and women who have made this country great have been molded.*

10. *The tenth fold is a tribute to father, for he, too, has given his sons and daughters for the defense of our country since they were first born.*

11. *The eleventh fold, in the eyes of a Hebrew citizen, represents the lower portion of the seal of King David and King Solomon, and glorifies, in their eyes, the God of Abraham, Isaac, and Jacob.*

12. *The twelfth fold, in the eyes of a Christian citizen, represents an emblem of eternity and glorifies, in their eyes, God the Father, the Son, and Holy Ghost.*

When the flag is completely folded, the stars are uppermost, reminding us of our national motto, "In God we Trust."

After the flag is completely folded and tucked in, it takes on the appearance of a cocked hat, ever reminding us of the soldiers who served under General George Washington and the sailors and marines who served under Captain John Paul Jones who were followed by their comrades and shipmates in the Armed Forces of the United States, preserving for us the rights, privileges, and freedoms we enjoy today.

How whimsical to imagine this symbol of the end of a life as a *hat!*

My "cocked hat" is still in my possession. It still resides in the original triangular plastic envelope in which it was presented. It sits on a shelf in a cupboard. When shaken like a baby's rattle, the spent shells tucked inside make a jingling sound. I didn't keep this flag because of what it says in Section 8j of the

U.S. Flag Code: "The flag represents a living country and is itself considered a living thing." (This is why old, tattered flags are ceremoniously cremated.) I kept it because it's the only object I have that was close to Dave's body on his trip back from Vietnam in 1969.

It remains a powerful symbol of his return. A convoluted sentiment, perhaps, certainly not related to patriotism—I can't recognize myself among the explanations of those folds—but my ambiguity is no more inexplicable than the way we have canonized and glorified the act of war and military proliferation in our culture. Disentangling the web of ritual, tragedy, patriotism, war and sentimentality is not for sissies. I can say with honesty that the motivation to keep my flag, untouched, in a safe quiet place for more than forty years is a mystery. Even Dave might have said, "Don't keep that. Get rid of it. It's useless."

At the Infantry Museum, this small, intimate enclosure with its *cocked hat* behind glass in the center of the building is the only place that speaks directly to the cost of war. There are no pictures of caskets, or "cases," as they are referred to these days. As yet, there is no area in the building which acknowledges the *wounded and permanently maimed*, or those who return without limbs or without themselves otherwise intact.

Where are the tributes to those survivors with bionic arms and robotic legs who run marathons?

Where is the note that acknowledges the fact that since the wars in Iraq and Afghanistan, there is an average of one suicide per day among military personnel?

After experiencing the camaraderie of battle in this museum, it seems odd that our greeter is alone, that big bronze guy in the front, the statue of an infantryman. So much of the tone and theme throughout the exhibits repeat the notion of brotherhood and willingness to give one's life for a comrade in arms. Over and over the suggestion that you fight a war "with your brothers" underlies every scene. One leaves with the impression that war begets a "perfect union" rather than horror and chaos. The message is that war is necessary and that you perform it as part of a brotherhood. Survival is dependent on teamwork.

I can't argue with the brotherhood part. I've experienced the magic of meeting my "brothers" over and over at these reunions. They are as protective towards me as they are towards each other. I feel bathed in unconditional positive regard when I meet them now in different parts of the country and they have become a significant part of my healing from the loss of Dave and my desire to think deeper about my relationship with war and militarism. I would never have visited this museum without them and would have missed an opportunity to re-visit my former life. And—if I had to serve in war—I would be proud and feel safe if they were with me.

But I'm puzzled as I step out the door looking for Ike and bus 225 so we can head back to Atlanta for an evening of dinner and stories. After all the money that was spent on this museum, I wonder why they didn't spend a little more and put *two* bronze infantrymen out front, side by side. The war in Iraq alone cost more than two trillion dollars. He looks so lonely up there on his pedestal, as if he's going the last one hundred yards all by himself. This might sound like a half-cocked idea, but perhaps there's a message embedded in this lonesome figure. Otherwise, why wouldn't the creators of this memory of war have spent a few more bucks to splurge on another statue and given him a buddy? Perhaps he is the harbinger of the changing conditions of war.

In Michael Stephenson's historical account of death in combat in ground warfare, *The Last Full Measure: How Soldiers Die in Battle*, he states that soldiers die in the style of their times, and to a large extent, World War II was the last war in which opponents met each other face to face on the battlefield. In Vietnam, Iraq and Afghanistan, troops did not die by the hundreds in pitched battles, they died one man at a time, the victims mainly of mines, booby traps and other explosive devices. Protection on the battlefield is more a question today of body armor, impervious vehicles and those comrades who stay continually alert to what or who may be lethal. As Stephenson relates from his interviews with veterans, what happens to human beings in mechanized warfare today has absolutely no poetic or theoretical possibilities. It is a solitude of unimagined horror.

As we board our bus and I take one last glance at our bronze greeter, I'm reminded of Stephenson's words:

"War is about many things, but at its core it is about killing or getting killed. It is not chess, or a computer game, or a movie, or a book *about* death [or a museum]. It is, implacably and non-negotiably, the thing itself."

PART NINE
SECRETS THAT HEAL

---

*Secrets are rarely betrayed or discovered
according to any program our fear has sketched out.*
—George Eliot, *The Mill on the Floss* (1860)

I'm not great at keeping secrets, but the fact that I didn't speak outside my family about my decision regarding Dave's ashes and the burial of the letters for almost four decades was a personal record for me. I don't recommend secrets for their own sake. It was the effect of making a decision and creating my own ceremony that carried me safely for years in the peculiar silence that followed the Vietnam War. That private act was my initiation into my own grieving process. Survival after a traumatic experience is a kind of resistance. Rebuilding oneself takes time and confidence in intuition. It is not a calculated experience. In: *You Learn by Living,* Eleanor Roosevelt suggested that when you get to the end of your rope—tie a knot in it and hang on.

In the late 1990s something changed for me. Perhaps I'm like those pine trees in Montana that require a forest fire to crack open their spore-like seeds and grow. The fact that I've witnessed the deaths of my father, mother and brother in recent years—none of them easy passages—helped to wedge me out of my monastic attitude about earlier decisions, supposedly made for eternity. Choice is what makes us human and the courage to choose is also to begin, again and again.

Digging up the letters was not my first idea as I began to unearth memories. At first I wanted to write Dave a new letter. I wanted to re-open communication beyond just imagining him in the ether around me. I wanted to excavate my thoughts about him and our brief life together. I knew that his examples of leadership, companionship and excellence in all his aspirations had set forth a path for me, a pitch by which I could tune my life. How did he teach me so much in such a short time?

Perhaps it was his consistent humanity. One of the guys in Alpha Company recalls being wounded in the jungle, separated from the rest of the unit in the midst of a fire fight. He was able to reach Dave on the radio and Joe never forgot his calm voice over the crackling airwaves: "Don't worry. We'll come and get you." And he did.

I've grown up from the person Dave knew and perhaps he would recognize me. When I remarried, I even thought he would like my new husband. Dave would appreciate that I take care of myself and enjoy my life. Meeting the soldiers of Alpha Company cemented some small fissures in my healing because they reaffirmed that he actually had existed and was exactly the person I remembered. Everlasting life exists in the memories of those who know and love us.

The fact that we have been in new wars for the past ten years also spurred me on to reflect and write about the experience of loving and losing someone in war. When I started to write this story, I was not intending to dig up a coffin and describe its contents. I wanted to share my personal perspective that war is an unpredictable unfolding of miscalculations. I'm thankful that military conscription no longer exists. Dave chose a military life, but my son can grow up without ever being forced to go to war —at least for today and tomorrow. War leaves us transformed—but never unscathed.

"Why now? What are you looking for?" my son asks. He's pushing me to come up with a good reason as to why I would dig up the grave after forty years, why I've changed my mind.

"I've forgotten things. I always thought I would remember enough."

I'm still stumbling in my explanations. There is always a little voice inside saying, *Don't touch it. Leave it be.*

"Did you think about the coincidence of buying a house two doors down from McDougall's Funeral Home back in 1986 when we moved back to Mystic?" he asks. Noah is prodding me, but I appreciate his direct questions. His loving cross-examination feels good. He's charging me to think—and feel.

"No—I just liked the house—big and airy with lots of windows. But I like your idea. Maybe there was something lurking in my unconscious. I was trying not to think about the past in those days."

Now that it's out in the open, people do ask: *how could you do it? How could you bury all that?* Perhaps I was settling my affairs, putting things straight. I wasn't sure what would become of me. It was the best I could think to do at the time and

I meant it to last for eternity; it was the best solution for a wedding gown, West Point uniforms and regalia that might become someone's Halloween costume, the many volumes of his tiny date books full of daily minutiae, and a few hundred love letters written during four years.

In 1969, I had to think fast before the wheels of the military funeral machinery began to grind forward—and I never regretted my choice. Rather, the creativity of my solution nurtured me for years. That decision was the only *right thing* that happened that week following May 17, 1969. I still believe in what I did, but now after listening to stories I've never heard before about how he lived and how he died, something has changed. My old immutable plan has crumbled. What *did* I put in that coffin? And what might I learn from his letters? I'm ready to re-meet the past, I think.

Can I have a last interview with him through those letters?

November 1st, 2011. We are back at the cemetery, the place where this story began. Brian and the crew have found the latch and this is the moment of the unimaginable. I feel a fluttering in my chest of anxious anticipation, as if I'm just about to reach the summit of a mountain and gaze out at a fantastic view.

But, when finally the coffin was banged and pried open and the cover lifted back, there was no sound except cars speeding past on the road beyond the cemetery. Even the wind was quiet. There was a mild scuffling of boots against dirt as Moe and Jay jostled to balance on the edge of the hole. By chance they momentarily blocked my view of the interior as they propped the lid open. Our breath made wispy puffs of fog in the chilling air. Noah moved in with his camera. We were all like kids on Christmas morning, scanning for treasure as sunlight revealed the inside of the box for the first time in more than four decades. I imagined the coffin yawning and blinking like Rip Van Winkle.

The anticipation of my reunion with this precious cargo was contagious. Everyone was drawn forward in a palpable eagerness. I felt among friends. I'm almost there, almost home free. Have I really managed to turn back the clock? How did I wait all these years for this? But, I wasn't waiting—or was I?

Something was wrong.

I heard a muffled gasp somewhere. Perhaps John or Brian, leaning in from behind me. I squinted to focus on a view that I had never expected even though I thought I was ready for everything. In spite of what I saw, I kept looking for a white dress and green uniforms and gray cardboard boxes. There should be several gray cardboard boxes. But, now it was all gray - and smaller. My history was a clump, a miniaturized mountain of matter. The box had been full to the brim when I packed it in 1969. Now it seemed barely half full. Embarrassment, more accessible than sadness, welled up inside me for a second. What's this! Have I created an awful moment—for everyone?

The contents had not been spared the years and the intrusion of water. They had become a soggy rendering of the perfect, dry and beautiful things I had placed there.

I was instantly recalculating. Forty-two years. Yes. Things can happen. We are next to a river. We did have floods, perhaps three over the entire time period. The contents didn't look decayed, just transformed. Everything inside was sopping wet, but the water was gone. It had filled at some time with cold, fresh water (not salt water—I tasted it). There was no stagnant smell. The water had seeped in and out, leaving the form, the shape of the original mound of boxes, clothing, and photograph albums. Possibly it was the great flood that came from rain and snow melt in March, 2010 when most of the cemetery was underwater. *Had I missed my chance by only one year?* Based on the state of what I saw, the water had entered, remained for a time, and left slowly. At some point it had been an aquarium. I recalled Miss Havisham's table in *Great Expectations*, where the cake and place settings lay under a film of gauzy cobwebs after decades of suspended animation. Here, everything had settled down to a soaked, grayish mound of gunk with flecks of color here and there.

The fabric of Dave's green uniforms and my white wedding dress was discernible as a clump of something that formerly could be cloth. But it crumbled like wet cardboard at my touch. The sword from Dave's dress parade uniform at West Point still looked like a sword within a ragged waterlogged sheath (I didn't remember putting the sword in the coffin). The leather hat-box holding his uniform hats disintegrated when I touched it. The original shape of the piled contents had been compressed down to a smaller version of the old tableau, bearing only the outline of what I had placed in the box long ago. Now the remainder was like a long abandoned nest of some prehistoric creature.

Oh no! was the voice from my chest. I blinked in disbelief. "Can we replay this part," I wanted to say, staring at the frail mess. And, something else stirred in me: was it resignation, or more resistance? A powerful acknowledgement of what I had done; what I had assumed. I had expected the earth and the elements to respect my valuables and they had done what the earth does. It takes back, and turns decomposable things back into elements. I had trusted a shiny silver army issue coffin to be foolproof.

"What is that yellow stuff around the inside edges that looks like something from a packing crate?" I asked John.

He was leaning in towards the coffin with a look of stricken concentration. I didn't need to remind him that he thought everything would be dry and perfect. I saw the shock and drain of color from his face and wondered if I looked the same. With measured words in a calm voice he said that they used to pack the inside of coffins with a cellulose straw beneath the satin fabric to make it look soft and cloud-like.

This layer of *straw* two or three inches thick against the outer walls of the coffin was the only material that still looked intact. I remembered the puffy, quilted, shiny, white satin lining that surrounded Dave's head and shoulders when I went to identify his body. Now it had become bits of stringy gray tatters here and there. I never imagined that coffins were padded with straw. It was a medieval moment, as if staring into a time capsule from another century.

John said they use a plastic material these days, like Styrofoam. He also noted that there was some evidence of a white powder. "I can smell it," he said, and described an anti-mildew agent that Ed MacDougal had evidently sprinkled in before the burial. I couldn't discern a powder from all the other mess, but it did make me think that perhaps Mr. Ed had expected me to dig it up some day and had tried to help preserve the contents, even if he had warned me back in 1969:

"Remember. You can't dig this up."

Perhaps he thought I would change my mind a few days or months after the funeral. How loving the people around me were! How indulgent to accept and collaborate with me on this wild scheme as I struggled to manage my grief. Perhaps no one knew how leaky and frugal the box was. Coffin makers had to churn out more than 58,000 before the war ended based on the reported war dead.

I took out a recognizable but soaked scrapbook of mementos and pictures that was on the very top of everything. The cover fell away in wet chunks when I picked it up. The sodden pictures were muddy and barely preserved in plastic sleeves. There was a "dance card" that had been pasted on one page, a souvenir of the "Ring Hop" at West Point at which many couples announce their engagement, including us, and a photo of us taken in the center of a giant replica of the class ring. On my dance card Dave had written his name on every line for every dance.

Surprisingly, when I wiped away the mud on the photos, many were pictures of me. I had forgotten how much I needed to bury every reminder, every memory. I looked so young and so much prettier than I remember.

I tried to gently burrow down through the sopping detritus, but there was not even a whiff of the letters. The hundreds of letters written on thin airmail paper and the cardboard boxes that contained them had simply dissolved, probably because they were under the weight of everything else. No sign of even a postage stamp or an envelope—as if the words had been written on water and seeped out when the water departed.

I didn't spend long mucking around in the coffin—only five or ten minutes. It was too real, and too wet and cold to handle. The temperature was about 45 degrees with rain clouds thickening above. My fingers felt numb against the wet thickness of everything I touched. Moe started to dig around for me, uttering the names of things he recognized: "Here's a boot—here's a book—here's a little plastic box with gold buttons!" Somewhere he saw the word "Vietnam" and his voice fell to a whisper.

The rest watched in silence. Moe, who was used to digging and working with his hands, was trying to be helpful and kept pulling things out, but I didn't want to turn it all into a soup. It was already like an over-baked casserole. Touching items made them fall apart and I was overcome with the urge to stop this disturbance. It was almost compost now. I didn't want to turn it and aerate the mass of debris. Without handling, I could keep the shape of what it was and I could still imagine the layers of what I had originally placed there just as I have for years.

"This looks like pink silk," Moe said as he handed me something bright but unrecognizable. It was an eight-by-ten-inch, wet, flattened, clear plastic envelope containing fabric—perhaps a scarf or blouse that Dave had sent from Vietnam for Christmas or my birthday. Picking apart this pile and trying to discern what was there seemed counterintuitive to all that I have lived these past forty plus years; that only in memory and dreams do we still have what was. Nothing is lost here, just different.

I can hear my friend Chester, the renegade storytelling Methodist minister, standing here at the funeral in his black choir robe, reading from *The Prophet*:

And though death may hide me, and the greater silence enfold me, yet again will I seek your understanding.

I understand who Dave was and all his gifts. And today, in front of the results of my decision long ago, I understand and accept myself.

"We have to stop," I said. "Let's put it back. It needs to stay as it is—or was. I've seen enough."

Everyone in the little crew was quietly mournful, murmuring "oh dear" and "so sad." I wanted to reassure them. Suddenly I was in my mode of taking care of others. But that is part of healing, too, to re-find courage, to restore oneself step by step, to take care of the wounded, to find comfort in the restoration of peace, to be flexible, to try new things, to learn all we can and then to live.

I'm responsible for this, I thought. This was my idea, my choice and these are my consequences. *It's okay.* It's not perfect, but it has to be okay. I had never intended to dig this up. So, this is what it is. No different from yesterday, last year or 1969. It was the act of doing back then that mattered—and still matters today.

I turned to my crew, "Listen guys, I have a good imagination and now I have to use it to remember things as they were." I smiled at them because there was nothing else to do except laugh at my own audacity.

Privately, to my deepest self, I said, *How fabulous it would have been to see this as it was; to have this material to go back with and to dissect and analyze the years represented by these things, to have my interview with Dave, to spend time with him again.*

Yes. Yes. I'm glad I finally did it. Now I know. And each time I drive by the cemetery I don't have to wonder—and I'm ecstatic that I delivered him to the Eiger. That part of our story is still perfect.

I kept the sodden scrapbook as the only evidence of what I had done. The rest went back.

Noah and I watched Moe and Jay reclose the lid and lower the coffin back down with difficulty. Everyone stood quietly and stared down into the hole as if we could suddenly stop, rewind and start over. I understood that I would have to leave before they would start to refill the hole. We seldom see that part at funerals—the moving of the earth out and in.

Noah had discreetly moved around with his camera throughout. My brother Bob was in the background somewhere with his hands in his pockets and his arms tight against his body. It was 2:00pm, cloudy and cold on our All Saints' Day.

"Seeing that made me realize how fragile everything is," Bob said.

Bob, Noah and I got in the car and turned on the heater. I glanced back at the little crew at the gravesite. I felt empty and full at the same time. The emptiness was the keening echo from long ago, reminding me of how I had arrived at this unique, bizarre scene today. The fullness was the realization that, despite everything, I am surrounded by people who care about me, and this event today was carried out with dignity, respect and loving kindness by everyone who assisted me. Nothing has changed except the confirmation that we must keep courage handy.

"Let's go for lunch," I said. "Shouldn't we have a reception after the funeral?"

I wanted to be in a warm place away from this frigid grave-yard. I had dared to look back, to revisit an absolute decision made in a terrible time. I have survived and I'm still whole. It's time for communion with food and wine. It's time to be thankful for all we learn and share, and tell each other stories about where we find the gumption to survive, rebuild ourselves, and carry on.

Noah and I returned to the cemetery the next day to plant one hundred daffodil and narcissus bulbs in the now pliable earth above the grave. Hopefully they will bloom before Moe and Jay start mowing the grass next spring.

I can't recall all the questions Noah asked me as he filmed—before, during and after—except that they kept me moving and thinking throughout. The questions are captured and safe, though, along with my responses, on film. His interview grounded me and helped me to stay in the experience. One thing he asked at the end was if I realized how much I had been taking care of everyone else during the procedure. I did remember a moment when I worried that Moe was going to break down into a great sad, blubbering heap, tripping over the slab and end up spread eagle over the coffin. Perhaps I was projecting my own desire. I remember telling Moe that everything was okay, that I was okay. Perhaps I was channeling the nurses I remember who had to see the worst, do their best and keep working.

But I took care of myself, too. I wanted to stay calm and I did.

What I saw in the coffin shocked me. It was unexpected even though I tried to be without expectations. I can't linger on that image. I am the same person who I was long ago, a practical decider who also relies on intuition, the kindness of people around me, and the predilection to escape a bad situation as fast as I can. Without Noah's compassion and focus, I don't think I could have taken in what I saw. Perhaps I am in lockdown denial, but I'm apparently okay with no visible wounds.

Noah was able to say how affected he was by the image of the contents. But, he couldn't compare that to what things looked like when I packed the coffin over forty years ago. He saw only a decomposed pile. He said it looked putrefied and ancient which made it seem like it all happened a hundred years ago. I'm holding on to the original image even though the facts try to crowd in on me. But, it occurs to me today that this is what I've always done: accept the reality as fast as I can and keep the dream in a safe place.

After this experience, I did feel older for a time like a centenarian bird returned to look at her natal nest, and there was a shiver of the numbness I remember from long ago. My discovery on All Saints' Day was almost as hard to comprehend as what happened back in 1969, but this time I shared the experience deeply with my son. His questions and interest invites me to cherish and delve into what I have lived and what I am living. Communion with words and a good listener is the healing balm for grief.

I'm glad that this part of my life is on film. I can write and reflect about what I saw and what I feel now. And, when I'm ready, I can *see and hear* myself there.

Knowing the destiny of my treasure is more a parentheses in the story than an ending. Nothing is different. My original intention was for eternity. Now I know the letters are safe from all eyes, forever—including mine.

At the last reunion of Alpha Company, I told the guys about the letters and that I was thinking about digging them up. They were unanimous in their support. Cheering me on. They wanted to know what their beloved captain had written about them. But nothing has changed in that arena, either. There would be no surprises; they already know that the care and respect they felt for him was mutual, even without the evidence. We still have their stories and photographs. It was their writings on the Virtual Wall that brought Dave back to me like a message in a bottle.

I like to think that a rough-cut wisdom sustained me through my earlier life when I arrived at the beginning of adulthood, met incomprehensible tragedy and thought I had nothing left to live for. Sorrow does leave footprints, but healing is the courage just to continue, to begin again and again—many times over. I'm still standing, still believing. Hope works from within, rebuilding, even when we feel hopeless. It brings its own tools and works for free. Like a magic tailor who knows your size and shape, it repairs from the inside out.

About knowing, my mother repeated right up into her eighties that she felt the same as she had when she was twelve years old. I didn't understand what she meant until I became older. An earlier self at a precise age seems to form up firmly in the mind and survive, like an eternal chrysalis holding our youthful spirit.

I remember thinking that I was both *too young* and *not old enough*, that I would be able to understand things later if I could only outrun them while they were unfolding. Now I'm almost old enough. I can see in my mind's eye that young woman who climbed to the base of the north face of the Eiger wearing red sneakers, carrying a box of ashes in her backpack. I appreciate her quirky wisdom.

I aspire to live the words of Barry Stevens, Gestalt therapist and teacher. She said: "Don't push the river, it flows by itself."

It is in that same river that everything returns.

I credit Dave, his family, and mine, with my survival training—unwitting, at times, on their part because they never wished their loved one to endure grief and hardship as a lesson. The

fundamental lessons were simply part of growing up in a household where almost anything could happen; it was an apt training
ground for the ambushes in life. The adults around me were generous, complicated, confusing, annoying, arbitrary, even strange,
and I have an abiding love for them. They operated under tribal
membership rules rather than a child-rearing philosophy; they
steered me towards endurance against calamity as if they knew
what they were doing, and I'm grateful for their legacy. Their
intentions were based on love.

When I remarried on July 7, 2007 on a sailboat in the sparkling waters of Long Island Sound among several friends, I felt
the presence of Dave smiling through the clouds. He is with me
in all my beginnings—and never ending.

REMEMBRANCE

When our family connected with the members of Alpha Company of the 2/22 Infantry, we received many tributes to Dave through letters, emails and postings on the Vietnam Veterans Memorial Fund Virtual Wall. Here is a sample of some of those words and stories.

February 3, 1999 (posted on the Virtual Wall)
THANK YOU CAPTAIN
"The highest level of testimony to the greatness of David Crocker would be that in the five months of combat that I knew him, I never once heard a bad word said about him. And anyone who has been infantry knows how rare that history has been. His leadership qualities were textbook, but even though he was a West Point grad, he had a slight irreverence to the whole war and its' leadership that made you aware of the fact that he was one of us. He never faltered in his duties, and on the day of his death, some of the toughest, most hardened men in history wept like children. Thank you captain, for getting so many of us home. You are remembered many times a year in my household."
Dick Nash

March 5, 2002 (posted on the Virtual Wall)
MY HEROES HAVE ALWAYS BEEN COWBOYS
  "As a young, nineteen-year-old infantry squad leader, I found myself very much in need of a hero. I remember one day seeing Captain Crocker standing atop his APC directing the clearing of an area for a medical evacuation helicopter to come in and take out our wounded. He stood tall in the saddle like my boyhood cowboy heroes. Later that month he did likewise to medivac me. He was our "John Wayne," bigger than life to most of us. Thirty years later I still remember his leadership and compassion for every man in our company. I look back at photos of Vietnam and remember a man who helped me learn the lessons to get back home. He was a true hero. Rest in peace with Our Lord."
  Lon D. Oakley, Jr.

June 22, 2005 (email communication)
  "I remember Captain Crocker as the most liked and respected man/officer in Vietnam, or in the army. My first day in the field, as a new replacement in his Company, he took time to visit and ask a few questions about me, showing he genuinely cared about me as an individual. As I served with him, I soon found out that this was who Captain Crocker was. He truly cared more for his men than for himself. He would never ask his men to do anything or go anyplace he wouldn't be willing to go himself. He led us. He didn't ask us to lead and then for him to follow. He was leading us when he was killed. Many men (actually we were mostly still boys) openly cried because of the loss of a great leader and friend. Thank you for acknowledging my comments. You and your family should be proud of him. He was a brave warrior."
  Rich Jones

October 11, 2005 (email communication)

"I am very proud to say I served Captain Crocker in Vietnam from October 1968 until May 1969. I remember him for his remarkable leadership ability. It didn't matter if you were a private or a 1st sergeant; he respected us all the same. I had the pleasure of being his armored personnel carrier driver for a short period of time while his regular driver was on R & R. Even after 36 years, I remember him as if it was yesterday. God bless you all."

Charles "Butch" Jones

June 29, 2005 (email communication)

"I have several unfulfilled quests in my life and near the top of the list for 36 years has been trying to find your family so that I might relate to them the greatness of David Crocker as a commander of men in 1969. For so very long I kept my memories of Captain Dave in my own mind, thinking that "someday" I would try to find you and tell you of his greatness. I guess that day is here. There have never been anything except good thoughts about him from the first day we met. One quick but powerful anecdote I need to get out of the way so we can both cry a bit. Every single morning as the company would head out to our day's mission, Dave would do the required radio check with his four platoon leaders. Instead of "move out" or "let's go get em" or some other motivating phrase, his was always, "to the alps!" We platoon leaders knew what it meant, and it became our standard slogan for about anything that involved going forward. I was moved a great deal by finding out from you that he got there, and I know a great many other vets of our time together who will be equally moved when they find out. When he died it was the only time that Alpha 2/22nd Infantry had to be taken from the field because of the loss of just one man. He wasn't just one more man, he was the heart of one of the toughest outfits in army history, and it simply couldn't perform without him for several days."

Dick Nash

August 30, 2005 (email communication)

"I spent many days as a radio operator for David and witnessed a lot of his heroism. He was a true leader and admired by all who had the pleasure of meeting him. I sat beside him on our armored personnel carrier which he had painted "to the alps" on the side reflecting his love for mountain climbing. I was replaced by a conscientious objector who refused to carry a weapon. He was killed the same day by the same booby trap [as David]. That day will be forever emblazoned in my memory."

Bill Lipp

July 10, 2007 (email communication)

"I remember that Captain Crocker at first glance looked like a serious individual, which he was, but he had a mischievous side to him. He wasn't tall in stature but he was a giant. Everyone who knew him had the utmost respect for him. He was a leader not by rank alone. I cannot think of a single guy in our company that would not have followed him to hell if that is what he wanted. At times, it seemed like we made that trip but he always got us out safe. When I was driving the lead track and he was up on top, he would talk to me over the intercom in a reassuring voice to lower my stress level. I don't remember him being rattled by anything. Mostly what I remember was his genuine honesty to do what was expected of him. That meant he pressed us day after day but always as a leader and never as an individual who played it safe in the background. He had my respect from day one and I was never going to be a person to let him down. For some of his light-hearted moments, I recall on some of the slow hot nights hearing him calling in situation reports on the radio. He would make all kind of wild exaggerations while pretending to be someone other than himself. We never let on that we knew it was him, but we would talk about this unknown crazy person the next day in his presence. He would participate in some games with us on the slow days in the field. On some occasions, he played baseball with us. We had a wooden stick for a bat and a soda can for a ball. He was like a kid in a candy store one day when he drove our APC. In exchange for the driving lesson, I became captain for 10 seconds while my picture was taken with his shirt on. He was a genuine individual. I wish I could tell him today what he meant to me."

Phil Zablocki

REUNION

As much as we might think we are alone in the aftermath of tragic life events, there are many surrounding us who will find us if the heart is open.

The men of **Alpha Company of the 2/22 Infantry** found me by posting their words of tribute to Dave on the virtual Vietnam Memorial Wall. My regular reunions with them every eighteen months since 2006 have provided a consistent strengthening of my spirit with their stories, communications, friendship and support. Without them I would not have had the courage to visit the Wall at a reunion held in Washington, DC in 2008. Without them I would never have heard the first person stories of what a great leader Dave was until his death in Vietnam in 1969. Visit www.vietnamtripledeuce.org and www.22ndinfantry.org.

The members of the **Gold Star Wives (GSW) of America** have battled since their formation in 1947, with the support of Eleanor Roosevelt, to assure that spouses and family members of veterans are not forgotten. They have fought for pensions, health insurance, education benefits. They have pressed for acknowledgment of the costs of war such as the long-term impact of chemical exposure, psychological effects, handicaps and ultimately the recognition that someone they loved made a supreme sacrifice. The many chapters of GSW across the country and the

281

world carry out numerous volunteer efforts to keep the legacy of the sacrifices of military service alive. Find out who they are in your community and support them in their efforts. To learn more about the Gold Star Wives, visit www.goldstarwives.org.

PeaceTrees Vietnam is one of the rare and extraordinary responses to the consequences of war that makes us believe that humans might have a chance to survive on our planet. Since 1995 they have been working with Vietnamese people in the Quang Tri Province of Vietnam (a small area that received more bombs than all of Europe in World War II). They find and defuse unexploded ordinance before innocent adults and children are accidently killed or maimed. When the mines are removed, they plant indigenous trees. They provide land risk education, survivor assistance, civilian diplomacy trips, and a range of other supportive activities. Visit them at www.PeaceTreesVietnam.org.

These organizations, among many others, are examples of a response to the needs created by war. War has long tentacles that are difficult to disentangle for both the victims and the victors. People may be healed after war but they are never cured from its effects. One of the best ongoing treatments is the courage to listen, to speak, to share, and to tell your story. Elie Wiesel, a survivor of war and atrocities against humankind, has suggested that perhaps God made humans because he loved stories. The most important story will be the one you tell yourself.

GRATITUDE

My greatest thanks are to my son, Noah Bean, for his unflinching belief in my project and my writing. I thank my husband, Frédéric Walperswyler, for his constant reminder of the struggle to be a creator of an artistic work and not to give up. And, to Trudy Catterfeld, who understood with her abiding wisdom and made sure I saw this book through to completion.

I deeply appreciate the continued presence of David's family and their spouses and children in my life: His parents, Dave and Ruth Crocker, Sr., his brothers, Tom and John Crocker, and his sister Dotti Crocker Penny.

CPSIA information can be obtained at www.ICGtesting.com
Printed in the USA
BVOW05s0229260316

441847BV00001B/1/P